THE DOI

THE DONS

The History of Aberdeen Football Club
JACK WEBSTER

Stanley Paul

London   Sydney   Auckland   Johannesburg

Stanley Paul & Co. Ltd

An imprint of the Random Century Group

20 Vauxhall Bridge Road, London SW1V 2SA

Random Century Australia (Pty) Ltd
20 Alfred Street, Milsons Point, Sydney, NSW 2061

Random Century New Zealand Limited
191 Archers Road, PO Box 40–086, Glenfield, Auckland 10

Century Hutchinson South Africa (Pty) Ltd
PO Box 337, Bergvlei 2012, South Africa

First published 1978
Revised edition 1990

Phototypeset in 11/13 Times by Input Typesetting Limited, London

Printed and bound in Great Britain by
Mackays of Chatham Ltd, Chatham, Kent

British Library Cataloguing in Publication Data
available on request from the British Library

ISBN 0 09 174373 7

CONTENTS

Introduction 1

Dedicated to those who have given their loyalty to Aberdeen Football Club, not least my friend, the late Chris Anderson, fine player, sportsman, administrator who inspired so much of what is good about Pittodrie.

INTRODUCTION

It occurred to me one day in the mid 1970s that no one had ever written a history of Aberdeen Football Club. In terms of tangible success, it might have seemed there was precious little to write about; the less cynical view would be that silverware is not everything in this world and that there was a case for capturing the mood of high moments and low, the glamour of those well-spaced triumphs and the memory of some exquisite footballing talent which had graced the turf of Pittodrie Park down the years.

The seventy-fifth anniversary of the club, which would fall in 1978, seemed as good a milestone as any at which to encapsulate the fitful glory of the Dons, though I still have a letter from the directors of the day who thought I should wait until the centenary. My gentle reminder that some of us, not least the board themselves, might not be around in the year 2003 produced a silent blessing for a project which would be my own venture entirely and not an official history, as has sometimes been suggested. This would not be some cool, objective assessment but a totally subjective account by one devoted supporter among thousands, who had lived through the second half of the saga himself and would seek to absorb the first half from those who were there.

It was that earlier period which bore the urgency of finding witnesses who were still alive. It was difficult enough to find players from as far back as the First World War, let alone the founding days of 1903. For a variety of reasons, including a fire at the premises, there was little historic evidence forthcoming from Pittodrie itself and I would have to depend on two main sources of material – searching through old newspapers and talking to old players. The former task entailed laborious months in the depths of Woodside Public Library, trying to extract from the week-by-week events and the pronouncements of my journalistic

1

predecessors some form of historical pattern which would make logical sense.

That task alone produced 100,000 words of notes, which was more than the final book would merit. Into that fabric must be injected the personal remembrances of older men such as Matt Forsyth and W. K. Jackson, who were playing in the aftermath of the First World War. Some said the greatest Don of all was the legendary Benny Yorston of the 1920s. But Benny was dead, said some. Or was he? The great search was on. And by the time it had finished nearly two years later, I had sweated my way through an ordeal which carried no thoughts of commercial opportunism but would more properly be identified as a labour of love. In the absence of further achievement in my life, I would happily settle for an epitaph which said that I had rescued the history of the Dons which, because of the vanishing witnesses, could not have been written even a few years later.

When the book was published in 1978, there was a launching celebration at the Capitol Cinema, attended by a glittering array of Pittodrie stars down the century. One man came quietly among the throng and said very little because, as the most recent employee of the club, he had so far done nothing. He could only hope, he said modestly, to emulate those distinguished people from the past. How could we have known, in celebrating seventy-five years of Aberdeen Football Club on a rain-sodden night, that the real history of the Dons was about to be created by the newcomer in our midst? In welcoming the new manager, Alex Ferguson, how could we possibly have guessed that the Golden Era of Pittodrie lay just around the corner?

It is one of the maddening fascinations of history that it begins to run out of date the moment it is written. With much pleasure, however, I now address myself to updating that original story of the Dons which gains a whole new perspective in the light of all that has happened in the most incredible decade of all.

1
GLAMOROUS NIGHT

Against a dark and leaden Scandinavian sky, the electronic score-board flashed out its magical message of confirmation that Aberdeen Football Club had indeed won the European Cup Winners' Cup. The event itself, still shrouded in a deep sense of unreality, had slipped into history just a few minutes earlier, but there we stood, all 12,000 of us from Scotland, gazing down on that sodden sward in rapt disbelief that our most optimistic football dream had actually come true.

Was there some way to convince a befuddled brain that the scoreboard's insistent ABERDEEN 2–REAL MADRID 1 was a reality and not some cruel joke which would soon disappear in the storms of that incredible night? Yes, yes, it had happened, we finally managed to convince ourselves, and as the heavens opened their floodgates and wept tears of joy for all things Aberdonian, they were merely reflecting those earthly scenes inside the Ullevi Stadium of Gothenburg, where delirium had reached its zenith.

When that final whistle blew, we reached for new ways of expressing it, denied help from any precedent. We danced and sang, hugged people we didn't know and called upon reserves of voice, stamina and emotion we hardly knew we possessed. The rain could pour till all hell was sizzling in steam but we would stand there and try to capture in our minds and absorb into our beings for ever the greatest moment in the history of Aberdeen Football Club.

The date was Wednesday 11 May 1983. Everything else that had happened in eighty eventful years became less than significant when set against the spectacle we had just been privileged to witness, that Cup Winners' Cup Final in which the Dons had taken on the greatest name in world football – and beaten it!

Any dismay that the supreme occasion had been visited by atro-cious weather was soon replaced by the thought that the crash and flash of the thunderstorm which immediately preceded the game were no more than nature's own spectacular setting for the most dramatic night most of us would ever see. As can happen in European finals, one gnawing regret was the disappointing turnout of Swedish people to augment the 12,000 Aberdonians and 3000 Spaniards. Live television, plus the weather, had kept the crowd to under 20,000, but the swelling chests of the Scots did their best to create an illusion of numbers. No such illusion was necessary for the noise level. Aberdonians bellowed like their native bulls – except for those who could raise no sound at all. I shall carry for ever the memory of solid, sober Scotsmen struck dumb with emotion.

How could I forget Joe Mitchell from Coburty of Rosehearty, hardened from a lifetime of bestriding the furrowed fields of Buchan, allowing the tears to flow freely down his weather-beaten cheeks? So, too, did Aberdeen's biggest bookmaker of the time, Bobby Morrison (now a Dons director), whose ducts might have been encouraged by the fortune he had just lost against loyal Aberdonian bets, although his obvious emotion was purer than that. We had waited a lifetime for this moment, and now that it had arrived we were unwilling to let the Ullevi Stadium's magic slip out of our grasp that night. Was there perhaps some secret way to bottle an atmosphere and preserve it for ever?

When the stewards finally ushered us out, we embarked on such a night of revelry as most of us had never known, drinking, dancing and celebrating in a Swedish rhapsody that reverberated throughout the city. I found my way to the team headquarters at the Buchan-sounding Hotel Farshatt, fifteen miles from Gothenburg, in time to watch the victorious Dons arriving for their celebration. Well-heeled Swedes dining in the restaurant rose to applaud the victors as they passed through to their reception room. Back in the city, people were bathing in the fountains in the manner of Trafalgar Square at Hogmanay. Every hotel in Gothenburg was filled with Aberdonians, among them the Europa, which tended to be the focal point of Dons activity.

Tomorrow would bring its own revelations – a welcome-home to defy the wildest imagination – as Alex Ferguson led his team back to Aberdeen, accompanied by the fifty aeroplanes and hundreds of cars which had carried the supporters to Sweden. It was the culmination of five years' work by the young man from Govan to stretch the horizons of Pittodrie beyond the limits of Scottish football. Considering that the Dons had once gone for forty-three years without a reward of any kind, there had been a time when any national trophy was a cause for rejoicing. Now there had been a re-drawing of perspectives – and who could tell what else lay ahead?

From that memorable May night of 1983, the name of Gothenburg has been established in the standard vocabulary of Aberdonians, coming to mean 'a high point of experience, the greatest night of your life – or just pure magic!'. As virtual unknowns in the greater arenas of Europe, the men from the North-east had not only broken a monotonous mould of Scottish football (by which I mean that divine right of Rangers and Celtic to win everything) but had also demolished all obstacles at the top of European football as well, to take their place among the elite. Just as a certain chemistry, brewed up by manager Alex Ferguson, had produced a team which would take its tally to ten major trophies in seven seasons, so had the fates decreed that this would be their finest hour.

The history books can reveal in cold print the story of an Aberdeen victory as famous as any. The emotional details, however, are more carefully hidden in the hearts and minds of those who will always be able to say 'I was there!'

2
A MILESTONE

Through nine decades, the pounding feet of football loyalty have vibrated down the breadth of Merkland Road East as the faithful headed for Pittodrie Park with as much dedication as pilgrims on the road to Mecca. For this is *their* Mecca, shrine of sporting worship in the Granite City, where many a silent prayer has been offered up to the gods above, when brilliant unpredictables like Harry Yorston or Paddy Buckley were faced with an open goal and were liable either to burst the net or to send what the scribes used to call 'the leather sphere' in the general direction of heaven.

There was a time when I used to walk the whole way from Union Street, not so much to save the bus fare but to absorb and savour the mounting excitement of the occasion. In that period of post-war enthusiasm, when the average working man had not yet stretched his horizons from the only known pastime of the 1920s and 1930s, it seemed inconceivable that a chap could even contemplate spending his Saturday afternoons anywhere else if there was a match at Pittodrie. We would survey the odd one (and regard him as a very odd one) here and there who would be digging his garden or preparing for an enforced expedition with his wife to Isaac Benzie's, and wonder what brand of insanity might possess the poor creature. Mind you, depending on the performance of the day, we were not above re-assessing our opinions by a quarter to five and considering that the man maybe wasn't so daft after all! But such is the enduring quality of football optimism that thoughts of possible disappointment seldom entered your head on the great trek to Pittodrie. Tramcars would clank past, some heading straight along King Street to the Bridge of Don but most were specials, turning right into Pittodrie Street to unload their catch in Ardarroch Road before completing the square up Merkland Road East and back up King Street to the Castlegate for another load. If you were walking down King Street you would pass that long, thin fellow with the half-moon face at a gate on the left-hand side, just watching the folk go by, and he would still be there when you came back. For all you knew, he maybe stood there all the rest of the week as well, a protective tree of a man with roots in his boots, silently feeding on the sight of the saps who passed beneath his branches on a Saturday afternoon. I don't suppose he ever saw a football match, for his role in life was to observe the observers.

On each alternate Saturday, when the Dons were playing their away games and there was no First Division football nearer than Dundee (and what self-respecting Aberdonian would want to go there!), Aberdeen seemed a bare and barren place to live in, a city without heart or soul, an Arctic citadel to be tolerated with difficulty until the following Saturday when life would flow again through the urban arteries, sending the pining fanatic once again down Merkland Road with the bounce of optimism and excitement that keeps men and women going in this troubled world of ours. Home or away, we would regurgitate it all from the columns of the *Green Final* over the tea hour, confirming what we had just seen at Pittodrie or hanging upon the words of James Forbes as he re-created dramas fought out on the foreign fields of Glasgow or some other primitive spot of the Darkest South.

It is akin to a fever, this football enthusiasm, often infectious, usually incurable and binding men, women and children to one particular club in a loyalty and affection which become an integral part of their lives. In some districts of Glasgow or Liverpool it becomes the only escape from drabness, the only possible rub with success. A European victory in Lisbon or Rome becomes a victory in the anonymous living rooms of Parkhead or Merseyside docklands. To me, the wonder of it is that football loyalty in less likely places survives through a history of predictable failure. What have they ever had to cheer about on the slopes of Stenhousemuir, and is there any reasonable prospect of improvement? Yet, in asking such a question we may be forgetting that loyalty, in its purest form, is more in evidence in defeat than in victory. Certainly, in the Pittodrie experience, it survived through the first forty-three years of the club's existence without knowing the reward of a single success at national level.

It was not until 1946 that the League Cup came hurtling north to Aberdeen after a memorable victory over Rangers at Hampden Park, gained with a last-kick goal by left-half George Taylor. Then came the Scottish Cup in 1947, to be followed by the greatest national honour, the Scottish League Championship, in 1955. In that same year the Dons won the League Cup, but that was followed by a gap of fifteen years before the Scottish Cup came again in 1970, and another six years before the League Cup victory of 1976. In terms of tangible success, it took the victory bells of the Second World War to spark off the Pittodrie story. But old men with dew in their eyes will tell you that the story began a long, long time before that. Who needed silver trophies when you had memories of Donald Colman or Alec Jackson, Benny Yorston or Willie Mills? They may not have won medals but they were, in themselves, an array of glittering prizes in the minds of those who were privileged to see them. One day there will be no remaining witness to their greatness.

3
THE BLACK-AND-GOLD

Aberdeen Football Club as we know it today came into existence in 1903, a latecomer to the big-time scene of Scottish football which had been developing through the last quarter of the nineteenth century. It had become obvious that a city the size of Aberdeen should be involved at national level, and the way to achieve it was surely a merger between a number of the smaller local clubs.

The precise origins of Aberdeen FC become a little confusing to the public mind because of the fact that there was already in existence a club of the same name, and that club was one of three which amalgamated for the new formation of 1903.

Let us briefly, then, follow that limb of the story back to an October afternoon in 1881 when a dozen people gathered in the Albert Hall in Correction Wynd to form the very first Aberdeen Football Club. The meeting had been called by three teachers at Woodside Public School who were determined, it was reported, 'to start the dribbling game in Aberdeen'. Eight of those present were teachers, two were bookbinders and the others were a medical student and a tailor. They elected Mr W. Stewart, a Woodside teacher, to be the secretary and despatched him forthwith to buy a dozen maroon jerseys, two balls and one inflator. Thus they brought the dribbling game to the North-east of Scotland and played it wherever the opportunity arose – at the Links, at Hayton, then on Holburn cricket ground and, more permanently, on a beautiful setting at the Chanonry, by which time they had discarded the maroon jerseys and become known as the 'Whites'. A picture of the day shows the team in typical Victorian pose, complete with white jerseys and knickerbockers and in some cases sporting bowler hats.

By the late 1890s, however, the club was being forced to vacate its Chanonry setting and the search for a new ground began. Close by the old North Turnpike Road, which we now know as King Street, the former Gallows Marsh had been converted into a dung hill for police horses, which were stabled in those days at Poynernook Road. The land upon which the dung hill stood had been leased to the city by Mr Knight Erskine of Pittodrie, in the Chapel of Garioch, but in February 1899 its tenancy was transferred to Aberdeen Football Club on condition that the Whites restored the ground to its former agricultural state, repaired the cart road and removed or utilised the old rubbish heap which stood on the ground. With great spirit the club set about its task, levelling the ground, raising a terrace at the east end and holding a bazaar to raise the minimum requirement of £550. By the end of the summer of 1899 everything was ready for the grand opening of the enclosure. Pittodrie Park was a new name on Aberdeen lips (Pittodrie is a Celtic place-name which can mean 'the place of manure'!) and the crowds who flocked to that first game against Dumbarton, some of them on tramcars which ran a shuttle service from Market Street, found themselves caught up in a festive atmosphere, with music provided by the pipe band of the 1st Volunteer Battalion, the Gordon Highlanders.

Aberdeen won that day, but the appearance of a brand-new football ground in the city merely emphasised the fact that they were by no means the best team in town. In the Northern League of the day they invariably had to play third fiddle to Orion, who were known as the 'Stripes' and played at Cattofield, and Victoria United, who were the 'Blues' and played at Central Park. Wouldn't it make sense for these three clubs to band together and become one major club which could take the Granite City out of its Grampian isolation and into the mainstream of Scottish football? There was bickering among the three but the logic of pooling their resources and making an assault on the Scottish League finally triumphed at a meeting in Aberdeen Trades Hall on 26 March 1903, when the chairman was Mr John Clarke, lecturer in education at Aberdeen University. The gathering agreed to the formation of a limited liability company, with a capital of £1500, taking over at valuation the removable assets of the three clubs involved. There was no guarantee, of course, that they would gain admission to the Scottish League or that they could afford the £50 a week required to survive, but the move had to be made and the club came into being officially on 18 April 1903. The constitution set out 'to promote the practice and play of football, cricket, lacrosse, lawn tennis, hockey, bowling, cycle-riding, running, jumping and the physical training and development of the human frame', a breadth of vision which might have given the loud-mouths a chance to say, on a bad day, that the footballers didn't know which game they were supposed to be playing!

This new version of Aberdeen Football Club first showed its face at Pittodrie Park on 15 August 1903, a dull afternoon when Stenhousemuir came north to share in a 1–1 draw. For the first season Aberdeen FC had to content themselves with a place in the old Northern League, a secondary affair which took in an area from Aberdeen to Fife and included teams like Montrose, Dunfermline, St Johnstone, Forfar, Dundee A and Lochgelly United.

Solid Aberdonians were not ready to be bowled over by the new arrangement, however, and the directors were soon under fire for the poor results. A letter to the *Evening Express* came from a disgruntled gentleman who complained: 'Twice since the season opened have I seen members of the team dawdling about the town, apparently doing nothing. Now, lads, a football life does not last very long and Satan finds some mischief, so try and get something to do during the day.' Some excitement, however, was generated by the signing of Bert Shinner from Middlesbrough, an early idol at Pittodrie, and Duncan McNicol from Arsenal who became one of the best backs the club ever had. McNicol was of a tall and magnificent build and was reported to take the ball from opponents with ease and grace. At the scoring of one of his early goals, 'hats and sticks were thrown in the air'. The team won the Aberdeenshire Cup that season and, when they were drawn against Arbroath in the Qualifying Cup, the mob of Aberdonians who travelled south for the game caused such chaotic scenes at the local railway station that they promptly built a better one!

Towards the end of that first season the directors turned their minds to the possibility of gaining entry to the First Division. The Scottish League of that time consisted of two divisions of fourteen teams each, but they had not yet arrived at a system of promotion and relegation. Instead, the top twelve clubs in the First Division were asked to vote on who should make up their numbers, choosing between the two bottom clubs and the two who topped the Second Division. To complicate matters that season, Aberdeen FC was asking to be considered and Jimmy Philip, who had been appointed first manager, was despatched on a canvassing trip with the plausible argument that a city as important as Aberdeen should surely be represented in the principal showcase of Scottish football.

Meanwhile, the Spring Holiday of 1904 brought north the popular attraction of Newcastle United, which gave the Pittodrie fans a chance to see those legendary figures of their day, Bobby Templeton and R. S. McColl, the former Queen's Parker who later became famous for his chain of sweet shops. Newcastle won 7–1, which was not so surprising since Aberdeen had managed to finish only third in the mediocrity of the Northern League. So what chance the First Division?

It was the custom of those days for crowds to gather outside the newspaper offices to gain first news of major events. Many years ago, old Willie Benton gave me a vivid description of the scenes outside the *Aberdeen Journal* office in Broad Street when he, as the office boy, came out to post up the bills announcing the Relief of Mafeking in 1901. In much the same way, crowds gathered in Broad Street on the day when the Scottish League was voting on whether or not to admit Aberdeen FC to the First Division. Such was the fanaticism of the time.

Jimmy Philip had returned from his expedition to the south with the promise of enough support to carry the day but, when the news came through to the crowds outside the offices of the *Evening Express* and *Evening Gazette*, there was an outburst of boos and groans. The promise of support had not materialised and, instead, Aberdeen FC was elected to the Second Division in the company of Hamilton Academicals, Clyde, Leith Athletic, St Bernard, Falkirk, East Stirlingshire, Abercorn, Ayr United, Albion Rovers, Raith Rovers and Arthurlie. It was better than nothing and the onus was now on the club to prove that it was worthy of the top grade. That could be done only by producing a winning team and to that end Willie McAuley and Jimmy Robertson had already been signed from Middlesbrough and the Teesside club had also produced the former Celtic goalkeeper Rab Macfarlane for a total treble fee of £210. Rab turned out to be one of the characters of the game, indulging in a free exchange of banter with the crowd behind his goal. On one occasion, when he failed to get in the way of a fierce shot which landed in the back of the net, a wag roared out 'Hey Rab, foo did ye come to lose that goal?' Picking himself up from the ground, Rab looked round the post and shouted back 'Better tae lose a goal than a goalkeeper!' In the build-up of a team which would take them to the top, Aberdeen also signed Ecky Halkett from Dundee, who was to become captain before being killed in the First World War.

At the first annual general meeting in July 1904, Councillor Alexander Milne (whose son Vic later became a popular centre-half as well as a doctor) announced an income of £1927 which, together with the profits from the bar, left a surplus of £319 11s 9d. The directors recommended a dividend of ten per cent. That bar, incidentally, was in existence for twenty years before someone discovered that it was not legally licensed! At the start of the season 1904–05 the big talking point was the departure from the old white jerseys, which had given the original club its nickname, and the introduction of a new-fangled black and gold strip which threatened to drive the old faithful to distraction. They became known as the 'Black-and-Gold Brigade' or, more appropriately, the 'Wasps', a name which was accurate in its description but highly unpopular with the players because it gave a ready weapon to the terracing wits on those off-days when there was little sign of sting in their play. The team which had shaped up into a recognisable eleven was emerging as: Macfarlane; Willox, J. Mackie; Halkett, Strang, Low; Knowles, Mackay, G. McNicol, Ellis, Johnstone. By now the Pittodrie Reserves had taken the place of their seniors in the old Northern League.

As in the previous season at Arbroath, the Qualifying Cup became a cause for great enthusiasm in 1904–05. Aberdeen were drawn to play at Cowdenbeath and the Fife team were firm favourites to win. Once again the crowds gathered outside the newspaper offices, and when the word came through that Aberdeen had won, 'staid and sober men hugged each other in their ecstasy. Reckless partisans threw their go-to-meeting hats in the air and everybody, with one voice, "let her rip" at the fullest pitch of their lungs.' Quite disgraceful behaviour in 1904 – and all because of a win over Cowdenbeath. Crowds thronged the Joint Station for the team's return and in the enthusiasm of the period nearly all the share capital was snapped up and Aberdeen Football Club bought over Pittodrie for the sum of £5668. They also signed Johnny Edgar from Arsenal, another great favourite with the supporters, and prepared for the semi-final of that Qualifying Cup which seemed capable of arousing such emotion in those days.

The opponents were Clyde, who came to Pittodrie for the tie and brought with them, in the customary way, their own linesman. The poor fellow took dogs' abuse from the home crowd, though one commentator did agree that the man 'would have tried the patience of a Job-and-a-half'. During that game the Clyde skipper interrupted proceedings to hand over a note to Aberdeen captain McNicol, protesting that a certain player was ineligible for the match. Aberdeen won and the SFA did not uphold the protest. The Qualifying Cup euphoria reached its climax at Dens Park, Dundee, on 26 November 1904, when Aberdeen actually won the trophy with a 2–0 victory over Renton, a club which had taken its place in football history by winning the Scottish Cup in 1888 and being hailed as 'champions of the world'. The team on duty that day was: Macfarlane; Murray, D. McNicol; Halkett, Strang, Low; Robertson, G. McNicol, A. Lowe, McAuley, Ritchie. The 1500 Aberdonians who travelled to Dundee on a Caledonian Railway special saw their team slithering about in the snow during the first half. But trainer Peter Simpson had a change of boots awaiting them at half-time and that more than anything paved the way for victory. The cup was handed over in Wood's Hotel, Dundee, before Aberdeen returned to a city which was out in full ecstatic force, carrying players shoulder-high from the station through the streets and keeping up the din far into the night. Players and officials celebrated in the old Palace Hotel, which stood at the corner of Union Street and Bridge Street (a site now occupied by C & A) and which was the social hub of Aberdeen until it was burned down in 1941.

In contrast to the scientific build-up to Cup-ties today, isn't it rather appealing to find that the training preparation for a major game in those days consisted of a tramcar ride to Mannofield and a brisk walk to Culter and back to the terminus? That Qualifying Cup win may seem a modest enough achievement but it did play its part in demonstrating that the emerging club in Aberdeen was capable of winning something, which was a better advertisement than its League position at the end of the 1904–05 season. To finish seventh out of twelve teams in the Scottish Second Division was bound to raise doubts about whether Aberdeen Football Club was ready to take the place it so earnestly pursued in the First Division. But that did not prevent the manager and directors renewing their efforts to drum up support and submitting their application once again. Seven other clubs were also forward with applications to join the First Division, including Motherwell and Morton who had ended up at the bottom of the division, and Clyde and Falkirk who were champions and runners-up in Division Two.

Aberdeen pinned their faith on having friends at court and, when the League meeting was held on 22 May 1905, Celtic sought to ease the dilemma by proposing that the League be extended from fourteen teams to sixteen teams. That opened the way for four teams to gain a place in the top division – but who? When it came to voting, Aberdeen were top of the poll. Motherwell and Morton were re-elected and Falkirk landed the fourth place, which was rough justice on Clyde, considering they had just won the Second Division championship ahead of Falkirk.

Their ambition now realised, the Aberdeen directors were over-joyed and went all out to improve the quality of both the ground and the team. The board of that time consisted of Councillor Milne as chairman, with James Rae, James Weir, John Mackay, Harry Wyllie, Willie Jaffrey and Tom Duncan, who was the last survivor.

The terracing was extended and due notice was taken of the burgh surveyor who had been scathing about the condition of the old Orion grandstand which had been transplanted from Cattofield. A new pavilion at the north-east corner was fitted with two large dressing rooms and an ornamental front. Indeed, you might have been excused for expecting a cricket team to emerge, such was the shape and style of the place with its balcony where gentlemen used to recline on a Saturday afternoon as if they were watching a Test Match at Lord's.

On the playing side, the staff of twenty-seven now included the great Willie Lennie, former Queen's Park, Dundee and Rangers player who had gone to Fulham but failed to settle. Willie was a brilliant left-winger who seldom played off form and later became the very first Aberdeen player to be capped for Scotland.

In the crystallising of the new football club the names of men who would shape its destiny inevitably emerged and the first man of influence was Jimmy Philip, the original manager, whose first four-teen months of work earned him the princely sum of £116 3s 4d.

4
PHILIP IN CHARGE

Jimmy Philip was in business as a wood-turner when he was given the job as part-time manager of Aberdeen Football Club in 1903. Among all the managers who have guided the Pittodrie fortunes, he was the only one who could call himself an Aberdonian until the arrival of Jocky Scott as co-manager in 1988. His son George, who lived in Counteswells Road until his death in 1977, remembered the early days of the family home at 13 Erskine Street and how as a child he would be hurled to Pittodrie on the back of his father's bike. There he would examine, with the wonder of a child's eyes, the jerseys and boots of the men who filled them – names which were to take on a legendary ring: Donald Colman, Jock Hume, Rab Macfarlane, Bobby Hannah.

The choice of Jimmy Philip as manager was no random happening. From a broad base of sporting interest, he had a particularly far-seeing view about football. For example, he proposed the very first overseas tour by a Scottish international team, telling the SFA that he would foot the bill if there was a loss and that they could keep the profit if there was one. Also a talented referee, he was invited to officiate at the Olympic Games of 1912 in Stockholm. His son George kept the silver memento to prove it.

In our more sophisticated days of professionalism, such an invitation would be unthinkable. But attitudes were less rigid in those days; players were allowed to develop their own colour and personality without having to conform to some central pattern. And there were some characters! Can you imagine, for example, Alex Ferguson or Alex Smith putting up with the behaviour of a little Irishman called Flanagan, who was signed by Jimmy Philip from Maidstone in Kent? Flanagan worked for Sharpe's cream toffees and whether the sweetness of the job had anything to do with it must remain a matter of conjecture. The certainty of it was that he much preferred two drinks to one, in which respect he was neither the first nor the last among footballers, but his trouble was that he found it hard to keep the two pursuits apart. He would collect his pay at Pittodrie on a Friday and proceed to the nearest hostelry for a liquid consumption which landed him, as often as not, in the privacy of a police cell. It was nothing unusual for Jimmy Philip to bail him out on a Saturday morning, bring him back to his senses and produce him in the dressing room in time for the kick-off. To his eternal credit, Flanagan could go out there and play down that left wing with all the assurance of a man who had spent his Friday evening at a temperance meeting. There was colour, if not stability, in some of those old-time worthies. But there was one popular Don of that period before the First World War whose colour was invariably black. For Bobby Hannah worked as a coal-dunter at the harbour, finishing his shift at one o'clock and catching a tramcar to Pittodrie, still covered in coal-dust. He was one of the few professional players in the history of football who had to be put into a bath *before* the game! Bobby had a kind of two-footed tackle which was all his own. He also had one particular experience which hardly bears re-telling. In a game with Rangers, the full-blooded boot of the famous Tommy Cairns connected with his private parts and that, painfully and understandably, put a virtual end to the top-class career of Bobby Hannah, though he was to turn up later in America.

Meanwhile, Jimmy Philip, the wood-turner from Erskine Street, guided Aberdeen FC into the mainstream of Scottish football. The Black-and-Golds, who had not yet been called the Dons, made their entry to the Scottish First Division in a match against Partick Thistle at Pittodrie on Saturday 19 August 1905. The graceful Duncan McNicol was absent through injury, which explains why the team which lined up for that historic debut was: Macfarlane; Murray and Brebner; Halkett, Strang and Low; Robertson, Henderson, Ward, McAuley and Lennie. Aberdeen went under 1–0 but had to wait just another fortnight to register their first win in the top division – a 2–0 result against Kilmarnock at Pittodrie. The season saw them finish in twelfth position of a sixteen-team league. During that first season, Bailie Milne, who had been chairman since the new club was formed in 1903, resigned through pressure of business and was succeeded by a Mr Harry Wyllie. Mr William Philip, a local painter who had been associated with the old Victoria United in 1888, joined the board.

The popular Duncan McNicol did not recover from that injury

and by season 1906–07 had given up the game, later to become the professional at Murcar golf course. The movement of players, that eternal and inevitable feature of the football scene, had already begun. Willie McAuley was transferred to Falkirk and goalkeeper Rab Macfarlane had turned down terms, so the manager went off and signed a big-name keeper of the time, Willie Stead from Southampton. Meanwhile, however, he had fixed up a promising local goalie, Cody Mutch from Inverurie, who turned out to be the star of the pre-season trial match – and Willie Stead never played at Pittodrie again! Cody later distinguished himself with Huddersfield. Jimmy Philip was never afraid to carry his spotting missions right into the heart of English football, and on one of those occasions he came back with Charlie O'Hagan, the Irish internationalist who played for Middlesbrough. Charlie was a real broth of a boy who loved the popularity which came to him through the Aberdeen crowd. As an inside-left, he teamed up with the great Willie Lennie and there would be a strong case for saying that it was the best left-wing partnership ever seen at Pittodrie. They became such an attraction in themselves that football followers in other parts of Scotland would turn out to an Aberdeen match just to watch the beautiful rhythms of O'Hagan and Lennie.

Season 1906–07 ended with the Black-and-Golds in twelfth position, a repeat of the previous year, and in the close season which followed they were to lose Henry Low, who had been a fine servant from the start but who was now on his way to Sunderland. That merely signalled the arrival of other names which were to write themselves indelibly into the Pittodrie story. The first to arrive was a young man from the West Lothian club of Broxburn Athletic, distinctive from the start because he was inseparable from his clay pipe. His name was Jock Hume and few could have guessed that he would become one half of a famous full-back partnership which remained the backbone of the Aberdeen defence for fourteen years. He also became one of the characters of Pittodrie.

When he finally left Aberdeen in 1921 he became player–coach to Darwen, a small town near Blackburn, then played for Arbroath and Peterhead before emigrating to America where he became trainer to Brooklyn Wanderers. Some say that it was on his recommendation that Aberdeen later signed the incomparable Alec Jackson, whom he played against when the latter was with Bethlehem Steel. Jock finally turned to refereeing and for twelve years was honoured with the handling of games at New York's

West Point Military Academy. That was where they had buried General George Custer, of Last Stand fame, and there were no doubt a few who wanted to 'dig a hole' for the Scots referee as well. But the solid figure of Jock Hume was not for intimidating. He finally returned to Aberdeen and died in 1962.

If Jock Hume was destined to be one half of a famous partnership, the other half appeared with even less of a hint that glory lay ahead. In the latter part of 1907, unheralded and unsung, a man of small build and modest manner slipped quietly into Pittodrie to become one of the most influential figures in the entire story of Aberdeen Football Club. The fact that he needs a chapter to himself indicates that his name was Donald Colman.

5
DONALD COLMAN

Donald Colman was surely one of the most remarkable men in the whole history of the game. Those people who remember him still glow with reverence at the mention of his name, such was the power of this quietly impressive gentleman.

Colman was born in Renton, Dunbartonshire, in 1878 and the first surprising fact about him is that his name was not Donald Colman at all. It was Donald Cunningham. Well brought up in a poor but proud home, young Donald spent a lot of time at his grandmother's, fired with a passion for football, which was not regarded as a sensible choice of career in those far-off days. So, when he first put pen to paper in local junior circles, he guarded his identity from the anticipated disapproval of his father by adopting his granny's surname. In later years, when he had made a career of football, his mother suggested that he should resume his own name, but by then it was all too well established and it stuck with him until he died of tuberculosis in Aberdeen in 1942, aged sixty-four. In the years between, he chalked up a career which is hard to believe.

As a boy, Colman (for that is what we shall call him) had carried the hamper for his local Renton team, which gained fame by winning the Scottish Cup. He played at full-back for Glasgow Perthshire, Tontine Athletic, Renton and Glasgow Maryhill (the team which had produced Willie Lennie), and developed into a player of some class, gaining a record number of junior international caps. But Colman was a man of small build and senior clubs fought shy of him. Sunderland tried him out against Hibernian but the Roker Park boss, Tom Watson, handed him his expenses, patted his head and said, 'You're a first-class little back but be advised by me, my mannie, you stay with the juniors. You're too little for senior football.'

What part that played in hindering his career is hard to say but Donald Colman did remain in junior football until he was twenty-seven. Finally, in 1905, he was given the chance to turn senior and signed for Motherwell but that lasted for only two seasons before he was considered to have entered the twilight of a mediocre career. The Fir Park club gave him a free transfer and that seemed to be the end of the line for Donald Colman.

Incredibly, at the age of twenty-nine, it was just the start. Two of his former team-mates at Maryhill, Jimmy Muir and Dinger Drain, were by then at Pittodrie and Donald travelled north with them one day for want of anything better to do. It was Jimmy Muir who asked for a quiet word with Aberdeen manager Jimmy Philip and said, 'Why not give Donald a run?' To his everlasting credit, Philip took a gamble and before the 1907–08 season was ended the Motherwell discard was established in the Aberdeen team, succeeding at last as a senior footballer when approaching his thirtieth birthday – and about to embark on a partnership of Colman and Hume which would last for nearly fourteen years. By the age of thirty-three he was being hailed as the best right-back in Scotland and in that same year his recognition was complete when he won the triple honour of being capped against England, Ireland and Wales. Where had Aberdeen found this man and, having been found, was there no stopping him? The football world was, understandably, baffled. Two years later he was still going strong for Aberdeen and Scotland and it took the outbreak of the First World War to prise him out of football and spirit him away to the battlefields of France. When the war ended Donald Colman returned to Pittodrie and, lo and beyond, he was still playing for Aberdeen in 1920 at the age of forty-two!

After that he 'voluntarily severed his connection' with the club, as befitted a gentleman; but this remarkable tale is far from over. Still a bachelor, Colman went off home to the Vale of Leven but only to become player–manager of Dumbarton, and the records show that he was still turning out as a player when he was forty-seven. At the risk of breaking the chronology of this story, let us follow through the rest of the Colman saga in all its revelations.

By 1931 another Dunbartonshire man and former Pittodrie player, Paddy Travers, was well established as manager of Aberdeen. He needed a trainer-coach to succeed the late Billy Russell and what better candidate than you-know-who? Then fifty-three, Donald Colman re-enters the Pittodrie story to begin a chapter which was perhaps more glorious than the first because it was a chapter of influence and innovation. Players who came under his guidance still marvel at his brilliant football mind which was capped by a delightful personality and a healthy, manly outlook on life which allowed no room for rough language. During that remarkable career, Colman was developing a philosophy about how to play football which was far ahead of his time and proves that some of the so-called recent thinking about the game is not so recent after all. In his playing days at Aberdeen he was friendly with a Mr Gordon Deans, who had business connections in Norway. When those Pittodrie days ended in 1920, he established a link with football in the land of the midnight sun and for the next ten years spent the close season telling the Norwegians how he thought the game should be played. By 1930 he was the uncrowned king of Norwegian soccer. During that same period, he was lecturing about football in Glasgow, advocating the use of the 'open space', running off the ball and experimenting with possession football.

He went to endless trouble to mould football boots to fit the feet, buying them slightly too small then working on the leather until it expanded to a suppleness which covered the foot like a sensitive glove. He worked his Aberdeen players into an awareness of two-footed play, training them with one boot and one sand-shoe to drill them into the use of that reluctant foot. His methods were a revelation to people who thought you just went out and kicked a ball to the best of your ability – and an inspiration to those players who were benefiting from it all.

But the inventive mind of Donald Colman ranged beyond the manipulation of a ball. Like every Scot of the time, he was deeply upset by the tragedy of Celtic goalkeeper John Thomson, who died after colliding with Sam English of Rangers in a game at Ibrox in 1931. But Colman was not the kind of man merely to sit down and mourn. He determined to do something about it, in the hope that that kind of tragedy would never happen again. He invented a headgear for goalkeepers but unfortunately it turned out to be too cumbersome and in the end had to be abandoned. Some of his other inventions were eminently more successful. It was Donald Colman, for example, who created the trainer's dugout – the very first one in Britain, probably in the world. Until that time, trainers had sat on a bench by the touchline, like the Continentals today. But Colman not only wanted to give shelter, he wanted to study footwork from a worm's eye view. There he would sit with a notebook and scribble out a running assessment of every game, pinpointing the good and the bad, so that mistakes could be sorted out during the Monday post-mortem. His Pittodrie dugout caused tremendous interest when Everton came to play Aberdeen in a friendly in the 1930s, and the Goodison Park official went back to Liverpool and built the first one in England.

Colman, as you will have gathered, was a perfectionist, an artistic full-back who was also a boxing enthusiast and a most accomplished dancer in everything from ballroom to Scottish country dancing. It was all to do with footwork, balance and rhythm and there was one Aberdeen player above all others whom he privately idolised because he personified his own dreams of football at its artistic best. Fair-mindedness would never have allowed him to show favouritism among his players but I am indebted for the information to his daughter Edna, now Mrs Brown of Summerhill Terrace, and his only son Donald (Cunningham, of course) who became a lecturer in English at Aberdeen College of Education. Who was that very special player? It will not surprise those fans of the 1930s to learn that it was Willie Mills, another product of the Vale of Leven and the perfect example of all that Colman had tried to teach. His admiration for Mills survived a criticism that he should have clinched the Scottish Cup Final for Aberdeen in 1937. Saddened as he was by the defeat, he resorted to the more human reaction of blaming the referee! Though Donald Colman was born in 1878, he did not marry until 1924 when he was forty-six, keeping up his reputation as a late starter. One outcome was that his family came late in his life and Donald and Edna are still fresh and lively people. Their time with their father was all too short, for he fell victim to tuberculosis which was still a major killer up to the Second World War; but they remember as children accompanying him to Pittodrie to help in the marking of the pitch. They lingered with him and absorbed a great deal of the man, fondly remembering, for example, his talent as a singer and finally rationalising their love and admiration into a single statement: 'He was just a wonderful father.' What better epitaph for Donald Colman, the man who proved that fairy-tales can be real? It is certain that no finer human being ever crossed the threshold of Pittodrie.

6
A RIGHT OLD RIOT

The arrival of Donald Colman did more than anything to bring a stability to the fledgling football club of Aberdeen and by the time that season had reached into March 1908, the Pittodrie team was heading for its first major experience in the upper echelons of Scottish football, the Scottish Cup semi-final.

There were no neutral venues for the penultimate stage in those days, so you can imagine the excitement when the game was announced for Pittodrie, especially since the opponents were to be Celtic. It was the year when Aberdeen had a player capped for the very first time in outside-left Willie Lennie, but the well-established club from Parkhead, already twenty years in existence, was brimful of international players, on top of which they were the Scottish Cup holders.

So the interest built up to an unprecedented pitch of enthusiasm as Pittodrie prepared for its first-ever 20,000 crowd on 21 March 1908. Celtic came north amid much publicity to stay at the Murtle Hydro and on the eve of the game both teams attended a performance at the Palace Theatre, Aberdeen. On the big day, the band of the Royal Engineers was there in all its glory to play for half an hour before the kick-off and the team which took the field was: Macfarlane; Colman and Hume; Halkett, McIntosh and Low; McDonald, Muir, Murray, O'Hagan and Lennie. It had all the ingredients of a great game but, alas, it turned out to be an anti-climax of dirty play in which, according to the commentators of the time, Aberdeen got the heavy end. It was duly reported that Charlie O'Hagan was fouled six times in five minutes and when the popular Irishman protested, the referee threatened to send him off. This roused the anger of the crowd and the referee held up the game and went across to lecture them too! When Celtic had scored the only goal of the game and it was all over, a hostile crowd pelted the visitors with stones for what they felt had been an exhibition of dirty tactics.

So crowd trouble is not entirely new. It was in that same period, for example, that there was a notorious crowd riot during a Rangers–Celtic game at Hampden and the patrons of Pittodrie were themselves no angels when it came to turning their anger into violence. In that same year of the Celtic visit, Hearts came to Pittodrie for what Aberdeen thought was a North-east Cup tie. Hearts, who arrived late, apparently told the referee that they were here for a friendly and he took the liberty of cutting the second half to thirty minutes. The crowd checked its pocket-watch and, in a state of bewilderment, invaded the field, smashed the pavilion windows, tore down advertising hoardings, pulled the King Street gate off its hinges and – shades of Wembley 1977 – tried to uproot the goalposts! In the following season, a referee abandoned a game with Kilmarnock because of snow and a dissatisfied crowd again attacked the Pittodrie pavilion. It took Donald Colman to come out from the dressing room and explain the position before they could be pacified.

Their favourite goalkeeper, Rab Macfarlane, had now left Aberdeen but they had taken kindly to local lad Cody Mutch, who had developed into a top-class keeper. What's more, the team was occupying the top of the Scottish League for the first time and, in the gathering interest, there were more and more women turning up at Pittodrie. Until 1908 they had been admitted free of charge but with their numbers increasing to significant proportions there was little sense in turning chivalry into insanity when a few bawbees could be collected from their presence. So the ladies were charged for admittance to the grandstand, such as it was.

Superstition was rife in those days and, in the fortnightly journey to the south, the Aberdeen players would never cross the Tay or Forth railway bridges without casting their coins. On his way to the Joint Station, Colman would never pass a certain blind beggar without giving him some money. Aberdeen fans swore that a particular Cup tie in the south was lost because their train killed a black cat at Cove. A local versifier wrote to the *Evening Express*:

> Poor cat, we mourn your awful fate
> No more will you be seen
> But why, I ask, should your demise
> Bring woe to Aberdeen?

In 1910 Aberdeen FC paid out its first benefit, to a man who had also brought its first international honour, the popular Willie Lennie. He collected a sum of £150. Wilfie Low had gone off to Newcastle and Aberdeen received, in part exchange, a splendid right-winger called Jimmy Soye, but that was only the start of a series of comings and goings. They also acquired W. D. Nichol, an Englishman serving in the Seaforths who became known as the 'Thunderbolt' for the power of his shot. Charlie O'Hagan refused Aberdeen's top terms and ended up with Morton, while the Pittodrie management replaced him with a name which was going to figure largely in the subsequent affairs of the club. Patrick Travers came from Clyde to establish a left wing of Travers and Lennie, which became just as effective as the O'Hagan–Lennie partnership had been. Later, when he had played for Celtic, coached in Norway and trained Dumbarton, he returned as Aberdeen's second manager when Jimmy Philip gave up in 1924.

But in that close season of 1910 his thoughts were only on playing football and among the new arrivals was one of his former teammates at Shawfield, centre-half Jock Wyllie. It did not take the Pittodrie crowds long to realize that in Big Jock they had a new personality, a real capture, a man who was robust but nimble and with a head of iron which he used to fine effect as he moved up to meet corner kicks. As a measure of Big Jock's heading power, he is reputed on one memorable occasion to have scored with a header from the half-way line! After two years, Jock went to Bradford City but did not take any more kindly to English football than the Pittodrie faithfuls did to losing him. So the discomfort all round was resolved to everyone's satisfaction when he was welcomed back with open arms.

Football in those days produced incidents which would be unthinkable today. Just picture the situation at Pittodrie on 3 September 1910, in a game with Hamilton Academicals, when the ball was kicked into one of the garden plots adjoining the popular-side terracing. A youth who went to retrieve it was warned off by a woman who was as indignant as she was substantial. Then Peter Simpson, the trainer, made an attempt but he too was driven into retreat. The mirth of the spectators, now standing with their backs to the pitch, reached its peak when a policeman went to bring some order to the situation and the formidable madam grabbed hold of him and bodily threw him out. Finally, somebody tumbled on the wisdom of producing another ball.

Two weeks later Aberdeen, who had not saved a single point at Ibrox in five seasons of First Division football, went to Glasgow in determined mood and collected them both, an accomplishment which raised new pride in the Granite City. The team which broke the Ibrox duck was: King; Colman and Hume; Wilson, Wyllie and Millar; Soye, McIntosh, Murray, Travers and Lennie. That was Colman's hundredth game since joining the club in 1907 and in that time he had missed only one.

Still with unusual incidents, spectators were baffled one Saturday to see Arthur King, who had taken over in goal from Cody Mutch, grabbing a ball from the Falkirk left-winger while standing well inside his goal-net area. It did not seem possible from that angle. Falkirk claimed a goal but the referee discovered that the ball had reached King's hands after bursting through the side netting.

Aberdeen were now top of the Scottish League, with some spectacular goals coming from outside-right Jimmy Soye, and they were soon the target team for others to beat. Incentives were not uncommon in those days and when the team travelled to play Partick Thistle, one of the Firhill players mentioned that they were on a £4 bonus if they could be the first team to beat Aberdeen that season. The Pittodrie players hastily confronted chairman Tom Duncan with a request for a similar bonus and, while he could not commit his board to this kind of undertaking, he did promise some reward if they put up a good show. In the event, Partick's players collected their £4 bonus and the men from the north were awarded an extra ten shillings for their first defeat of the season on the grounds that they had put up a plucky fight.

The commercialism of 1910 had little to learn from the modern day. In that same year a Greenock butcher was offering a lamb to any Morton player who could score a goal in a game against Rangers. With a liking for a tender chop, former Pittodrie player Charlie O'Hagan went out and scored five goals for Morton and collected his small flock of sheep – and a poorer but wiser Greenock butcher restricted his generosity to cutlets thereafter!

Rangers were then due at Pittodrie, having been beaten by Aberdeen at Ibrox that season but never having lost a game in the Granite City. The question of whether Aberdeen could bring off the double was unresolved with three minutes left to play and still no scoring. Then Willie Lennie took a corner kick on the left and Angus McIntosh came up to head home the winner. At last Rangers had been beaten at Pittodrie. Neutral linesmen came into force on

New Year's Day 1911 and soon it was Celtic's turn to appear at Pittodrie. They too came a cropper, with a last-minute goal from Jimmy Soye, who regarded it as the best he had ever scored – and Jimmy scored some remarkable ones. So Aberdeen had notched up an Old Firm double, largely inspired by Donald Colman, now in his thirty-third year but just at the start of an international career. He was growing in stature by the week, a small body with a shrewd brain and a brave heart, impressing the wider public and sparking off a rash of verses like:

> We hae a back in Aberdeen
> His like this toun has never seen
> For sterling pluck and judgement keen
> There's nane can match wi' Donald.

There was a promise in the spring of 1911 when Aberdeen once again found themselves in the semi-final of the Scottish Cup, due to play Celtic at Parkhead this time, and still joint League leaders with Rangers. But the Old Firm took the respective titles, and the best that could be said of Aberdeen was that they were making their mark on Scottish football and that their success was being noticed on the Continent. The sequel to that was an invitation to tour the romantic lands of Bohemia, Moravia and Poland and off they set to play eight games in two weeks, with a total strength of only twelve players. They lost the first game but won the other seven and full-back Jock Hume distinguished himself when he was drafted to centre-forward and scored eighteen goals!

Back home there was disappointment that Paddy Travers, who had business interests in Glasgow, was being transferred to Celtic along with W. D. Nichol. But the most notable incident of 1911–12 was that, after stone-throwing at an Aberdeen–Rangers match in which the visitors' half-back, Jimmy Gordon, was said to have been set upon by spectators and was saved only by the intervention of Aberdeen players, the SFA decided to close Pittodrie for two weeks. In fact, the punishment was ineffective since Aberdeen were due to play away from home on both the weeks in question.

It was in that close season that Jock Wyllie was transferred to Bradford City for £300, a move which caused ructions in the board-room despite the consolation that Paddy Travers was returning from Celtic. On the national scene there was an imaginative move to cater for the supporters who were unable to see football on a

Saturday; the six top teams – Rangers, Celtic, Aberdeen, Dundee, Hearts and Hibernian – formed themselves into an Inter-City League, with midweek games. But the clubs themselves failed to sustain a noble concept, fielding under-strength teams who were inclined to treat the games as friendlies, and the whole thing flopped and disappeared as quickly as it had arisen. More substantially, Aberdeen had now established a second team to play in the Highland League along with Buckie Thistle, Elgin City, Forres Mechanics, the 93rd (Argyll and Sutherland Highlanders) and the four Inverness clubs, Clachnacuddin, Caledonian, Thistle and Citadel.

In the First Division, however, Aberdeen were in the doldrums and, in the general unrest, there was talk of transfers. Manchester City came north waving a cheque for £1000 to secure the signature of the illustrious Colman but Donald drew himself to his full height and, with touching loyalty, made it patently plain that he had no wish to leave Pittodrie and that was that.

7
ENTER THE 'DONS'

So far in the story from 1903 I have not spoken of the 'Dons', because the popular term of today had not yet found its way into the local vocabulary. People have argued down the years about how the players of Aberdeen Football Club came to be known in that way. There are those who say that it comes from the educational use of the word, pointing to the fact that eight of the twelve people who formed the original club in 1881 were school teachers, and that another don of education, Mr John Clarke, was chairman when the present club was created in 1903. It is an interesting theory but I believe it has no foundation. While they may speak of dons at Oxford or Cambridge, it is not a word which found much favour in the fishyards of Torry or the sharny byres of Buchan. More likely it arose as a simple contraction of 'Aberdonian', turning it firstly into 'Come on the 'Donians' and then 'Come on the Dons!'

If there is doubt about how it arose, at least there was one man who claimed he could pinpoint the day when it was first used in print in the local press. The meticulous George Sleigh, who was a sports writer with *Aberdeen Journal* in the earlier part of the century, maintained that it first appeared, for some unaccountable reason, after an Aberdeen–Celtic game at Pittodrie on 15 February 1913. Before then they were the 'Black-and-Golds' or the 'Wasps'.

But now they were the 'Dons', celebrating the occasion with a 3–0 win over Celtic in a game which marked the very first appearance of one of the worthies of his day, Dod Brewster from Mugiemoss, whose signature was obtained just an hour before a Sunderland man arrived on his doorstep.

Throughout this period that other popular Don, the incomparable Donald Colman, was playing with splendid consistency despite his thirty-five years and there was local disappointment when he was chosen only as a reserve against Ireland in Dublin. On the morning of the game, however, the selectors decided not only to include him in the team but to appoint him captain and Colman, the legend who found international fame in the twilight of his career, strode out to play yet another magnificent match and to lead Scotland to a 2–1 victory, maintaining his record of never having played in a losing Scottish side.

In that season 1912–13 the Dons utilised twenty-one players whose names, for the record, were: Arthur King, Andy Greig, Donald Colman, Jock Hume, Bobby Hannah, Stewart Davidson, George Wilson, Jock McConnell, Dod Brewster, Fred Watson, Willie Low, Jimmy Soye, Pat Travers, Davie Main, Johnny Wood, Willie Lennie, Johnny Scorgie, Joe Walker, Willie Milne, Bertie Murray and Angus McIntosh. Financially the Dons were running through a lean spell and were in no position to go into the buying market.

Both Colman and Hume had turned down offers to tempt them away but Stewart Davidson left for Middlesbrough, Willie Milne went to Third Lanark and goalkeeper Arthur King went to Spurs, having taken a lot of barracking from a section of the crowd. Meanwhile, there had been the cry to bring back Jock Wyllie, who was sorely missed, and it was then that manager Jimmy Philip and director William Philip were despatched to see what they could do. Jock was then captain of Bradford City but they managed to bring him back. After eight years, Pittodrie's first internationalist, Willie Lennie, had been transferred to Falkirk for what seemed like the ridiculous fee of £30, and public unrest about the poor form of the team was reflected in the number of letters which poured into the newspaper offices. With a show of public-spiritedness, the editor of the *Evening Express* announced that he had been receiving a lot of critical mail but that, in view of the club's lowly position and poor attendances, he did not think that it was in the interests of the game in Aberdeen to publish it. In the spring of 1914 flagging interest was revived with a benefit game for Johnny Edgar in which the team of the day faced a selection of former Dons and won 4–2. The line-up that April day was: Present – Greig; Colman and Hannah; Chatwin, J. J. Simpson and Low; Wyllie, Walker, Main, Travers and Scorgie; Former – Rab Macfarlane; George Macfarlane, Jimmy Gault; Ecky Halkett, Wilfie Low, Henry Low; D. Taylor (Argyll), Bertie Murray, Dr Jock Sangster, Charlie O'Hagan and Willie Lennie.

In the close season of 1914, Paddy Travers went back to his

native Dumbarton and Aberdeen signed a new personality, a goal-keeper from Tyneside who had been with Newcastle and Sunderland. His name was George Anderson, a man who was soon taken to the hearts of the Pittodrie crowd and later became a leading citizen of Aberdeen – town councillor, businessman and wartime manager, before becoming mastermind of Dundee and projecting the talent of the famous Billy Steel. Another signing of that time was Bert MacLachlan, whose wish to return from Aston Villa to Scotland was picked up by the keen intelligence service at Pittodrie. Bert, who was a cousin of future manager Davie Halliday, settled down at left-half and later became captain in a period of the 1920s which was to produce some of the top names in the Pittodrie story. For the moment, Bobby Archibald arrived from Third Lanark and John Robertson, a city tinsmith and a good judge of a player, joined the board and later became chairman.

But the assassination at Sarajevo had sparked off the First World War and if a lifestyle which had survived for centuries was about to be destroyed forever, then little wonder that the equilibrium of organized football began to feel the ripples. Fearing that the game might have to be suspended altogether, the Scottish Football Association consulted the War Office and it was agreed that they should carry on as long as possible. But the players were members of the Territorials and some were off to the war. Bobby Hannah was mobilised for the 7th Gordons and Alec Wright for the 4th Battalion. There was fleeting excitement for the visit of a Queen's Park team which included an outside-right called Alan Morton, before he transferred to the other wing and became the Wee Blue Devil of Ibrox, the most venerated Rangers player of all time. In the movement and uncertainty of wartime, the Gordon Highlanders appearing in Aberdeen jerseys included Mungo Hutton, later to become a famous Scottish referee as well as Aberdeen scout in the west of Scotland. As the nation began to feel the effect of war, the crowds fell away and there was a need for cuts in club spending. The League and the Players' Union agreed that footballers receiving £2 10s per week and over would take a reduction of twenty-five per cent. The Scottish Cup was abandoned and by 1916, with events leading up to the unspeakable horrors of the Somme, the war news was so bad that the public could raise little enthusiasm for football. Mourning armbands became a regular feature, reflecting the fate of young men in the glaur and stench and din of some foreign field, too far removed from the swaying corn-parks of Aberdeenshire.

The first of the black bands was for John Mackay, a Dons director and quartermaster in one of the Aberdeen companies of the Royal Engineers, who was killed in Flanders. Then came CSM Charlie Neilson from Ellon, an outside-left who was killed with the 5th Gordons. The war had brought an unfamiliar look to the team as well as chaotic incidents, like missing a connection to Kilmarnock, having to change on the train and running on to the field twenty-five minutes late, only to be beaten 7–0. But there was the friendliness and helpfulness which became features of both world wars. For example, Raith Rovers arrived at Pittodrie without a goalkeeper at a time when they were bottom of the League and the Dons were second from bottom. The home team obligingly gave Raith Rovers the services of Andy Greig for the day – and he helped to inflict defeat on his own team!

The Dons struggled on through the turmoil of war but finally the burden became too much and it was agreed that Aberdeen, Dundee and Raith Rovers should drop out of competitive football until conditions improved. From 1917 until 1919 there was no senior football in Aberdeen and the club turned its attention to the local amateur league, giving it a great deal of help and encouragement. Much of the success of that competition was due to a man called Billy Russell, who must surely have done more than most people to foster the game of football in Aberdeen. As a motivator in all grades of the game, he laboured with a devotion which helped inestimably to promote football in the public mind of the North-east. Eventually he gave up his job as a foreman tinsmith to become the Dons' trainer.

With the war now drawn to an end in what was called a victory, though the trail of human destruction left precious little room for celebration, Aberdeen Football Club began to pick up the threads of normality again. Appropriately, the very first player they signed after the First World War was to become one of the most famous of all Dons. His name was Jock Hutton, the most jovial chap who ever wore a football jersey. Later generations will conjure up a more accurate picture of the man if I say he was very much the build and style of Don Emery, only 5 ft 8 in in height but reckoned to be well in excess of fifteen stone, though his actual weight was never published, for diplomatic reasons. He did not use that massive bulk and strength to unfair advantage, though there were occasions when he executed a perfectly fair shoulder charge and opposing players were launched with all the lift-off of a guided missile. But

Jock was a happy, likeable man romping through a game with the same jolly abandon he showed in life. Money, they said, burned holes in his pocket, yet Jock would come up smiling even when he couldn't lay his hands on a shilling.

For all his size, Jock was regarded as a soft and kindly soul and not a little gullible. On the payroll at Pittodrie in the 1920s was a real wee Glasgow joker called Johnny Paton, who sometimes spent the weekend at home after a game in the south, returning to Pittodrie on the Monday morning. He would arrive back with a special greeting for Jock, saying, 'I have something here to interest you, Jock – a gold watch.' And Jock would look at it and say, 'How much?' and the wee fellow would reply, 'Ach, £3 to you.' Three days later the 'gold' would peel off, which was no more than you could have expected from a so-called bargain which had been picked up at the Barrowlands of Glasgow on the Sunday. But all that happened later.

When Partick Thistle came north on 21 April 1919 for a friendly which was intended to help Aberdeen FC restore its contact with the game, Aberdeen fielded the sturdy youngster from Bellshill Athletic. He played the game with a scarf round his neck, but whatever mirth that aroused, the Pittodrie crowd were soon much more engrossed in the actual performance of the young man. Jock Hutton may have been destined to be Scotland's right-back but he was fielded at inside-left that day, opening the scoring with a perfect header, then rounding several Partick players to score again with a fierce shot which had everyone talking. That cannonball kick was soon to become the hallmark of Hutton's play. Manager Jimmy Philip realised after the game that he hadn't signed him and hastened to Motherwell on the Monday morning, thankful that the Partick Thistle party, with whom Jock had travelled south, had not discovered that he was not already an Aberdeen player.

So the war was finally behind them and at the annual general meeting of 1 August 1919 chairman Tom Duncan reported that thirty-three players and officials of Aberdeen Football Club had served in the forces and eight of them had died: Dr J. Ellis Milne, John Mackay, Herbert Murray, the brothers Charlie and J. H. Neilson, John Munro, Angus McLeod and Fred Watson.

The Scottish League gave £1130 towards the on-costs for the two blank seasons and the club decided to increase the share capital from £1500 to £5000, bringing in many new shareholders.

Big-time football in Aberdeen resumed on 16 August 1919 with a Scottish League game against Albion Rovers, a game for which the club dared to introduce the shilling gate, which represented a doubling of the entrance money but did not deter 9000 people from turning out to see an Aberdeen victory. The team on that historic return was: Anderson; Hannah, Hume; Wright, Brewster, MacLachlan; C. G. Watson, Caie, Hutton, Robertson, Archibald. Jacky Connon, one of the best local players ever seen at Pittodrie, was also edging his way into the team and Jock Hutton was soon to be moved to full-back.

The wider world had been turned inside out in history's greatest upset and football was suffering no less from a sense of lost continuity, but if there was one event which could restore a touch of normality to the slopes of Pittodrie, it would surely be the return of Donald Colman. Demobilised from the forces, he had fulfilled a coaching engagement in Norway and by the end of 1919 was back in Aberdeen, now past his best (which was not surprising when you consider that he was by then forty-one) but still a stabilising influence and a welcome link with an age which had gone for ever.

If Colman was back, another Pittodrie favourite was on his way to fresh pastures. The New Year's Day game (the rest of Scotland calls it Ne'erday, but not us!) against Dundee was Dod Brewster's last for the Dons before he was transferred to Everton for an Aberdeen record fee of £1500, and that marked the start of a new series of transfers which enabled the Dons to improve their ground and build a new stand. Dod became a big favourite in English football and a year later was capped for Scotland against England at Hampden, playing alongside Stewart Davidson, another former Don who was by then captain of Middlesbrough.

Aberdeen's first Scottish Cup tie after the war was at Cowdenbeath on 27 January 1920, a day which produced yet another illustration of hooliganism on the soccer slopes of Scotland. Aberdeen's line-up at Cowdenbeath was: Anderson; Colman, Hume; Wright, Robertson, MacLachlan; Grant, W. Wyllie, Connon, Hutton, Archibald.

In the closing minutes of that Scottish Cup tie the Dons were a goal up when the home team claimed a penalty. The referee's refusal brought hundreds of Cowdenbeath supporters swarming on to the pitch and there was fighting and shouting everywhere. The Dons found their way to the pavilion barred by an angry crowd but the crisis produced its own hero in the shape of a gigantic sailor who jumped down from the stand and assumed the role of Popeye, the Pittodrie protector, cleaving a way to the dressing room with threatening fists. Goalkeeper George Anderson had farthest to come and became isolated in an ugly scene from which he emerged so badly mauled that he had to be carried to the pavilion in a state of collapse.

Meanwhile, burly Jock Hutton was employing the granite structure of his frame to rescue referee Stevenson, whose penalty decision had caused the riot. Mr Stevenson decided there was no time to resume the game anyway and the Dons were thankful to escape from the Fife town without further injury, through now to another round of the Scottish Cup in which they were drawn away from home against Gala Fairydean.

For a financial consideration, however, the Border team agreed to switch the venue to Pittodrie and that game on 7 February 1920, which drew a crowd of 15,000, was the first Scottish Cup tie seen at Pittodrie since 1914. A month later, in a game against Raith Rovers, the Dons produced a lanky centre-half, an amateur called Victor E. Milne, a medical student of Aberdeen University and a player whose performance soon had the spectators waxing enthusiastic. When he signed as a professional for the following season he was completing a half-back line of Wright, Milne and MacLachlan which subsequent players like Willie Cooper would claim to be the finest half-line ever seen at Pittodrie. As it happened, Vic Milne was the son of that early chairman of the club, Bailie Milne, and football was by no means his only interest. Playing cricket for Aberdeenshire was just one of his many sporting outlets, though football claimed him in the end and he became a big name in England after joining Aston Villa, and retained his connection in later life by becoming doctor to the Birmingham club.

In that year of 1920 Donald Colman was forty-two, long past the limit of a normal football lifespan but still in harness at Pittodrie. Indeed, any suggestion of a free transfer would have been an unthinkable act of indecency towards a man of such stature. So it was left to the great little man himself to bow out gracefully, before embarking seriously on his next big task – fostering the game of football in Norway. His partner of so many seasons, Jock Hume, departed to become player–coach of Darwen, a Lancashire club, and the veteran Jock Wyllie, for whom Colman had a great affection, went to Forfar.

The feeling that an era had ended spread from dressing room to board-room where there were ructions among the directors, ending with the resignation of Tom Duncan, who had been chairman for fourteen years. The row centred around manager Jimmy Philip, who had reverted to part-time managership during the First World War. In restoring the job to a full-time one, some directors felt that it should be advertised but the majority decided to offer it to Philip who had, after all, been there since 1903. Perhaps that was long enough in the eyes of some directors, but in any case he was offered his former status at a salary of £350 and he did not hesitate to accept it. Tom Duncan was replaced as chairman by another man called Philip, this time William.

8
BLACKWELL'S UMBRELLA

The legendary Donald Colman had played his last game for Aberdeen against Kilmarnock at Rugby Park on 21 April 1920 and, with the departure of his full-back partner Jock Hume as well, the Dons were faced with the long-forgotten task of finding full-backs. But luck was on their side when they found a junior internationalist from Glasgow Perthshire called Matt Forsyth. When it was also discovered that the young Hutton was really a full-back and not a forward, they came up with a new partnership of Hutton and Forsyth, which turned out to be just as successful, if not as long-lived, as that of Colman and Hume.

Forsyth had a fine football brain, much in the style of Colman, cool and calculating and the perfect contrast to the rumbustious Hutton, whose later international career owed much to the influence of Forsyth. Matt had come back from the First World War, where he was fighting on the Somme, and was keenly pursued by English clubs but his mother was a widow and his deal with Aberdeen allowed him to stay in Glasgow and travel up for games on the Friday night. Working for a firm which acted as an agent for the London and North-Eastern Railway, he was able to get a cheap ticket. As a player he was stylish and adventurous, introducing to his play the 'overlap' when neither the word nor the idea had gained currency. Indeed, full-backs who ever dared to cross the half-way line in those days were liable to be carpeted for their indiscretion! Matt trained with Third Lanark and travelled up with them for a game at Pittodrie. During the match he came forward on one of his adventures and unleashed a tremendous shot towards Jimmy Brownlie, that rugged and memorable character who used to keep goal for the Hi-Hi. The big keeper rose to meet it and caught his hand between the crossbar and the ball. On the journey back to Glasgow, Matt was walking down the train corridor when a voice boomed out: 'Hey, young man; I want a word with you.' A slightly apprehensive Forsyth stuck his head into the Brownlie compartment. 'What the hell d'ye think you are – a centre-foward? In future, stay back where you belong, at left-back!' the big goalie demanded, stabbing a fractured finger in the direction of the Dons player.

But not all the rumblings of big Jimmy could stifle the class of Matt Forsyth, who was the perfect thinking partner for Hutton. He smiled when he recalled the likeable warmth of big Jock and said, 'As often as not, his hefty clearances came straight back from where he had sent them.'

The pity of it was that a player like Forsyth did not get the same international recognition as Jock Hutton, who had seven caps during his years at Pittodrie and several more after he left. Matt, by comparison, had the doubtful consolation of being a Scottish reserve on no fewer than thirteen occasions!

Matt had been a schoolboy witness of the first big Ibrox disaster at the start of the century and was present again at Hampden in 1909 when the Rangers–Celtic Scottish Cup Final ended in a riot, the crowd calling for extra time, invading the field, ripping up the goalposts and generally wrecking the place. He worked for the Admiralty for many years at Scapa Flow and then in London but finally returned to Aberdeen, a lively octogenarian regaling a circle of friends with tales of long ago. Indeed, making friends had always been a talent of Matt Forsyth, who had a strong touch of the theatrical personality. He knew Harry Lauder, Marie Lloyd and not least Dr Walford Bodie, the man from Macduff who became world famous for his extraordinary hypnotic powers. He also befriended that great jockey, Steve Donoghue, during his visits to the Scottish racecourses and went to see him winning the Epsom Derby of 1922 on the back of Captain Cuttle.

Apart from Forsyth, there were other personalities gathering at Pittodrie in the transition to a new era, including Sandy Grosert, later a dentist in the city, who came back from Hibs with a high reputation, having previously played for the Dons as an amateur. In his unpaid days at Pittodrie, Sandy had an unwritten stipulation in his agreement that the manager would provide him with a bottle of stout after his Saturday games – and Jimmy Philip fulfilled his bargain.

There was also an attempt to gather up as many of the promising local youngsters as possible and these included Andy Rankin from

Banks o'Dee (one of the best players ever to come from the Aberdeen junior ranks), George Sutherland, Alec Wright, Victor Milne, Arthur Robertson, Clarence Watt (Clarty), Walter Grant, Jacky Connon and Bobby Yule.

With size and strength, that combination of Wright, Milne and MacLachlan was establishing itself as a brilliant half-back line. A young goalkeeper arrived from Scunthorpe to play a trial game and was soon to become popularly entrenched as Harry Blackwell, worthy successor to George Anderson and the first leg of a back division which rolled off every North-eastern tongue as 'Blackwell, Hutton and Forsyth'. Out Bucksburn way, young Alec Moir was scoring forty goals for Mugiemoss in one season and a man from Leeds United arrived in Aberdeen one Friday night to complete the signing transaction first thing next morning. Word reached manager Jimmy Philip, who headed out Great Northern Road at one o'clock in the morning to contact Moir and sign him on the spot. He played many fine games for Aberdeen but never did make the position of centre-forward his own.

Jimmy Smith was brought from Rangers to be hailed by the Pittodrie crowds as their best left-winger since Willie Lennie, and behind the scenes Pat Travers was engaged as coach, having finished his own playing career and returned to his native Dumbarton as trainer to the local football team. Travers, like his former Pittodrie team-mate Donald Colman, was far from finished with Aberdeen Football Club.

Meanwhile, in that season of 1920–22 the system of promotion and relegation had been introduced to Scottish football. Hearts came to Pittodrie desperately needing a win to escape the Second Division and they got it, in a game which sparked off criticism that Aberdeen 'lay down' to make sure that the valuable asset of the Edinburgh club would not be lost to the top division. The Tynecastle team, in fact, continued to escape relegation for another fifty-five years until 1977, when it reduced to an elite of three – Rangers, Celtic and Aberdeen – the number of Scottish clubs which have yet to go down.

But of all the Pittodrie talking points of the early 1920s, there was none so notorious as the Scottish Cup third-round tie of 1923. That was the occasion when the Dons were drawn against Peterhead in what turned out to be the craziest game of football ever seen at Pittodrie, or anywhere else for that matter. For a start, it was due to be played at Peterhead but Aberdeen persuaded the Blue

Mogganers to give up their ground rights in exchange for a hard-driven bargain of a £250 guarantee, plus travelling expenses for players and directors and a visit of the Aberdeen League team to Peterhead before the end of the season. In anticipation of defeat, the Highland League team was making sure that there would be ample compensation. But matters were not so simple as that. News of the terms brought an immediate demand from the Peterhead players to be paid £10 a man. The club dug in its heels, refused to pay the money except for a win, and finally fielded a team which was without eight of its regular players. As small consolation, the management had been able to sign Jock Hume, the former Dons stalwart, just before the game but the rest were simply a motley gathering scraped together for the occasion. Among them were C. P. Murray and J. T. Wiseman, secretary and captain of the Aberdeen University side, who gave rise to the kind of complications which would produce heart attacks at the headquarters of the Scottish Football Association today. Murray and Wiseman had to be listed under false names because they had already played in the qualifying stages of the Scottish Cup earlier that season – against Peterhead! However, small matters like an illegal team did not deter them in those more colourful times. The two players were widely recognised for their true identities and, if by some mischance Peterhead had won that game, Aberdeen captain Bert MacLachlan was fully primed, as he later confirmed, to lodge a protest about Peterhead's unlawful team before the game ended.

In the event, that was hardly necessary. Aberdeen's 5–0 lead at half-time became 13–0 before the end, by which time two Peterhead players, Buchan and McRobbie, had retired to the pavilion suffering from exposure! The game was played on a day of gale-force wind and rain so bad that, over in Advocates Park, the strong-going Port Glasgow conceded their Scottish Junior Cup tie to the popular Aberdeen club Richmond half-way through the second half rather than suffer any more.

Back at Pittodrie the fixture was farcical enough without the weather, but the Aberdeen goalkeeper, Harry Blackwell, set a new fashion between the sticks by wearing a waterproof coat – and raising a spectator's umbrella – which he removed on the one and only occasion when Peterhead ventured within shooting distance of his goal.

A gallant crowd of 3241 huddled together for the miserable occasion, having paid a total of £181 8s 11d at the gate, a sum which left Aberdeen well out of pocket with the deal. The teams that day, as published in the morning papers (and note how the papers relieved themselves of responsibility for the false names), were: Aberdeen – Blackwell; Hutton, Forsyth; MacLachlan, Milne, Robertson; Middleton, Thomson, Grant, Rankin and Smith. Peterhead ('as supplied') – Drysdale; J. K. Allan, Hume; F. Thomson, J. Buchan, G. Slessor; W. Hutcheson, G. Allan, A. McRobbie, A. Hall and W. Milne.

The goals, for the interest of those with masochistic tendencies, were scored by Grant (3), Thomson (4), Milne (3), Rankin, Middleton and Smith. They would have done better to have saved some of the goals for the fourth round, because they promptly went out of the Cup at the hands of Hibs.

9
HUTTON'S CURE

Just as Donald Colman had played in all three home internationals in season 1910–11, Jock Hutton was similarly capped in 1922–23 when Scotland won the Championship with wins over Ireland and Wales and a draw with England at Hampden.

The Wales game was played that year at Paisley and it was known in advance that Hutton was quietly worried about facing up to the famous Ted Vizard, Bolton Wanderers' outside-left. On the forenoon of the game, Aberdeen sports writer George Sleigh met Jock walking in Argyle Street, Glasgow, asked how he was feeling and was given the rather confidential information that he was suffering from a dose of diarrhoea. Suspecting the reason, George suggested a glass of good port wine as a known cure for the internal disruption and Jock was more than receptive to the idea. But Scotland's right-back could hardly be seen in a pub on the day of a big game, so the two of them found a quiet retreat and George administered a good stiff dose of his recommended medicine. Jock said he felt much the better for that and proceeded to the game. In fact, Vizard was pulled out of the Welsh team at the last minute due to injury, while Jock played a splendid game and went on to establish himself in a distinguished international career, diarrhoea or no diarrhoea!

Meanwhile, the staffing position at Pittodrie was far from settled. Centre-half Vic Milne, by then a doctor and a man commanding great respect, was on the move to Aston Villa, leaving behind not only the football scene of Pittodrie but the cricketing fraternity of the Aberdeenshire club for whom he had been a sound bat and an effective change bowler. But if they were losing a doctor, the Dons directors replaced him with a budding minister, Jimmy Jackson from Motherwell, who took up his divinity studies in Aberdeen and later played for Liverpool before taking over a Presbyterian church in the north of England. Stewart Davidson, who had gone to Middlesbrough in 1911, came back in 1923, clearly past his best but still a good influence on those around him. By now the Dons had shaped into a formation of: Blackwell; Hutton, Forsyth; Davidson, J. Jackson, MacLachlan; Moir, Grant, Miller, Rankin and Smith.

But the movement of players had far from stopped (does it ever in football?). Jock Edward, a Glasgow junior, arrived in Aberdeen, where he had several fine seasons before moving to Portsmouth, later returning as player–coach to Huntly and settling in business in Torry, like his close friend Harry Blackwell. Among the other arrivals was little Johnny Paton (the one who sold the watch to Jock Hutton), an amusing little fellow who had played for Celtic and Third Lanark and could dribble through a defence with a bundle of tricks in his boots. His humour conveyed itself to the crowds who enjoyed his antics, but it was not always appreciated by the referees. On a bitterly cold day he took the field in a game to be refereed by David Calder (brother of the famous Bobby, later Aberdeen's chief scout). Rubbing his hands together before the start, Johnny nodded to the referee with Glasgow perkiness and said, 'I'm cauld, ref – but you're Calder.' Mr Calder looked around to see if anyone was within earshot then told him: 'Watch it, you little bugger, or I'll send you off the park!'

Manager Philip was as eager as ever to catch local talent and, indeed, his enthusiasm landed him in trouble. There had been a delay in signing Alex Ross from the local Richmond club and Dundee stepped in to sign him on a Sunday. Next morning the lad informed Mr Philip of the move but mentioned that the signing had not been witnessed. Philip's eyes brightened. What was more, he reckoned that a Sunday signature was illegal and promptly persuaded the player to sign for Aberdeen instead, dashing off to Glasgow to register him and to announce to the press that he would play for the Aberdeen reserves on Saturday. Ross returned the signing-on fee to Dundee, who were furious about it. Not unnaturally they reported the matter to the SFA who held an inquiry and declared that the lad from Richmond was a Dundee player. He was severely censured and Aberdeen Football Club was fined £100, though the Association accepted Philip's explanation about his understanding of a Sunday contract.

With twenty years of history now behind them, the Dons were still searching for a national prize and hopes were rising in season 1923–24 when they reached the semi-final of the Scottish Cup for the fourth time. They had been there in 1908 and 1911, beaten both times by Celtic, and again in 1922 when Morton won through to the final. This time it was Hibernian who provided the opposition at Dens Park, Dundee, and a goalless draw was followed by a replay at Dens, followed by extra time which still produced no goals. As the marathon continued, Hibs managed to score one goal amid protests that the talented Tim Dunn, later to become a Wembley Wizard, had steadied the ball with his hand. But the goal stood and Hibs went through to the Scottish Cup Final, leaving Aberdeen fans to wonder when they were ever to savour the sweet smell of success. On top of all that, the club itself was running into trouble. Between those Scottish Cup replays the Dons had to play Queen's Park, who were deep in relegation trouble, and the team which took the field was without Hutton, Forsyth, Davidson, Miller, Rankin and Smith. It could have been argued that they were saving their players for the gruelling Cup tie but the blunt criticism was that they were trying to help Queens. Charles Forbes, a future chairman, was playing for Aberdeen in a team which showed no lack of effort to win the game. But Queen's Park were the victors and Clyde Football Club, who were also in relegation trouble, lodged a complaint that Aberdeen had purposely fielded a weakened team. Jimmy Philip said his players had been left out on doctor's orders but that did not satisfy the League Committee and the Dons were fined another £100. At the end of that season Queen's did escape and poor old Clyde went down.

In May 1924 Aberdeen toured Germany and the big talking point on their return was the resignation of manager Philip, the local wood-turner who had been given the part-time appointment in 1903 and had guided the club through its formative years. He had brought the city of Aberdeen into the mainstream of Scottish football, harnessed the talents of great players such as Colman and Hume and the club's first internationalist, the inimitable Willie Lennie; he had restored life after the barren period of the Great War, and had taken the club into the 'Roaring Twenties' with the famous full-back partnership of Hutton and Forsyth. Admittedly there was no silver to show for his efforts but then it takes a long time to establish a structure of tradition in football and Aberdeen had had less time than most. Under the guidance of Jimmy Philip, the Dons had come through their first twenty-one years; they had come of age and were now maturing, though it was to be another twenty-one years and more before any kind of trophy was to grace the Pittodrie sideboard. Yet, much as we rejoice in the winning of cups and flags, it is the personalities and the performances at least as much as the prizes which tend to linger in the mind when the period has passed into the grey mists of history.

Colman and Hume, Hutton and Forsyth won nothing at all at club level and the same fate was to befall other great Dons such as Benny Yorston, Willie Mills and Matt Armstrong as well as those famous half-lines of Wright–Milne–MacLachlan and Black–McLaren–Hill. There was not a medal between them. Yet every one of those names stirred a glow in the hearts of Dons supporters according to their ages.

Jimmy Philip became a director after he retired. He also became interested in the MacGregor clan and its annual gathering and it was during a MacGregor day in Belfast that he was involved in a road accident and died in 1930. In those earlier days his son George had shown an interest in playing football but was diverted by the caution of a father who pointed to the dangers of committing everything to football and having nothing to fall back on when the playing days were over. 'Look at the people who were once footballers and who ended up as sandwich-board men on Union Street,' he used to point out to young George. 'No, son, you should go to sea.' And George did and carved a fine career for himself, becoming captain of an oil tanker before returning to dry land and taking over the Crown Bar in Woodside. So Jimmy Philip was gone and the choice as his successor was almost predictably Patrick Travers, the Dumbarton man of stocky build and pawky humour who had played for Aberdeen and Celtic, trained his home-town team and finally returned to coach Aberdeen. In that summer of 1924 he was about to embark on a fourteen-year reign as Pittodrie boss which would produce its own tragedy and high drama, as well as an array of memorable footballers.

Before his departure Jimmy Philip had begun negotiations for a transfer which would bring to Pittodrie one of Scottish football's greatest personalities. The fact that the deal was completed by Paddy Travers was appropriate, if only for the fact that the player had originated in his own Dunbartonshire. The first hint of it all came at the annual general meeting when chairman William Philip announced that two forwards of whom much was expected would soon be joining the club. Pittodrie fans could hardly wait to hear the good news.

10
THE JACKSON FOUR

When the mystery was unwrapped and the two newcomers to Pittodrie were revealed as the brothers Alec and Walter Jackson, there was little more than a shrug of anti-climax since their identities seemed to produce no particular cause for excitement. Yet there can be no apology for devoting a whole chapter to the name of Jackson, if only because the younger brother Alec turned out to be one of the legends of Scottish football, as sleek and delightful a figure as ever graced the game and a member of that immortal elite which will for ever be remembered as the Wembley Wizards.

Alec Jackson was the youngest of five brothers from the small community of Renton in Dunbartonshire. The eldest, John, had emigrated to America while Walter took up professional football with Kilmarnock and Alec went to Dumbarton, where he played with such confidence that he suggested to his team-mates, when he was only seventeen, that they should hold a celebration reunion on the evening after his first game for Scotland. But the promised land of the United States was calling and Walter and Alec Jackson decided to follow brother John, attracted by an early attempt to introduce football to the land of baseball. The Americans were offering well-paid jobs to people who could also play football and the Jacksons landed with Bethlehem Steel of Pennsylvania, whose senior executives included a fervent Welshman called W. Luther Lewis, the main inspiration of soccer in America. Jock Hume was by then with Brooklyn Wanderers and he is credited with sending back reports to Aberdeen about the tremendous talents of young Alec Jackson. Simultaneously, however, word was filtering through the Dumbarton connections of Donald Colman and Paddy Travers that the Jacksons were not so settled in the New World that they could not be lured back to the old country. Aberdeen wasted no time in making contact and the popular story has been that they wanted Walter, who refused to come without his young brother, and that the Dons directors agreed, only to find that the boy who had been foisted upon them emerged as one of Scotland's greatest players. It is an attractive story but the fact that it is not true was confirmed by the Jacksons' nephews, John and William, from Renton. Alec was the target and he was the one who wanted his brother as company.

The two of them duly arrived in the city and were conveyed to the Caledonian Hotel in Union Terrace, which has often been the centre of backroom activity connected with Aberdeen Football Club. It did not take Paddy Travers long to complete the deal and sign up the Jacksons for less than £1000, one of the best pieces of football business ever transacted. It is always difficult to acquire the full flavour of a figure from the past and those of us who never saw him must depend on the words and judgements of those who did. Fortunately, the evidence about Alec Jackson is everywhere. It does him poor justice to say that he was tall, lithe, swift and beautifully proportioned, but one of his contemporaries comes nearer to the colour of his personality when he says that he had laughter in his eyes as well as magic in his feet, a real dandy of a man who was suave of manner and was blessed with a soft West Highland lilt. Jackson's father had originally hailed from Fittie, and now the son was back delighting the crowd with his artistry. Luther Lewis had given Alec a return ticket when he left America, with an open invitation to go back, but although he kept it in his wallet for a long time, it became patently clear that his future lay in the land where football was well established and understood.

In no time at all he was an automatic choice for the Scottish team at outside-right, chosen in 1925, at the age of nineteen, to play against England at Hampden in the first team since 1895 to be drawn entirely from home clubs. The Scots took the Sassenachs apart that day in a 2–0 victory which told little of their superiority. In the company of men such as Meiklejohn, McMullan and Morton, the man of the match was unanimously declared to be Alec Jackson, the teenage cavalier from Pittodrie, a boy with the dash and flair and charisma of a superstar, twinkling in the football firmament in a manner which seemed to say he had an appetite for life as well as his chosen sport. In recognition of his performance that day they presented him with the ball.

In the black-and-gold of Aberdeen he went to Kilmarnock one Saturday and found that his team-mates were playing mostly to the left wing and suffering a 2–0 defeat at half-time. During the interval Jackson teased his colleagues: 'If you would play more to the right-hand side of the park, we might win this game you know.' A cocky devil, eh? But the Aberdeen players quietly took the hint nevertheless, knowing that it would take the Jackson genius to turn the game. So they played to his wing and he responded with three magnificent goals which gave the Dons a 3–2 victory. As the players returned to the dressing room he just winked and said, 'I tell't ye!'

The Jackson brothers had made their Pittodrie debut against Rangers on 23 August 1924, when the crowd had the novelty of seeing the great Alan Morton falling back into defence to help his team-mates cope with the new menace of the right-winger. Little Johnny Paton and Walter Grant had had to make way for the newcomers but Paton later returned to the team where he formed an effective combination with the Jacksons, sandwiched between them at inside-right. Aberdeen's signings were far from finished. Jock McHale arrived, a strong and robust player who knew the game better than most and later had an inspiring influence on the rest of the team.

With Jimmy Jackson still playing in the half-back line, the Dons had three players with the same surname all appearing in the team together. As if that were not enough of a headache for the corre-spondents of the day, Paddy Travers added to the confusion by heading for his home territory in the Vale of Leven and signing a fourth! This time it was Willie Jackson, more often known as W. K. or 'Stonewall', who came from the same little district as Alec and Walter but was no relation. As well as four Jacksons there were also two Bruces in the Aberdeen team, which had taken new shape as: Blackwell; D. Bruce, Forsyth; J. Jackson, Hutton, MacLachlan; A. Jackson, W. Jackson, W. K. Jackson, R. Bruce and Smith.

But the idolatry was reserved for the thoroughbred on the right wing, who was sometimes compared in later years to Stanley Mat-thews. The high point of his career was to come in 1928, when he was chosen to play for Scotland against England at Wembley. The Scottish team was immersed in criticism from the start when it was discovered that the selectors had left out such names as Andy Cunningham, Bob McPhail, Jimmy McGrory, Willie McStay and the formidable Jock Hutton, who had by then moved from his great days at Pittodrie to Blackburn Rovers. Eight of those chosen were by then playing in English football, including Jackson, and a cartoonist of the time produced a drawing of the three home players, Jack Harkness of Queen's Park, Tim Dunn of Hibs and Alan Morton of Rangers, heading south by train with one of them saying: 'If only we had another one we could have a game of solo!' The Scots team which gathered at the Regent Palace Hotel in London's Piccadilly Circus included little Alec James of Preston North End whose rougher mould was in sharp contrast to the smoothness of Jackson, often described as the Jack Buchanan of football. There was in fact a needle-sharp jealousy between James and Jackson, both with an ambition to be a superstar of the London scene, which they achieved later when James went to Arsenal and Jackson went to Chelsea. Both revelled in the limelight but it was the former Don who scored a point on the morning of the Scotland–England game when he and goalkeeper Harkness came down to the lounge of the Regent Palace. As they sat down for a cup of tea, Jackson employed an old trick much favoured by Harry Lauder on his visits to the Waldorf Astoria Hotel in New York. He summoned a page-boy and said: 'Here's half-a-crown, son. I want you to go through the hotel paging "Mister Alec Jackson".' Half-a-crown was a sizeable sum in those days and the delighted page-boy performed his duty with loud diligence. 'Paging Mr Alec Jackson – Mister Alec Jackson.' Heads turned in search of a famous football name and the mischievous Alec grinned in sheer delight as he nudged Jack Harkness and said, 'I bet James will be wild about this.'

By the time the much-criticised Scottish team reached Wembley Stadium on that historic day, the two potential kings were prepared to back their self-confidence with a bet as to which of them would score first, not that the team was given much chance of scoring at all. Out they went to the hallowed turf of Wembley in a downpour of rain to play a game of football which will be talked about for as long as Scotsmen have the breath of a boast in their lungs. Careering on the right with guile and gaiety, it was Alec Jackson who collected the winnings when he met an Alan Morton cross with a flashing header to put Scotland ahead in just three minutes. It was the first of a Jackson hat-trick, but the doughty James was not to be left out of it and he scored two more to make it 5–1 in the most famous Scottish victory of all. An ecstatic Scottish crowd became soaked as much on the inside as on the outside. In any case, who cared about a drop of rain on such a day as this?

Before that, however, Jackson had played with consistent brilliance through the season of 1924–25 which, ironically, turned out to be a thoroughly bad one for the Dons. They were lying equal bottom with five other clubs on the last day of the season, when they were hosts to a Motherwell team which was in the same plight. Would Aberdeen go down? A crowd of 15,000 was there to see and to cheer wildly when Walter Jackson shot home the opening goal. Then it was the turn of Jimmy Jackson to clinch victory and the reports of the match said he was 'enthusiastically hugged by his delighted colleagues' – 1925 that was! – 'and around the arena bedlam was let loose'.

So the Dons survived and so did Motherwell, as the crazy mathematics of goal average were worked out. With the skills of Alec Jackson clearly cut out for better company, there was a limit to how long the Dons could keep him, so it was hardly a surprise when he headed off south. Manager Travers was later to recall that Jackson, in fact, had no sooner settled on 'Deeside', as he liked to call the North-east, than there was a series of English raids across the 'Tweed', as he liked to call the border, for the purpose of seeing 'this human greyhound', as he liked to call Jackson. The privilege of signing him fell to the illustrious Herbert Chapman, later to mastermind Arsenal but at that time boss of Huddersfield Town, a team which may have little rating in the 1990s but which dominated English football during the 1920s. It won the First Division championship three times in a row and counted among its supporters a boy called Harold Wilson, a future tenant of No. 10 Downing Street. Huddersfield lured away more Pittodrie players in due time and lowered its popularity with Aberdonians even further in the 1950s when it snapped up a bespectacled boy from his classroom at Powis School before local people had had the chance to get to know that his name was Denis Law.

So Jackson was off on the golden trail to England for a fee of around £4500, a transfer which could not have taken place in the 1990s for less than millions. The silken skills were gone, leaving a feeling of desolation in many a Pittodrie heart. The indelible impression he made upon the football consciousness of Aberdeen is surely all the more remarkable when you consider that he had been and gone from a Pittodrie career before his twentieth birthday, a career which lasted for less than a year but which was to assure him of legendary status in the Granite City.

Jackson helped Huddersfield to the championship of the English First Division but London was still his target and it was no surprise when he moved to Chelsea for £8500 and became the highest-paid man in football, one of the very first to lend his name to advertising. London life suited his personality. For £5 a time he appeared on several days a week in the sports department of a big London shop, while a fashionable hairdresser used to pay him to come in for his morning shave. As one of the early superstars of sport, he was soon spreading his interests outside football, taking over a popular public house in St Martin's Lane, London, and entering a partnership to run the Queen's Hotel in Leicester Square just before the war. Indeed, his outside interests took him prematurely out of the game when there were still some years of football left in him; but footballers are naturally tempted to make some provision for their later years, although in the case of Alec Jackson those years were limited. The war was upon us and he became a major and a welfare officer with the Middle East forces. Soon after the war had ended Jackson, now a heftier version of the slim, high-cheek-boned thoroughbred who had graced the touchlines of Pittodrie Park, was driving along the dusty roads near Cairo when he was killed in a crash.

Death is no respecter of genius and it came to Alec Jackson with all the swiftness which had characterised his life and movement – and for which he himself is remembered, even to this day, by older men with moisture in their eyes.

11
TRAVERS' TRAVELS

If the Aberdeen directors had relieved the confusion of surnames by transferring Alec Jackson to Huddersfield, they eased the commentators' problems still further by selling Jimmy Jackson, the Pittodrie padre, to Liverpool. When challenged about these sales by angry shareholders at the annual general meeting, chairman William Philip said that both players had complained about the kind of criticism they received from some spectators and pressmen and that this was the main cause of their departure. If this was truly the case then it does confirm the view that Pittodrie supporters are among the hardest to please. If the immortal Alec Jackson was not to the liking of some people, what did that leave for lesser mortals? Maybe we are a thrawn, ill-to-please lot after all!

Two of the four Jacksons had now gone and within a few months Alec's brother Walter was crossing the border to Preston North End, leaving W. K. alone to carry on the name. W. K. Jackson arrived at Pittodrie in February 1925, having played for Everton before returning to play for the Vale of Leven in the Scottish Second Division and to work at the Singer sewing-machine factory in Clydebank. He was a kindly and considerate player in the father-figure mould, who would nurture younger ones and take the weight off their shoulders. Another of the same type was Bob McDermid, who came to Aberdeen after being in dispute with Rangers and established himself as a tireless workhorse in the Dons' forward line and a natural choice as trainer when his playing days were over.

W. K. Jackson took over at right-back when Jock Hutton was transferred to Blackburn in 1926 and later moved to left-back to accommodate an up-and-coming youngster called Willie Cooper. He was also keeping a fatherly eye on another local boy, Dick Donald, whose father ran a well-known chain of cinemas as well as His Majesty's Theatre, the ice rink and Donald's Dancing Academy. On leaving school, son Dick was put in charge of the Cinema House at the corner of Union Terrace and Skene Terrace, a career which ran parallel to his football and produced a generosity of free tickets for his team-mates at Pittodrie. Playing in front of W. K. Jackson, Dick Donald was having one of those games when very little comes right. After one particular move the considerate Jackson sought to save the youngster from discouragement by calling, 'Hard luck, Dick'. His voice carried to the terracing, where there is very little regard for human feeling. One wag heard the remark and called back 'Hard luck, ma erse! Ye're just wantin' a ticket for the picters!' On another occasion, playing against Motherwell, W. K. said to a Fir Park player of his acquaintance: 'Don't be too hard on young Donald. He's a newcomer to the team.' By half-time the same young lad had taken the Motherwell defence apart with one of his finest-ever performances and poor Willie Jackson had to thole an earful from the Motherwell player whom he had asked to show consideration! Jackson was eventually laid low with double pneumonia and pleurisy, which gave an opening to another Pittodrie favourite, Charlie 'Oor ba' McGill, the man who was inclined to claim that every ball which went out of play was an Aberdeen ball. Jackson had already made provision for his future with a shop in Rosemount, where his son carried on the family business while W. K. confined himself to the bowling green. He suffered the agonies of many a former footballer who tried to become a spectator and found the frustration of merely watching unbearable. In Willie's case he would land himself in arguments until finally he joined that majority group of ex-professionals who would not go near a football match any more.

But Willie, like every former Don I talked to, was filled with memories of warm fellowship at Pittodrie. It was a good place to be. Paddy Travers and Donald Colman were men of power and authority who were solidly behind their players but demanded respect in return. You had to be at Pittodrie very strictly to a time-table before the game and when internationalist Alec Cheyne turned up minutes late one day he found that a reserve player had already been alerted and was in fact stripped. There was still time for Cheyne to change but, in fairness to the reserve and as a lesson to the first-team man, the position was not to be reversed. Travers had a way with him. Coming back from Hamilton one Saturday, the Dons players were having dinner on the Glasgow to Aberdeen train and after they had finished they sat on in the dining car. The team that day had included a young lad with an Italian name who was playing a trial. 'I believe you are a bit of a singer,' said Travers. 'How about giving us a song?' So the lad obliged, singing arias from operas, and turned out to have a beautiful voice. Travers was genuinely full of praise for the performance, then took him aside and said, 'You stick to singing, son. You'll do better at that than you will at football.' It was as tactful a way as any of telling him that his career at Pittodrie was over.

With three of the Jacksons gone, Paddy Travers went out to make good the deficiencies and pursued the former Celtic personality player Tommy McInally, who had moved to Third Lanark. Just when he was about to sign for Aberdeen, however, he rejoined Celtic. But Travers did manage to sign another Third Lanark player, Alec Reid, for whom he paid Aberdeen's biggest fee to date of £2,000 and Reid came into the team at outside-right and played with such skill that the crowd felt a little less aggrieved about the departure of Alec Jackson. Bob McDermid, too, had come to add quality to a team that had had to start that season of 1925–26 with the new offside law. This said that a player was offside unless there were at least two opponents between him and the goal when the ball was last played. Previously, the requirement had been three players.

Matt Forsyth's benefit match that year was an occasion for some excusable nostalgia, particularly when the players who took the field included not only manager Paddy Travers but the indestructible Donald Colman, still turning on the soccer style at the age of forty-seven! That was to be Forsyth's last season at Pittodrie before transferring his services to Forres Mechanics in the Highland League. Jock Hutton, who was still very much in the midst of his international career, was transferred just a few months later to Blackburn, where he became as much a local favourite as he had been in Aberdeen. Pittodrie looked a good deal emptier without the dominant bulk of the likeable Jock but it was not inappropriate that he should go when his partner had gone. With other famous couplings like Colman and Hume before them, and Cooper and McGill or Armstrong and Mills to come, the names of Hutton and Forsyth went together as inseparably as Rolls and Royce and sometimes just as smoothly.

When Jock's playing days were finally over he landed a manager's job in Ireland but the first player he signed had already been signed by another club and Jock's reign was not of the extended variety! People argue as to whether he was just a hefty kicker or a man of wider skills but the balance of my inquiry shows that Jock was, in fact, a considerable footballer. What no one argues about is that he was one of the most jovial and popular figures ever seen at Pittodrie.

Just as the Jacksons, the Forsyths and the Huttons had now departed the scene, there were new talents creeping quietly upon the fringes of Pittodrie, ready to burst forth as the idols whose names would dance from a North-east tongue with all the liveliness of the Feugh in spate. Alec Jackson's reign had been so brief that the appreciation of it tended to rumble on like distant thunder that lingers when the daze of the flash has passed away. The genius of Jackson was beyond dispute but there were soon to be two others who would stay longer and carve themselves just as deeply into the affections of the Pittodrie faithful. One was Alec Cheyne. The other will take the vote of many old-timers as the greatest Don of all. His name was Benny Yorston.

12
BENNY – THE GREATEST?

Down the trendy length of the King's Road in Chelsea, where youth paraded in a trail of psychedelic fashion, I went in pursuit of a legend. Some said he was the greatest Don of them all and most believed that he was long since dead. But suddenly there came the word that Benny Yorston was still alive and living somewhere in Chelsea.

Furnished with an address which turned out to be as erroneous as it sounded, I headed for London with something of the air of a Sherlock Holmes of soccer. The particular district of Chelsea was suitably called World's End, which seemed as good a place as any to begin the search. Finally I tracked down a block of flats which bore a slight similarity to the address in my pocket and climbed stairs on a random quest for anyone called Yorston.

'Try that door there,' said a Cockney woman with curlers. So I did – and listened with fascination to the short step of the man who was coming to answer the door. There he stood in open-necked shirt and cardigan with a belt holding up his trousers, a pale, rotund little fellow with short-short thighs but a tongue that was still as recognisably Aberdeen as the Great Northern Road where he grew up. Yes, it was Benny Yorston all right, recovering from a heart attack suffered in January 1977 and apologising for the fact that a wartime knock on the head had affected his memory.

Benny Yorston grew up at 68 Great Northern Road, Aberdeen, as one of six children attending Kittybrewster School. As a twelve-year-old he had played at Pittodrie in the schools' championship and was scoring goals galore even then, and thinking nothing about it. Born in 1905, he had gone to Webster's College for a secretarial course in shorthand and typing. Benny happened to know George Philip, son of the Aberdeen manager, who told him that his father needed someone to help out in the office at Pittodrie. Would he like the job? So Benny Yorston, who was playing for Mugiemoss, took up work under manager Philip who gave him a run in the Dons' Highland League team and paid him a combined wage of £6 a week, of which he gave £5 to his mother.

Yorston escaped the Pittodrie net for a while, however, and played for Montrose where the club chairman was desperate that they should win the Scottish Alliance Cup. In his enthusiasm, he said to Benny: 'I'll give you ten pounds for every goal you score.' Benny replied: 'Ten pounds? You must have more money than brains.' So out he went and scored four of those glorious goals which were later to become characteristic of Benny Yorston, collecting the promised total of £40 from the Montrose chairman and eliciting from his bewildered mother the question: 'What bank have you been robbing?'

That well-known referee Peter Craigmyle, who had no hesitation in nominating little Benny as the Don who stood out in his memory above all others, had seen him play at Montrose and told the Aberdeen directors that they had better snap him up at once. They did, at a fee of less than Benny collected for his four goals!

He proceeded to become the big name of the late 1920s and early 1930s, one of the smallest footballers of his day but capable of out-jumping the tallest centre-half and hitting his head on the crossbar if he was not careful. In four seasons he scored 102 goals, including a Dons record of thirty-eight League and eight Scottish Cup goals in the 1929–30 season – and he could score them with left foot, right foot or head, and often from the most incredible angles. Little wonder that he became the idol of his day, setting up a tradition of smallish centre-forwards which was to be followed by men such as Paddy Moore, Matt Armstrong, Stan Williams, Paddy Buckley and the man of the 1970s who echoed much of Yorston's idolatry of the 1920s, Joe Harper. Though the fans adored him, his colleagues on the park felt that he turned on his brilliance only when he was in the mood for it. But none denied him his supremacy on the day, as the leader of that dashing forward-line which read: Love, Cheyne, Yorston, McDermid and Smith.

Mention of Alec Cheyne, who had arrived from Shettleston in 1926, stirs memories of a beautifully deceptive body-swerve and a footwork artistry which made him a worthy choice for the Scottish team to play England at Hampden in 1929. He could hardly have guessed as he travelled south for his big event that he was about to write himself into the history books of football as the player who started the famous Hampden Roar. Indeed, he was the reserve that day and came into the team only because of a late withdrawal. Cheyne was to have the privilege of playing as inside partner to Alec Jackson, who had left Aberdeen just before he arrived. Alas, the right-winger was carried off with a broken arm before half-time and removed to the Victoria Infirmary in Glasgow. There was no substituting in those days so Scotland prepared to play the second half with ten men. A hasty dressing-room conference produced the emergency plan that Cheyne would take the right wing and, as often as possible, carry the ball to the English corner flag, even running it out for a throw-in if necessary. It was more a question of keeping it in the English half and trying to save the game rather than win it. There was only a minute left to play when one of Alec's forays on the right produced a corner off the body of Ernie Blenkinsop. Alec took the kick himself. Over came the ball from the right, curving in on the crossbar – and dropping into the far corner of the net. A goal direct from a corner! The only score of the game – and just a minute left for play. The eyes of 110,512 Scottish fans were turned upon the big clock which graced Hampden at that time, aware that the English scarcely had time to equalise. So the Scots set up a mighty roar which was designed to keep their team inspired until the final whistle. That roar did not flag by a single decibel before the referee drew breath for the last blast of his whistle – and not for a long time after it.

Just a year after thrashing the English in the famous Wembley Wizards game of 1928, the Scots had won again, by a narrower margin this time but with only ten men – and by a single goal in a million which would stand to the credit of a real Pittodrie favourite. Not only had Alec Cheyne brought a unique decider to an international match but he had given birth to the Hampden Roar, a sound which rings out even today as a thunderous symbol of Scottish support.

But the story does not end there. Along Battlefield Road, less than a mile from Hampden Park, Alec Jackson was under chloroform at the Victoria Infirmary having his broken arm repaired. I was indebted to the late Jack Harkness, Scotland's goalkeeper of the time, for the story which was told by a nurse some time after the event. According to the nurse, who was standing at Jackson's side, the roar from Hampden resounded throughout the Victoria Infirmary and the mighty Jackson, still under sedation, sat bolt upright in a sudden burst of consciousness and called out 'Nurse, that's the winning goal for Scotland!' Then he lapsed back into unconsciousness. The last note to that memorable day is that the English defenders complained that Hughie Gallacher had stood on their goalkeeper's foot and prevented him from rising to Cheyne's shot. But then, there is always somebody ready to spoil a good story!

Back in Aberdeen, manager Travers loved to recall that goal for years to follow and was capable of indignation when anyone suggested that it was a fluke. 'Cheyne was a master of the corner-kick,' he would remind them. 'I have seen him practise flag-kick after flag-kick until he was satisfied that he had the right angle. Like Jackson, he was the idol of Pittodrie for his artistic footwork.' Indeed, Travers' contention was borne out in the Scottish Cup of the following season when the Dons met Nithsdale Wanderers and Alec Cheyne scored two goals – both of them directly from corner kicks! Such feats of accuracy, incidentally, had not been recognised as legal in the football rules until 1928–29, when the law was changed in time for Alec Cheyne's moment of international fame.

The Aberdeen directors made a determined bid to keep their talented inside-man but, with Chelsea in pursuit, he refused to be re-engaged and off he went to Stamford Bridge for an Aberdeen record fee of £6000. There he teamed up with Alec Jackson to continue that right-wing partnership which had lasted for less than forty-five minutes in the 'Cheyne International' of 1929.

13
McLAREN'S LUCK

In the summer of 1927, Aberdeen Football Club blazed the trail to South Africa with a tour which did much to popularise the round-ball game in a country where rugby dominated. It was a lengthy tour and a memorable experience for the players in an age when travel was little known to the average citizen. Their opponents were mostly of British stock and wherever they went the Dons were fêted and fussed over, not to mention sunburned by such a climate as they had never experienced before. Goalkeeper Harry Blackwell, the Englishman who never blunted his native accent, was the only man with cause to doubt the wisdom of the trip when he found himself the victim of travel sickness. Otherwise the main problem was to master the lightness of the ball and once that was achieved the tour was a resounding success from the footballing point of view as well as the social. It also revealed the full genius of young Benny Yorston, who was the leading scorer in South Africa and thereafter established himself in the League side. The players who undertook the adventurous journey, along with chairman William Philip and manager Paddy Travers, were: Harry Blackwell, Duff Bruce, Malcolm Muir, Willie Jackson, George Ritchie, Mike Cosgrove, Jock Edward, Sam Spencer, Jock McHale, Bob McDermid, Alec Cheyne, Bobby Bruce, Tommy McLeod, Andy Love and Benny Yorston.

Paddy Travers had never been slow to express his enthusiasm when he discovered a player who promised excitement. Having found little Bobby Bruce during a holiday soon after he became manager at Pittodrie, he wrote to a friend that he had seen a player with the name of Robert Bruce, who was likely to make his mark in Scottish football just as his namesake had done in Scottish history. It was an ambitious comparison but Robert the Bruce of Pittodrie did in fact develop into a most accomplished and entertaining forward.

Unfortunately he followed the well-worn path to England after four distinguished seasons, by which time he was still just twenty-one years of age. His departure for Middlesbrough was one of many lucrative deals which put a smile on the face of the Pittodrie bank manager from the mid to late 1920s. The great Dod Brewster had gone to Everton, Dr Victor Milne to Aston Villa, Alec Wright to Hearts, Alec Jackson to Huddersfield, brother Walter to Preston, Tom Pirie to Cardiff, Jimmy Jackson to Liverpool, Jock Hutton to Blackburn and Andy Rankin to Cowdenbeath. The annual general meeting of 1928 was told that, whereas the club had once owed the bank £16,000, they were now completely in the clear and had a positive balance of £2700. A concrete wall had been built around the pitch and an ornamental granite front had been built at the Merkland Road end. After the sale of Bobby Bruce, the club bought the ground behind the new grandstand which became the car park and later the all-weather training pitch. When Alec Jackson used to pay a visit to the city he would torment Paddy Travers about the new grandstand which he, Jackson, had 'bought' for the club with his transfer fee. Club captain Bert MacLachlan, who had been a mainstay of the team since he arrived from Aston Villa in 1914, bowed out in the late 1920s because of a persistent groin injury, and his leadership was sorely missed.

In the eternal regeneration of football talent, however, Paddy Travers was finding his replacements. Scots exile Jimmy Black had come back from the gathering gloom of the Depression in America and developed into a top-class midfield man, interrupted only by an extraordinary suspension. Jimmy had played for the American club called Springfield, which went defunct, but another club took over the assets and declared that Black was included among these assets. Word that the American Football Association had suspended him indefinitely reached Scotland and the Scottish Football Association was asked to confirm the action. As both associations were members of the international body, the SFA had no option but the matter was eventually sorted out and the suspension lifted after three weeks.

Travers signed Duggie Livingstone from Plymouth Argyle, Hugh McLaren from Nithsdale Wanderers and Frank Hill, who had been making a name for himself with Forfar. Although he was not aware of it at the time, the Dons' boss now had on his books a half-back line which would mould itself into one of the best in Britain, with the familiar ring of Black, McLaren and Hill. McLaren, however, was unlikely to find an early opportunity at centre-half, where the powerful Jock McHale was still a dominant figure, but his exclusion from the Aberdeen team led to an extraordinary piece of luck. Kilmarnock were doing well in the Scottish Cup of 1929 but they were short of a centre-half and asked if they could borrow McLaren for the duration of their Cup run. Since the player had not been committed to the Cup as an Aberdeen player, the laws of the day allowed him to be loaned and the Dons management agreed. Whereas Aberdeen went out of the Cup, Kilmarnock marched on to a triumphant final and Hugh McLaren, still an Aberdeen player, collected a Scottish Cup-winner's medal and returned to Pittodrie to await his big-team chance! The ever-active Travers beat off the challenge of Rangers, Liverpool and Blackburn to sign Davie Warnock, a talented outside-right from the local Banks o' Dee, who played some brilliant football for Aberdeen without getting full credit for his efforts. In the same year Travers was down in Glasgow signing the great Celtic and Scotland outside-left, Adam McLean, who came north to play out his veteran years in much the same way as that other great performer, Tommy Pearson, was to do nearly twenty years later. He also signed Bobby Fraser from Albion Rovers.

In the autumn of 1930 Aberdeen mourned its first football manager, Jimmy Philip, who by then had become a club director, and his death was followed closely by that of Billy Russell, the esteemed trainer. Billy's death signalled the return of the irrepressible Donald Colman, by now fifty-three and, having finally put his playing days behind him at Dumbarton, ready to embark on a whole new and distinguished career as coach at Aberdeen, in the company of his old friend and colleague, Paddy Travers. Paddy described the return as 'a source of general satisfaction to Deeside'. It was 1931 and the Travers–Colman combination had scarcely had time to settle down when they and the football public were struck by a sensational event so tightly veiled in mystery that it has not been properly explained to this day. There were legal difficulties in doing so, but perhaps I can shed some light on the matter.

14
THE GREAT MYSTERY

A first hint of the great Pittodrie mystery reached the North-east breakfast tables on the morning of 18 November 1931, when a curious story on the sports pages of the *Press and Journal* halted many a spoonful of porridge in mid-flight. Under the headline 'Dons' Drastic Changes', the report went as follows:

Surprising changes have been made in the Aberdeen team to oppose Falkirk at Brockville on Saturday. Three of the recognised stalwarts, McLaren, Hill and Yorston, have been relegated to the reserve team. Last night, Mr Travers, the club manager, declined to enter into the circumstances which have led to the players mentioned being dropped but admitted that it was on account of 'some domestic trouble'.

In the more publicity-conscious days of a later age there would no doubt be some probing reporter who would come up with a clarification of the 'domestic trouble', but in 1931 puzzled Aberdonians could only turn it over in their minds and proceed to other pages, where they found that big crowds had flocked to Marischal College to listen to John Buchan, the novelist, talking about 'Truth and Accuracy'. Raggie Morrison's, that Aberdeen institution which graced St Nicholas street where the more sophisticated Marks and Spencer store now stands, was advertising ladies' woollen combinations (soiled) for 1s 9d – less than nine pence today – frocks for 5s (25 pence) and real mink marmot coats for £14 10s. Well, well!

But sports fans cared less about Raggie Morrison's and the 'Truth and Accuracy' of John Buchan's speech than they did about the truth behind the mystifying events at Pittodrie. On the following Saturday, an under-strength Dons team was beaten at Falkirk by three goals to one and they were also despatched from the Scottish Cup by Arbroath. By now the situation had escalated, as they would have said at a later date, and the names of more players were drawn into the mystery. David Galloway, a winger who had come from Raith Rovers just a few months earlier, and Jimmy Black, the right-half who had come back from America, were also out of the team, though Black had been classed as injured. The Dons were now without one of the finest half-back lines in British football as well as the centre-forward who had recently been Scotland's top scorer.

On Friday 4 December 1931, the *Press and Journal* was still mystified. It reported:

The continued omission of McLaren, Hill, Yorston and Galloway from the Aberdeen team has given rise to much conjecture in football circles as to when they will be seen in their places again. Inquiries made have elicited that none of the players is on the open-to-transfer list but it is understood that the Aberdeen club directors are willing to consider offers for them and for Black, who is meantime suffering from a knee injury. All are players of ripe experience and, until omitted a fortnight ago – Galloway dropped out three weeks ago – were regarded as indispensable to the first eleven. Hill, who was previously with Forfar Athletic, has played several times at left-half for Scotland. McLaren, centre-half, in his fourth season at Pittodrie, came from Nithsdale Wanderers and is the possessor of a Scottish Cup badge which he won while on loan to Kilmarnock from Aberdeen in 1928–9. Black, right-half, played for the Scottish League against the Irish League this season. He has been three seasons at Pittodrie and before going to America was with Cowdenbeath. Yorston is a junior internationalist and three seasons ago headed the Scottish League list of goal-scorers. Galloway joined Aberdeen from Raith Rovers a few months ago.

Through all the latter weeks of 1931 the mystery remained. Manager Travers, a shrewd man in most respects, was no doubt doing his best to protect as many people as possible when he sealed his lips against comment of any kind. But if ever there was a classic case of how silence can damage innocent people, this was it. He should have known that a football club so much in the public eye cannot hope to drop a collection of star players – they never did play for the first team again – and escape public attention or the exaggerations of the public tongue.

Rumours were rampant and every conceivable explanation was offered, including the inevitable charge of some form of corruption. No charges were ever brought. The directors were split and confused over the issue but Travers had satisfied himself that there were certain of his players who would never pull on a first-team jersey again – and they never did. Nor is there any evidence that anyone raised a protest about Travers' decision.

Swiftly and abruptly, great names disappeared from the Pittodrie first team for ever, to play in the reserves until suitable transfers could be arranged. On 19 January 1932, the manager of Sunderland, a Mr Cochrane, came up with an offer of £500 for Benny Yorston, but there was no chance of landing one of the greatest goal-scorers in the game for such a paltry sum, even in those far-off days when money still had some value. The Dons set a figure of £2500, Sunderland raised their offer to £1500 and, in the customary manner of compromise, the two sides finally met in the North British Hotel in Edinburgh on Friday 22 January 1932, when Yorston became a Roker Park player for £2000.

At the Tivoli Theatre in Aberdeen that evening Albert Sandler was soothing local disappointment with his haunting violin. North-east sports enthusiasts of those days had the choice of football or occasional rugby at Pittodrie and one of the attractions of that bleak winter was a visit from the talented Springboks to play a match against the North of Scotland. But an air of sadness was hovering down Merkland Road East and the *Press and Journal* of Saturday 5 March, 1932, announced that Black, McLaren, Hill and Galloway had all expressed a desire to be transferred and that the club was prepared to accede to their requests. 'It will be remembered,' said the paper, 'that these four players, along with Yorston, were relegated to the reserve side in the middle of November owing, stated the Pittodrie club, to "domestic troubles".'

So, totally without an explanation to the public, those players did depart at the earliest opportunity, Hill for example going on to a successful career with Arsenal and ending up as manager of Burnley. Jimmy Black died a young man, protesting his innocence to the end, I am told. David Galloway died in the late 1970s, just after Benny Yorston, who was the only one I managed to talk to. I have found no trace of McLaren so the only one I know to be alive in 1990 is Frank Hill, whose nephew of the same name is a postman in Forfar. Frank went to coach in California, became a baseball referee and ran a chip shop. In the hope of casting some light on the Pittodrie Mystery, I wrote to him several years ago but there was no response. Since then he has suffered a stroke, is confined to a wheelchair and is, according to his nephew, incapable of communication.

That left me with Benny Yorston, who had gone on to rescue Sunderland from relegation to the English Second Division. Sometimes he was on a bonus of £10 a goal, an experience reminiscent of his brief sojourn with Montrose. He later moved to Middlesbrough and steered them clear of relegation as well. When the war was over he went into the business of rooming flats in London's South Kensington.

And what about the events which preceded his departure from Aberdeen? Had there been corruption? I leave you with his own statement, made just a few months before his death in November 1977: 'I don't know anything about corruption at Pittodrie. I would not have become involved. My father was the skipper of a boat and, if I had been involved in anything like that, he would have taken me to sea and thrown me overboard.' Mrs Yorston, formerly Hilda Mitchell from Aberdeen, denied all knowledge of the 1931 incident and the couple said they were glad to have the opportunity to say so. For all his greatness and popularity as a player, Benny's words had the hollow ring of untruthfulness. How could he have failed to know what I was speaking about? Only concern that I might precipitate another heart attack prevented me from pushing the point more forcibly.

From the Pittodrie dressing room of the time I gained the gist of what happened and I can now reveal it in print for the very first time, nearly sixty years later.

A number of players, it seems, decided to place a fixed-odds bet with Will Jamieson, the Aberdeen bookmaker, to the effect that the Dons would be drawing at half-time and winning at full-time. They were betting on matters which were, to some extent, in their own hands and were therefore laying themselves open to charges of corruption. Of course they were hoping to win the game in the end but, if there was any attempt to arrange the half-time score as a draw, that in itself could endanger the final result.

A perusal of the scores in that particular period of 1931 shows that there was, indeed, a remarkable coincidence of matches in which any such bet would have been successful. My own investigations revealed that, whatever the sinister implications, at least one of those half-time draws was pure coincidence. But it illustrates how easily an innocent person could be drawn into the net of suspicion. In that Dundee United game, Aberdeen were leading

2–1 just before half-time when Willie Cooper, as honest a servant as Aberdeen ever knew, gave away a penalty, which levelled the half-time score. It was only later that Willie discovered, to his horror, that he might have been seen as part of a plan to achieve the draw. He was, of course, totally innocent.

Allegations of corruption in football are extremely difficult to prove and we shall probably never know how far along the path of proof the investigation reached. Indeed, nothing might ever have been known of the matter if someone had not approached another Aberdeen player of the time, former Celtic and Scotland outside-left Adam McLean, who was playing out his veteran days at Pittodrie. Certain information was imparted to him, with the suggestion that he should participate. McLean's alarm was conveyed to at least one other player and the matter came to a head at half-time one day. By now convinced of manipulation, he left the field, making it known that he was not part of any plot. His words came to the ears of manager Travers and Donald Colman, who had returned that year as coach, and they began their own investigation. No police involvement is recorded but whatever the manager discovered was enough to convince him that five of his star players would not pull on a first-team jersey again. The rest was shrouded in a veil of secrecy and, until now, the general public have never been offered a word of explanation.

By coincidence, Percy Dickie left Aberdeen for St Johnstone in the aftermath of the incident and he could recall his anger when he discovered that the unfortunate timing of his move had aroused some suspicion. There was too much scope for innocent people to be hurt. Percy, in fact, had been one of the most colourful characters ever seen at Pittodrie, his crinkly face bristling with humour. Did any player ever exude so much sheer joy in the playing of football? He would play up to the crowd, who responded to him with the kind of theatrical rapport which develops between a comedian and his audience. He had been a Sunnybank Schoolboy who played for Mugiemoss before joining the Dons in 1929, at the age of twenty-two. After St Johnstone he went to Blackburn Rovers, where he became a favourite with the crowd, but the Second World War spirited him off to be a physical training instructor in the scheme instituted by Sir Stanley Rous, secretary of the Football Association. He played for Leicester City, Chelsea and Manchester United then returned to Pittodrie at the end of the war, by then a man in his late thirties but still the same old Percy. He bought a licensed shop in Bankhead, which bore his distinctive name over the door, and when his playing days at Pittodrie were over he continued his career with Peterhead in that immediate post-war period when the Buchan club was dominant in the Highland League.

Percy had belonged to that period of the early 1930s when players still turned out as if they were dressed for an occasion. Some players, such as W. K. Jackson, were known to appear in bowler hats and others, like Hugh McLaren, were known to convert W. K.'s bowler into a soft hat by putting a dent down the middle of it!

Donald Colman was back in full flight as coach, still bristling with ideas about football and footballers. He believed in total attention to the physical condition of his men and used to administer a body-building mixture of sherry, one tablespoonful of honey and a raw egg. More sharply, however, there are players like Willie Cooper who can still remember the taste of the Gregory mixture which Colman insisted upon for a weekly flushing of the bowels. Percy would queue up for his Wednesday dose, protesting that there was nothing wrong with his inner workings. He was, after all, a plumber by trade! Rumblings from the intestinal regions were matched by a rising rumble of discontent from the players until Frankie Hill finally took it up with the directors and there was an agreement that the Gregory mixture would be discontinued.

Another of the guiding influences at Pittodrie in that same period was club secretary Alan Robertson, a man who knew everything about money but absolutely nothing about football. He was organist at Rosemount kirk, where Percy Dickie was associated with the Boys' Brigade, and he would advise young players about how to handle their money. Percy's first shares – in Mitchell and Muil – were acquired under the guidance of Alan Robertson. But football was another world to him. On rare occasions he would gaze out from the pavilion at the mysteries of the Pittodrie football field, rather like a bewildered bullock on the run from Kittybrewster mart. He would survey those curious contraptions which people with knowledge called goalposts and, on one occasion, with a genuine desire to enlighten himself about the purpose of the crossbars, he was known to ask, 'Fit are the jeesties for?'

15
SMITH, COOPER AND McGILL

It was deep in the Bronx of New York City that I unearthed a solid man from Fittie whose name will be remembered as the first leg of that defensive trio of Smith, Cooper and McGill. Steve Smith was well through his seventies and retired from the New York Telephone Company by the time we met. Summers were for the bustle of the skyscraper city and winters for the sunny shores of Florida, but the heart and the tongue were still for the fish houses and granite yards of his native city, the dray horses of Market Street and the old tramcars which clanked their way up to Holburn Junction and beyond.

Smith's connection with Pittodrie began in childhood, where the best of club loyalties are rooted. It was back in 1912 that he first raised his voice inside the ground, not only to cheer the team but to sell his wares, for little Steve was a chocolate boy at Pittodrie, with one eye on business and the other on a team which he could still rattle off as: Greig; Colman and Hume; Wilson, Wyllie and Miller; Soye, Main, Walker, O'Hagan and Lennie. As he wove his way among the crowds selling his chocolate the wee lad from Fittie was vowing to himself: 'I'll play out there for Aberdeen one day.' In fact his debut on the Pittodrie turf came quite soon as a member of the St Clement's School team playing Sunnybank in a schools final. But there was still a long way to go before he joined the elevated ranks of the Black-and-Golds. The next stage in his apprenticeship was to progress from chocolate boy to programme boy, collecting his supplies from Munro's of Crown Street on a Saturday morning, dashing back to Fittie for lunch before taking up his stance at Pittodrie.

It was, of course, a vastly different-looking Pittodrie from the stadium we know today. There was open terracing at both the King Street and Beach ends and the pavilion stood at the north-east corner, where the small East Stand is now situated – that wooden pavilion with its two storeys which reminded you of cricket. The grandstand, such as it was, stood next to the pavilion on the north side where the present stand is situated and along that same side, at the north-west corner, there was a beer hut where men downed their draught and argued but generally kept themselves in good order. On the opposite side of the ground, by the gasworks area, there was another small stand close down on the boundary wall by the half-way line, with open terracing on either side.

In the memory of former chairman Charles B. Forbes, who played for the club in the 1920s, the dressing rooms were of primitive proportions, with a six-foot-deep zinc bath into which the players had to immerse themselves in ice-cold water. More than fifty years later, Mr Forbes could raise a shudder at the thought of edging himself into that tub.

Steve Smith described to me the atmosphere of that vastly different world before it was turned upside down by the Great War – a neighbourly kind of world where everybody knew Dod Munro the groundsman and Peter Simpson the trainer. His own arrival at Pittodrie as goalkeeper, however, was still a long way off. He was playing for Hall Russell's in 1922–23 when he decided to emigrate to play for the Toronto All-Scots. From there he went to Chicago, where he joined up with two of his old Pittodrie heroes from the chocolate-boy days, Bobby Hannah and Joe Walker, who were playing out their days in North America. By then, that other great name from Aberdeen, Jock Hume, was established on the American scene and it was he who asked Steve to join the professional ranks of Brooklyn Wanderers. At that time there were Scots galore in American football, which had opened up a whole new field for the immigrant. That enthusiastic Welshman, W. Luther Lewis, who had signed the Jackson brothers, was building up his Bethlehem Steel team with men such as Bob McGregor, who had captained Morton to their Scottish Cup triumph of 1922. Lewis moved on to become president of Chicago Pneumatic, the parent company of the Fraserburgh Toolworks, and you can imagine his delight some years later when he came to visit his Scottish outpost and ran into none other than Bob McGregor, by then back in Scotland as player–manager at Bellslea Park – and working for Lewis's tool company in the Broch.

Those early days of American soccer, of course, ran right across the Prohibition period of the 1920s when thirsty Americans were driven to the furtive shadows of the speak-easies to secure their booze. As a poor relation of baseball, football had to make do with whatever dressing-room accommodation was nearest to a local park and, often enough, that turned out to be the basement quarters of these illicit dens.

So the 1920s of the Charleston and Prohibition and an energetic spirit of abandon went roaring towards the Wall Street crash of 1929 and, in the ensuing chaos, the American soccer scene fell apart. Many an exile was joining the trek to New York Harbor and among those looking for a boat around that period were names such as Alec Massie, bound for Hearts, Charlie McGill, who was to land with Aberdeen, and Jimmy Black, who had come a little earlier and was to become part of that famous Pittodrie half-back line – Black, McLaren and Hill. Steve Smith was there as well, joining a ship which eventually sailed up the Clyde and berthed at Merkland Wharf, Glasgow, that day in 1929 with no fewer than 150 Scottish footballers on board. It so happened Aberdeen had released that fine goalkeeper, Harry Blackwell, in the previous season and Paddy Travers now signed on two new keepers, Dave Cumming from Hall Russell's and that former Russell's man now back from America, Steve Smith. It was the latter who commanded the top spot and Cumming was allowed to go off to Arbroath, from which he was transferred to Middlesbrough and became Scotland's goalkeeper! But the Pittodrie faithful had no complaints about Smith in goal, as the last line of a defence which lined up as: W. K. Jackson and Falloon; Black, McLaren and Hill. In the reshuffle after the mysterious incident of 1931, Falloon became the centre-half and Cooper and McGill emerged as the full-backs in front of Smith – a full-back partnership, incidentally, which set up a Pittodrie record of 161 League games together without a single break.

With his American years behind him and approaching his thirtieth birthday, Steve was a latecomer to Scottish professional football, but he played on until 1935, developing a fine understanding with his two backs. In the Second World War he was drafted back to the familiar surroundings of Hall Russell's and looked after the Dons' A team at the same time. In 1947 he returned to the United States, took up his job with the New York Telephone Company once again, became an American citizen and later retired with fond memories of the place where once he had sold chocolates and dreamed dreams which were destined to come true.

Willie Cooper had signed for Aberdeen in 1927 for a fee of £20 and was paid £1 a week while he continued to play for his junior team, Mugiemoss. Willie, a square-cut man with leathery features, as crisp and solid and reliable a fellow as ever donned a football jersey, became a key figure in a team of the 1930s, which many an honest witness will declare was the best Aberdeen team they have ever seen. The names they will reel off as a piece of pleasurable poetry are: Smith; Cooper and McGill; Fraser, Falloon and Thomson; Beynon, McKenzie, Armstrong, Mills and Strauss.

That team became the settled formation of the mid 1930s after Paddy Travers had recovered from the events of 1931–32 and worked himself through a transition period of seeking out his new blend of talents. To make good the deficiencies of the 1932 transfers, he was now desperately searching for men of quality. Fortunately, he had been able to rely on servants like W. K. Jackson and Bob McDermid to 'father' his team through a difficult period. Eddie Falloon, a likeable little Irishman from Larne, had been successfully converted into a centre-half, one of the smallest ever seen on a football pitch. His height of only 5ft 4in proved to be of no disadvantage to him whatsoever as he would soar like a bouncing ball to out-jump the tallest opponents. Another little Irishman, Paddy Moore, had a brief but distinguished career at Pittodrie. He had come from Shamrock Rovers and had a style of his own, gliding the ball to unmarked colleagues and heading backwards and sideways with devastating effect. There was a strong connection at this time between Aberdeen and the Irish Free State. In a good relationship, the Dons had always freely released their players for international duty and the gratitude of the football authorities in Eire can be witnessed at Pittodrie to this day in the shape of a presentation harp.

Irishmen included, Aberdeen has always been a meeting point for various nationalities whether they be English, Welsh, South African, Scandinavian, Dutch or Hungarian. Herbert Currer had set the pattern for a flow of South Africans to Pittodrie and he was soon followed by fellow countryman Billy Strauss, a splendid left-winger with such a force of foot that he is credited literally with bursting the net on at least two occasions while playing for Aberdeen. A Strauss waltz down that left wing was one of the exquisite delights of watching football at Pittodrie during that decade, though his movement was not so much a waltz as a quickstep, and a very quick step indeed. While the South African took up the left wing, a Welshman called Jackie Beynon was signed from Doncaster

Rovers to patrol the right and he became a Pittodrie favourite for whom, alas, tragedy was not far off.

But of all the names of the 1930s, there are two which symbolise that decade, just as names like Hutton, Jackson and Yorston had been synonymous with the 1920s. The names were as inseparable as ham and eggs because they complemented each other in much the same way. They were, of course, Mills and Armstrong.

16
MILLS AND ARMSTRONG

For many, many people, Willie Mills was the symbol of sporting glamour in the 1930s – smart and good-looking, the type to attract the gaze and idolatry of the young even before he had kicked a ball. And when he did that, his personal appeal was translated into football terms, just as it had been ten years earlier with Alec Jackson, whose gaiety and appetite for living were reflected in his style of play. Willie's skill was so pure and precious to manager Travers that he once said of him: 'Just give me five minutes of the real Mills and I'm satisfied.' As with many another thoroughbred of the soccer stables, those five minutes could change the whole complexion of a football match and, when you teamed him up with the dash of Matt Armstrong at centre-forward, Aberdeen could boast one of the most deadly duos in British football. So there was glamour at the heels of Mills and Armstrong, with Matt being likened to the film star Ronald Colman and Mills being teased by Travers that he was too good-looking to be a boy. But it was the glamour of their football which mattered most and that was based on a twin-like understanding, developed during intensive afternoon sessions at Pittodrie under the supervision of Donald Colman, who was as fine a teacher as Scottish football had seen.

Indeed, it was said that Travers' early impression of Armstrong was not favourable and that it took Colman to convince him that he was a future internationalist. As far as Mills was concerned, Colman never wavered from the privately held view that he was the personification of all he had ever dreamed about in the perfectly balanced footballer. That view was in no way coloured by the fact that the boy had come from his own home corner and that he himself had played alongside Mills' father when they won the Scottish Junior Cup with Ashfield towards the end of the nineteenth century. Colman was far too fair and unbiased for that. He simply knew a great footballer when he saw one and Mills turned out to be one of the very best players ever seen at Pittodrie.

The boy from Bonhill, Dunbartonshire, had been recommended to Aberdeen by a local physical instructor, Mr Jim Baxter, and arrived at Pittodrie in 1932 as a lad of seventeen. He played his first game in the reserve team against Celtic at Pittodrie and on that same day the regular inside-left in the first team, Bob McDermid, was injured at Parkhead. Those were the days when replacements were drawn directly from the corresponding position in the reserve team so Willie Mills, at seventeen years of age, walked into the Aberdeen team exactly one week after his arrival and stayed there for the next six years. During that time he was credited by many people with having pioneered the long, sweeping pass, in an age where the tanner-ba' type of game was much more in vogue. Mills himself diverts a lot of that credit to Paddy Travers, who was thinking intelligently about the shape and form of the game long before the more recent era of track-suit managers with their method football and scientific manoeuvrings. Willie recalled Travers' influence: 'At a throw-in, for example, he would say, "Instead of getting the ball and sending it back to the wing-half, let it run past you, then turn and hit it across to the opposite wing, changing the whole focus of play." I had also watched Bob McPhail doing it with Rangers.'

So the teenage Mills was established in the Aberdeen team in 1932, earning a basic £5 a week (£4 in summer) with a bonus of £2 for a win and £1 for a draw. Set that against the tradesman's wage of £2 or £2 10s and you realise that the footballer was not badly off. Mills remembers that he could go down town to the city's top tailor and buy himself two of the best suits in Aberdeen for £5. It seemed like a golden world to the boy from the Vale of Leven who had spent his schooldays in the unemployment of the 1920s, when people had nothing to do but gather at public parks in places like Bonhill, young lads and old men alike, and kick a ball around. By the mid 1930s the Pittodrie wage had gone up to £7 a week, plus bonuses, and Mills was augmenting his income with a string of international appearances, including the Jubilee international against England and a place in the Scottish team which toured America in 1935. When he eventually left Aberdeen in 1938, his destination was none other than Huddersfield, that dominant team of pre-war England which had already lured away men such as Alec

Jackson. The fee was £6500 and the wage which attracted Mills was still only £8 a week.

But the war was only a year away and his career was cut short in an all too familiar way. Huddersfield told their players: 'Your contracts are finished, boys. You are on the dole.' At the end of the war Mills was playing for the British Army in Berlin, along with another name from Pittodrie, Charlie Gavin; then he returned to Aberdeen, by now in his thirties and with some of the best years of his football life totally wasted. He started training at Pittodrie again and went to Lossiemouth before teaming up with two of his former Aberdeen team-mates, Willie Cooper and Dave Warnock, at Huntly. Willie Mills still recalls the occasion during his Highland League days when Huntly had an important game written up by James Forbes of the *Evening Express*. His report in the *Green Final* was a splendid one, except for a printer's error. Thousands of people read that Saturday evening that Willie Mills collected the ball outside the penalty area – and *shit* high over the bar! Willie's only complaint is that he did not get his name in the *Guinness Book of Records* for such a feat of elevation.

Now in his mid seventies, Willie lives in Rubislaw Park Home. And there he ruminates about what it is that separates people in the great spectrum of talent. Within seconds of the starting-block, one sprinter is out in front. What puts him there? What secrets of power and transmission are shared between brain and limb? Willie tries to convey the feeling of a well-coordinated body, and then there is a pause as you remember that those legs which once accepted the dictates of a brilliant football brain are no longer accepting dictates at all. For the legs which carried Willie Mills through a memorable, if far too short, career are now riddled with arthritis and there is room only for talking about it and remembering his very special skills – and reflecting quietly on the devilish inevitability of age.

Until recently, Willie could at least count on a knock on the door and a cheery greeting from the other half of the Pittodrie partnership, his old buddy with the sleeked-back hair and neat moustache and the lively features creasing with good humour.

Matt Armstrong, born in Newton Stewart and reared in Port Glasgow, was provisionally signed by Celtic when a telegram arrived at his home one day in 1931 asking him to keep an appointment with someone at the Central Hotel, Glasgow. Matt turned up to find that the anonymous gentleman was none other than manager

Paddy Travers of Aberdeen, anxious to know if Celtic had taken up their option. They hadn't. After careful homework, Travers was able to point out to the lad that the option had expired on the previous night and that he was now completely free of any obligation. Matt thought he had better wait to see what manager Willie Maley of Celtic had to say but the production of fifty crisp pound notes convinced him that that was hardly necessary!

So he became an Aberdeen player, biding his time to succeed Paddy Moore at centre-forward and to strike up that telepathic partnership with Mills which stood for all that was skilful and exciting in the game of football. Matt could still savour the joy of it as he recalled the feats of his inside partner and told you: 'I have seen Willie do things with the heavy ball of our day which nobody could attempt today.'

Armstrong went on to fulfil the forecast of Donald Colman, playing for Scotland and the Scottish League on several occasions, including the Jubilee international when Scotland beat England 4–2 at Hampden Park and the Dons' centre scored a goal along with Jimmy Delaney, Tommy Walker and Aberdonian Dally Duncan of Derby County. His Pittodrie career ran through the 1930s to be broken by the war and, by the time that was over, he was reaching the veteran stage. His departure from Pittodrie, he could recall with a wry smile, followed an incident when he and a friend had a merry joust with Johnnie Walker and a brick was thrown through a window down Pittodrie way! Perhaps it was time to leave anyway, so Matt made his way to Queen of the South, then extended his career with Elgin City and Peterhead, still digging his hands deep inside his pants in characteristic fashion and pulling them up as if there were something defective in the elastic.

While playing for Elgin, Matt ran into one of those humorous incidents which tend to happen to such happy-go-lucky characters. One of his former mates at Pittodrie, Joe Devine, had succeeded where very few professional footballers ever do and had converted himself into a referee. Joe was in charge of an Elgin City match one Saturday when his old pal Matt committed a foul for which there was no alternative but a booking. Mr Devine called him over, produced the notebook and pencil and said in the customary and dead-pan fashion: 'Your name please?' Matt looked in astonishment as the minor farce was enacted and then, realising that Joe was only doing his job, sidled up to him and replied: 'My name? Tom f*****g Thumb!'

Matt became a car salesman before retiring and living at Kirk Brae, Cults, from which he ventured regularly to Pittodrie to cheer on the Dons and to be hailed by many an old-timer who warmed at the sight of him. He would meet old friends like Joe Devine and Ritchie Smith at the Carlton Bar or at Jimmy Wilson's. And he willingly put modesty aside to tell you that the greatest of all Aberdeen teams was: Johnstone; Cooper and McGill; Dunlop, Falloon and Thomson; Beynon, McKenzie, Armstrong, Mills and Strauss.

Until the 1980s at least, he was not alone in that view. But for these men and many thousands of North-east people there was one particular year of that era which stands out for high drama in the history of Aberdeen Football Club. It was 1937.

17
DRAMAS OF 1937

The story of Scottish football has been such a two-horse race that one wonders how it has managed to survive at all. If you consider that, during the forty-three years from 1904 to 1947, the Scottish League Championship was won by Motherwell once and on every other occasion by either Rangers or Celtic, you start to appreciate how farcical the position has been. The truth of the matter is that these two clubs have such power and resources, backed by such an inbuilt support through the various religious interests, that they should hardly ever be on the losing end. And they seldom are. They simply go on winning cups and flags almost as if by right and, in the more recent times of European competition, gaining their passport to continental battlegrounds with victories which are pretty hollow compared with those of the English clubs who seek the same goal.

It could well be argued that the greatest achievements in Scottish football are those of the teams other than the Old Firm who persevere against heavy odds and occasionally, but only occasionally, snatch the candy from the big boys. After thirty years and more in existence, there was still no candy for Aberdeen Football Club and the supporters were beginning to wonder if they were ever to know the sweet taste of actually winning something. Indeed, it became a standing joke for North-east bachelors, being teased about not having a wife, to reply that they would get married when the Dons won the Cup; that was intended to give them a possible escape route for life! But their celibacy came under sudden threat in 1937.

The Dons had started out on their Scottish Cup progression that year with a tie against Inverness Thistle on such a cold and miserable day that most of the players wore gloves, and Donald Colman rubbed down the Aberdonian limbs with whisky, a sacrilegious misuse according to players like Matt Armstrong, who declared that they would much rather have had it inside them. The biggest sufferer was goalkeeper George Johnstone, while Armstrong avoided the frostbite by rattling home a hat-trick in the Dons' 6–0 victory. In the second round, Third Lanark came to Pittodrie and were beaten 4–2. Among the stars of the Cathkin team that day were Scottish captain Jimmy Carabine and that truly great inside-right, Jimmy Mason. (Oh why did they have to go and destroy such a fine club as Third Lanark?) Billy Strauss scored twice that day.

Aberdeen coasted on with a third-round bye and won 2–1 against Hamilton in the fourth, Strauss and Armstrong scoring the goals. With mounting excitement, it was on to the semi-final with Morton at Easter Road, Edinburgh, just ninety minutes away from a historic moment in the history of Aberdeen FC.

Could this be the year? Were Aberdeen about to reach their very first Scottish Cup Final? Billy Strauss, that streak of lightning with the lethal shot, scored one, Matt Armstrong the other and, lo and behold, the Dons were on their way to Hampden Park for the Scottish Cup Final.

The excitement which ran the length of Union Street and far beyond was only a foretaste of the scenes outside Hampden Park on that Saturday, 24 April, when the crowds rolled up to see Aberdeen play Celtic in their first-ever final. Everyone knew they were two popular teams with a tradition of talented players but who could have foreseen that the crowd that day would set up an all-time record attendance for a club game in Britain? Just a week earlier, the biggest crowd ever to see a football match in Britain (149,547) had turned up at the same ground for the Scotland – England clash and no one imagined that there could be a repeat performance so soon. The turnstiles which clicked through this massive invasion of people from far and wide finally closed their doors when the figure had reached 146,433. But that was only part of the story. At least one gate was broken down and thousands of people streamed in to join the official figure, while a further 20,000 were left stranded outside. To get a proper perspective of the numbers who turned out with the intention of seeing Aberdeen and Celtic that day, one has to picture the present-day limit at Hampden Park – and more than double it. So they stood with their arms pinned to their sides, the green-and-white of Celtic, the black-and-gold of Aberdeen, awaiting the moment when they could greet the teams with more lung-power than has ever been known, before or since.

Willie Cooper and Bob Temple, who were the Aberdeen full-backs that day, later recalled to Alastair Macdonald of the *Press and Journal* the feeling of awe when they trotted out of the Hampden dressing room. Said Bob: 'There seemed to be nothing but a sea of tammies and pink faces and the sound started in the middle of the stand and moved right round the enclosure. I'll never forget it.' For two young men in particular, the run out to the Hampden pitch seemed like an impossible dream come true. For goalkeeper George Johnstone and right-half Frank Dunlop had been there just a year earlier as members of the Benburb team in the Scottish Junior Cup Final. They went straight to Aberdeen and here they were, back at Hampden in the senior Cup Final. One man for whom the occasion was a heartbreak before it started was South African left-winger Billy Strauss, who had done so much to make it possible with goals all the way to the semi-final. In that Morton game at Easter Road, Billy was badly injured and had to watch it from the sidelines, replaced by Johnny Lang. So the teams which lined up were: Aberdeen – Johnstone; Cooper and Temple; Dunlop, Falloon and Thomson; Beynon, McKenzie, Armstrong, Mills and Lang; Celtic – Kennaway; Hogg and Morrison; Geatons, Lyon, Paterson; Delaney, Buchan, McGrory, Crum and Murphy.

Northern hearts sank when Johnny Crum put Celtic ahead in ten minutes but there was hardly time to draw breath before the Dons went on the attack. From the centre, the ball went out to Jackie Beynon on the right wing and the Welshman went streaking off on his own. Matt Armstrong had a clear recollection of the thoughts running through his head: 'I remember seeing Jackie haring along the wing and I was saying to myself "Matt boy, you had better get up there fast to meet that ball when it comes across. If you don't you'll be in trouble." Fortunately, I made it in time to meet Jackie's low cross and I hit it first time into the Celtic net.'

But the glory was not to last. At the other end Celtic went ahead through Buchan, though Willie Cooper, not a man given to exaggeration, will swear to this day that the great Jimmy McGrory flicked the ball on with his hand before Buchan scored. That settled it and Cooper will still shake his head and tell you it was a terrible way to lose a Cup. Says Willie: 'We were so built up for that final and were playing so well at the time that it was a dreadful disappointment. In fact, it took me a long time to get over it.' Much as Willie shared the universal admiration of Donald Colman, he believes that his enthusiasm for physical fitness did much to lose that game. All week he had emphasised that the more running they did in training the less they would have to do in the final. But it was a week of heat and Cooper recalls that the Aberdeen players were drained of their energy before the great day came.

So players and supporters alike suffered a crushing sense of anti-climax as they headed back north, arguing over chances missed but unanimous on at least one point – that the presence of Billy Strauss would have made all the difference. The depth of disappointment was felt by none more than Paddy Travers. Despite all that he had done for the Dons since taking over in 1924, the great players he had spotted, signed and nurtured, the thought and imagination and colour he had brought to the Pittodrie scene, he had absolutely nothing to show for his efforts.

Two years later, however, there was to be a reward for the pawky Travers when his team won the Scottish Cup. But alas, it was not his Aberdeen team. By then, new directors had come to the Pittodrie board and Travers evidently felt he was not retaining the same power which he had previously enjoyed. So he moved in the unlikely direction of Shawfield and within a season had collected the trophy which had eluded him all those years. In the Clyde team which brought him the glory he had so richly deserved before, there was a man who had figured largely in his plans at Pittodrie. That great little centre-half, Eddie Falloon, had followed his old boss south and collected his Cup-winner's medal as a member of the Clyde team. Isn't it a funny old game?

The gloom of Pittodrie on that April weekend was compounded on the day after the Aberdeen–Celtic Cup Final when Dons director Bill Hay, a member of the lemonade family, collapsed and died while still in his forties. North-east folks tucked away their disappointment as summer approached and for the Pittodrie players there was the coming excitement of a tour to South Africa, a consolation much needed after a Cup Final which did not even offer the losers runners-up medals. The match programme is their only souvenir!

The Aberdeen party headed for Southampton to board the *Stirling Castle* for the voyage to South Africa. The heat of that southern land was a new experience to men accustomed to the blast of a nor'easter breaking across the Links to Pittodrie's field. But it was thoroughly familiar to Billy Strauss, now recovered from his injuries and going home to show his Aberdeen team-mates the land he had come from. But the joy was short-lived when Billy went down with illness and the problem of putting on the full Aberdeen side became even more difficult when the other winger, outside-right Jackie Beynon, was rushed to hospital in Johannesburg. The players knew that Jackie had sometimes been bothered with stomach trouble but his pains were diagnosed as appendicitis, which should not have been all that serious a matter though it would rule him out of the tour. Matt Armstrong went along to see him in hospital and when he came back that evening he told the Aberdeen party that Jackie was looking far from well. Paddy Travers came on the scene and was not at all pleased with Matt's remarks. Naturally, he did not want the rest of the players upset by what would normally be a routine operation and he told Armstrong he should not be speaking like that. But Matt was worried and his concern was well founded. Peritonitis had set in and Jackie Beynon died that night.

A helpless grief descended on the Aberdeen party, so far from home for the purpose of entertaining the South African people and now with little thought for anything but their dead colleague. Jackie had become such an integral part of their life together that they found it hard to believe he had been spirited away so swiftly. The tour would have to go on in the well-worn tradition but first of all they would have to bury Jackie that Saturday morning. The scenes in Johannesburg were almost without precedent. Traffic came to a standstill as people turned out in their thousands, including every exiled Welshman within travelling distance who had come to bring a touch of home to the farewell of as popular a Taffy as ever crossed the Scottish border. Up at the cemetery on the hillside, they gathered by the grave and raised their voices in such beautiful harmony as can come only from the soul of a Welshman. 'Land of My Fathers' they sang out loud and clear in a ceremony which etched itself forever in the minds of those who were there. Most of them had never seen him but he was a son of Wales, was he not? The Aberdeen team carried the coffin to the grave so far from the land of his fathers and from the grey streets of Aberdeen, his adopted city, where people shook their heads in disbelief. Wasn't it just a few weeks ago that they had watched him haring down the right wing at Hampden and sending over that low cross from which Matt Armstrong scored the equaliser? The Dons lowered their beloved friend and colleague into the grave, from which he was later uplifted and brought back to his permanent resting place in the valleys, from which his heart had never really departed.

'The players were broken-hearted, for Jackie was such a nice fellow,' Willie Mills recalled. 'I'll never forget the kindness of local people who felt deeply for us and couldn't do enough to help.' But broken hearts had to be patched over in the name of saving the tour and entertaining the people who had looked forward to seeing the much-publicised visitors from Scotland. So they played a match after the funeral and the tour continued, albeit beset with injury problems of one kind or another. The Dons were due to play Lourenço Marques but matters were further complicated when goalkeeper George Johnstone refused to play because the game was on a Sunday. It went ahead on a sand-pitch, with the Dons appearing in rubber boots. Within fifteen minutes, however, a tropical thunderstorm broke over the area and the sandy pitch became a quagmire, just the conditions to give the local team a 3–0 lead at half-time. The rubber boots had become a disaster and the main change at the interval was in footwear. Heavy boots and long studs were the secret weapon of the second half, which produced seven Aberdeen goals and a final victory of 7–3!

On a free day in Cape Town the Aberdeen party went along to watch a local football match and was greatly intrigued by a little fellow who was turning on the style for the railwaymen's team. He had already been following the Dons in South Africa, watching their style of play, studying their movements and wondering if he could emulate the skill of the Scots. His name lies ahead in the story of Pittodrie but he accepted an invitation to come to Scotland in the following year, 1938. The little fellow in the railway team at Cape Town gave his name as Alfred Stanley Williams.

18
HITLER'S WAR

Whatever clouds may have been gathering over Europe, the 1930s and Aberdeenshire seemed as good a time and place as any to be a child – a mellow decade of foxtrots, saxophones and fine summer days. And into the fabric of that childhood came the name of 'Pittodrie', the very sound of it playing a magical music on schoolboy heart-strings.

It carried a distant ring of romance and excitement for those who were just too young to make the formidable twenty-eight-mile journey from places like Maud. In the 1930s a visit of any kind to Aberdeen was an adventure for the country child, starting with tea and morning rolls at the Empress Café, near the Queen. That was when the Queen – Victoria that is – gave her name to the corner of Union Street and St Nicholas Street, where she stood in stony silence on her pedestal, thoroughly unamused, as the carthorses came trundling up Market Street and the trams rattled up towards Holburn Junction or down towards the Castlegate and the beach beyond.

Mothers would rummage in Raggie Morrison's (before local names like that had given way to multiples), then we would lunch at Isaac Benzie's in that delightful atmosphere where a palm court trio of piano, violin and cello would assist the broth, mince and tatties and semolina pudding with raisins in their progress along the digestive tract. Who remembers the tubby little fellow on the cello, Jackie Bromberg, who looked like a fatter version of Joe Loss? Afternoons were spent at the Capitol or the Astoria Cinema at Kittybrewster before fathers emerged from the Friday mart and we would leave behind the glamour of the city and head back to Buchan, with its nowt and neeps and bare frosty mornings, giving way in seasonal time to long summer days and Aikey Fair, to the rustle of hairst and the home-coming of the peats.

Pittodrie was still beyond my bounds but grown men brought home the tales of great names which came to stir their own delight; names like Billy Strauss, Willie Mills and Matt Armstrong. Curiously, one name above all others managed to register in the young mind, perhaps because the folklore of his feats in the late 1930s and early 1940s seemed to match the rounded ring of 'Johnny Pattillo'. Like many another Pittodrie performer, his name does not belong to any memorable formation, yet the middle parting, bow-legged run and natural flair of Pattillo made him the person who first engaged my loyalty to Aberdeen Football Club. From then on that loyalty has been a kind of disease for which medical science has not so far emerged with any known cure and from which most of us are content to remain eternal sufferers.

After the South African tour there was precious little time for any loyalty to take root before Hitler's war was taking shape. Folk said it couldn't happen; surely they had had enough with turning the world upside down once in a generation and nobody would be daft enough to do it again. But the grim reality finally broke upon us on that September Saturday of 1939, with Hitler's invasion of Poland. Like the rest of the country, the North-east was abuzz with activity. Those men who had joined the Territorial Army, perhaps in some sense of adventure, found that it was now for real. In our small towns and villages we watched as special trains from places like Peterhead and Fraserburgh collected the local contingents of Gordon Highlanders and rumbled through Strichen, Longside, Maud and Ellon to mass themselves at Bucksburn for whatever emergency lay ahead. Most of them were captured by Rommel at St Valéry in 1940 and spent the next five years in prison camps throughout Germany. Many employers took the gloomiest view and sacked their workers, a fate which more or less befell the Pittodrie players, whose contracts were terminated. People looked around and wondered what was going to happen next and, in the Phoney War which ensued, nothing much did for many months. So there was stagnation and uncertainty and, in the break-up of the playing structure at Pittodrie, Matt Armstrong, Billy Strauss and Andy Cowie went off to join the Royal Corps of Signals, reporting together to their depot at Canterbury. Others were called up for service.

The settled pattern of existence fell apart and football went with it. The area beneath the Pittodrie grandstand became an ARP (Air

Raid Precaution) post and the Dons were more or less shut out of their own home for a time.

But football, like life itself, had to go on in some shape or form as part of public entertainment and the administrators were trying to piece together some kind of organisation from the reigning chaos. Aberdeen FC played a major part in bringing into existence a Scottish North-Eastern League, which was really much wider than the name suggests. It included teams all down the east coast from Aberdeen and Arbroath to Dundee United and Raith Rovers, and included Rangers Reserves. The Dons chairman, William Mitchell, donated the Mitchell Bowl to augment the competition and the Dons themselves had a lot of success in that wartime period, winning the North-Eastern League and everything that was played for within the limitation of the emergency.

In the year before the war, of course, manager Paddy Travers had moved on to Clyde and Scottish Cup victory, and he had been replaced at Pittodrie by David Halliday, a Dumfries man who had been well known as a Dundee forward in his day. That invaluable coach and club legend, Donald Colman, applied for the manager's job when Travers left and his daughter Edna remembers the days of suspense in their home at 342 King Street as her dad and mum waited to hear about the post. It would make a big difference to their financial position. But Colman was by then approaching sixty and the directors considered that he was too old, a fact which Colman, the fitness fanatic, found hard to swallow.

Edna remembers her father's deep disappointment that he had been passed over, but he was not bitter; indeed, he cooperated to the full with David Halliday and the two men got on extremely well. If Colman was ever tempted to be bitter at all, it had been on an earlier occasion when he believed he had been done out of a benefit at Pittodrie, a situation which he blamed on one particular director. His daughter remembers that he never really forgave that man.

But the war was upon us and Mr Halliday had scarcely warmed the seat when he was himself diverted to the war effort. The job of caretaker managers fell jointly to Charles B. Forbes, the city schoolmaster who had played for the Dons in the 1920s, and that man of colourful ebullience, George Anderson, complete with bowler hat and carnation, who owned a sweet factory in Rosemount and had been a notable goalkeeper for Aberdeen in the early 1920s.

Together they faced up to the whole uncertainty of the situation, deprived of most of their own players but consoled by the large influx of soldiers and airmen who came to train in the North-east and who included a proportion of professional footballers. Random names which crossed our northern horizon and dallied to wear the Aberdeen colours for varying lengths of time included Dave Russell of Sheffield Wednesday, George Green of Huddersfield, Alex Dyer of Plymouth Argyle, Bobby Ancell and Jackie Dryden of Newcastle United and Joe Harvey of Bradford City. For my money, there were few better entertainers than that great little centre-forward from Crystal Palace, Ernie Waldron, who took no run at a penalty – and seldom missed.

But of all the wartime visitors, who were officially known as 'guests', there was one whose impact was greater than any other. George Anderson went up to Lossiemouth to cast an eye over an airman who was being hailed as a great discovery of English football. His name was Stanley Mortensen and he later became inside partner to that greatest of all dribbling wizards, Stanley Matthews, with whom he played for Blackpool in three FA Cup Finals after the war was over. In the last of these, in 1953, the veteran Matthews was making his final attempt to win an FA Cup-winner's medal. Blackpool were 3–1 down against Bolton Wanderers but the wizard himself inspired them to a memorable recovery against a team captained by Aberdonian Billy Moir, and in the final 4–3 victory Stan Mortensen scored a hat-trick.

More than ten years before that, however, George Anderson had lured him to Pittodrie, where his electrifying runs and cannonball shooting put him into the news over and over again. He arrived during season 1942–43 and played in the following season as well, averaging about a goal per game. One appearance in particular lingers in the minds of Aberdonians who had the privilege of seeing him. The Dons were playing a British Army team which was more or less an English international team in disguise. It included Cliff Britton of Everton, Stan Cullis of Wolves, Don Welsh of Charlton, Tommy Lawton of Everton, Jimmy Hagan of Sheffield United and the Compton brothers, Leslie and Denis – yes, the same Denis Compton of cricketing fame who had the rare distinction of playing for England at both football and cricket.

By half-time the Army were leading by four goals to one, but if they imagined that the contest was over they had reckoned without the great Mortensen, who was in the Aberdeen team that day along with players such as Tommy Walker of Hearts, Gordon Smith of

Hibs, and Jerry Dawson, Duggie Gray and Willie Waddell of Rangers. Having scored the first Dons goal, he went on to score three more, making it 5–4 for the Army at one stage. The fairy-tale seemed complete when he shot home a thirty-yard rocket which would round off a perfect draw but referee Peter Craigmyle blew for an infringement, which seemed like undue disregard for a true sense of occasion!

By 1947, when the Dons were approaching their second Scottish Cup Final, Mortensen had fulfilled all the early forecasts and was playing for England against Scotland at Wembley. Outside the stadium he ran into Charles B. Forbes, and Stanley, who enjoyed a bet, said: 'I've put my money on the Dons to win the Cup next week, Mr Forbes.' Then, more confidentially, the man who had always enjoyed his time at Pittodrie said: 'Any chance of Aberdeen coming to buy me?' Mr Forbes had to remind him that, much as the prospect would delight everyone at Pittodrie, the directors had no access to the Bank of England! And that, indeed, would have been necessary to meet the price of the Mortensen talents.

Charles Forbes was later to recall for me the pleasures and problems of wartime management: 'There were so many great performers around that George Anderson and I had to play them in trials to see who we wanted. In one of those games, there was a goalkeeper playing in the first half who did not seem to be good with high balls. So we left him out after half-time and chose one of the other contenders instead.' Imagine their embarrassment when they discovered that the man they had rejected as goalkeeper for Aberdeen was the great Ted Ditchburn, Tottenham Hotspur and England keeper!

But they soldiered on, Charles Forbes and George Anderson as joint managers, William Mitchell as chairman and John D. Robbie as secretary. The story goes that, during a wartime Cup tie, George Anderson kept running in to check with the club treasurer on how much they could afford as a bonus. From time to time he would run out to the edge of the pitch and shout: 'There's another pound in it for you, lads!' Such stories may benefit from exaggeration but they do illustrate the spirit of improvisation which was around at the time, as well as heightening the picture of the colourful George.

Thus Pittodrie marched on through its wartime emergency, with kaleidoscopic teams producing stars who would appear and disappear with equal swiftness, according to the movement of personnel or the secret needs of the war effort. It certainly brought fresh faces

Aberdeen team 1904, winners of Qualifying Cup. *Back row:* J. Philip (*manager*), A. Lowe, E. Halkett, T. Strang, R. Macfarlane, G. Ritchie, P. Simpson (*trainer*). *Front row:* J. Robertson, G. McNicol, R. Murray, D. McNicol, H. Low, W. McAulay

Jock Hutton, heavyweight back of the twenties

Alec Jackson – the Wembley Wizard

Aberdeen team 1928–29, with an array of local trophies. *Back row:* Merrie, Cooper, Donald (Dick), McHale, McLaren, McKenzie, Legge. *Middle row:* Ritchie (*assistant trainer*), Black, Smith, W. K. Jackson, Blackwell, Yuill, Love, McLeod, Livingstone, Russell (*trainer*). *Front row:* Robertson (*secretary*), Polland, Wilson, Falloon, McDermid (*captain*), Muir, Yorston, Cheyne, Hill, Travers (*manager*)

The Bonnet Brigade – a Cup-tie crowd of the 1930s heading down Merkland Road East

Aberdeen's 1937 tour of South Africa, pictured in Durban. *Back row:* Willie Cooper, Billy Scott (father of Dons' co-manager Jocky), Herbert Currer, Bob Temple, Billy Strauss. *Middle row:* Jackie Beynon (he died a few days later), Johnny McKenzie, Frank Dunlop, George Thomson, Eddie Falloon, Johnny Lang. *Front row:* skipper Bobby Fraser, S. V. Kimber (*South Africa team manager*), Frank Whitehead (*Dons' chairman*), manager Paddy Travers, trainer Donald Colman

Willie Mills and Matt Armstrong, deadly duo of the thirties, with Donald Colman

Dons win first major trophy – League Cup of 1946. *From left:* George Taylor (he scored winning goal), Andy Cowie, George Johnstone, Archie Baird, captain Frank Dunlop, Pat McKenna, George Hamilton, Alec Kiddie

Goal that won Scottish Cup for first time – against Hibs in 1947. Stan Williams' 'impossible angle' shot is watched by Archie Baird and Billy McCall of Aberdeen, Jimmy Kerr and Jock Govan of Hibs

The 1947 Cup winners arrive back at Joint Station. Joe McLaughlin manages to wear a soft hat

Golf outing 1950: Fred Martin, Chris Anderson, Frank Watson, Tommy Pearson

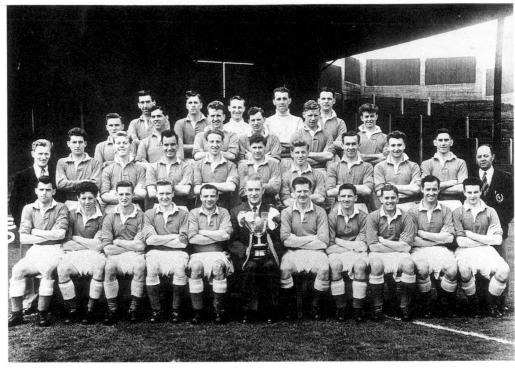

Dons celebrate first League Championship in 1955. They also won Reserve League and Second XI Cup. *Front row:* Allan, Davidson, Jimmy Brown, Paterson, Buckley, manager Halliday, Mitchell, Young, Yorston, Hamilton, Mulhall. *Second row:* D. Shaw (*trainer*), Ingram, Wilson, Glen, W. Smith, I. Smith, John Brown, Wishart, Allister Wallace, B. Alexander (*assistant trainer*). *Third row:* Clelland, O'Neil, Clunie, Hay, Scott, McNeill. *Back row:* Kelly, Dunbar, Morrison, Martin, Macfarlane. *Missing:* Leggat, Caldwell, Hather

Goal that won 1955 League Championship – Archie Glen's penalty at Shawfield

Scottish Cup Final, 1970 – a Derek McKay goal sinks Celtic. Despairing faces of Celtic's Hay, Williams and McNeill

The great Hungarian, Zoltan Varga (*centre*) with manager Bonthrone and Henning Boel

Moment of glory, 1970 – captain Martin Buchan with Scottish Cup

King Joe Harper, great goal-scorer of seventies

and excitement for the men on the terracing but the competition was necessarily of inferior quality and there was a general longing for the return of football life as they remembered it. Most of all, the supporters would engage each other at half-time and agree that they could be doing with men like Geordie Hamilton back from the war. 'Ay, ah wunner foo Geordie's daein'?' Just as genuinely, Hamilton and many others spread round the world were wondering how they were doing on their beloved terracings of Pittodrie Park.

19
HAMILTON–WILLIAMS
–BAIRD

The ten years between 1946 and 1956 were destined to be one of the greatest periods in the history of Aberdeen Football Club. In those years they were to carry off the Scottish League Championship and the Scottish Cup once and the Scottish League Cup twice, with three other appearances at Hampden Park in Cup Finals.

But nothing of that could be guessed when David Halliday came back from his wartime service. A man of quiet disposition, Halliday never did manage to communicate his personality to the average supporter, though, by deed rather than word, he turned out to be by far the most successful Pittodrie manager in the first seventy-five years of the club's history. The North-Eastern League was still in existence as he went about his task of re-occupying the seat he had taken up briefly seven years earlier and paving the way for the resumption of peacetime football.

For the basic structure of a post-war team, he could count on the talents of men who had been on the books before the war and would soon be returning. He was thinking of men like George Johnstone, Frank Dunlop, Andy Cowie, George Hamilton, Stanley Williams, Archie Baird and, of course, Willie Cooper, who had managed to play during the war because he had been returned to his trade as a marine engineer in Aberdeen. These men in turn were marking time before demobilisation and sometimes taking stock of how they had come to be Aberdeen players in the first place. To every man there is a story. Let us linger with a few of them.

George Hamilton, who belongs to that elite of great Dons, was playing for his local Ayrshire team of Irvine Meadow when Rangers invited him to play two trials before deciding that he was on the light side. Instead of the marble hall of Ibrox, the lad with the skilful feet and head and endless appetite for the game landed in the less fashionable surroundings of Palmerston Park, Dumfries, in season 1937–38. He soon made a big impression on Queen of the South spectator Billy Halliday, who remembered that his brother, just recently ensconced as Aberdeen manager, needed someone to replace Willie Mills, who was on his way to Huddersfield. So he tipped off David who hastened to Dumfries, and the first that Hamilton heard of it was when he was summoned from bed one morning and told to be at Palmerston Park by ten o'clock. He was introduced to the Aberdeen boss, who promptly signed him for £3000. He arrived in the season of 1938–39 in time to play his part in beating Chelsea in the Empire Exhibition Trophy, a contest run in connection with Scotland's biggest-ever organised event, which was staged at Bellahouston Park, Glasgow, in 1938. The Dons eventually went out in the semi-final to Everton.

The Pittodrie crowd was not slow to realise that it had the makings of a very special player in the twenty-year-old from Irvine but, once again, he belonged to that generation which was to have the heart cut out of its career by the Second World War. It is a tribute to his talents that he made such an impact at Aberdeen even though his career did not really get under way until he was twenty-seven. In the confusion of 1939, George went back to the local shipyard at Irvine, guested for Ayr and was finally called up in October 1940 for service with the Royal Engineers. He was a driver in the North African campaign but managed to play some army football, forming a right wing with that Englishman of immortal fame, Tom Finney. George had sailed abroad from Tail o' the Bank at Greenock and, in the German torpedoing of troop ships, his two closest friends had died; so the young Hamilton developed a new appreciation of life which also affected his attitude to football. As he told me later: 'I used to wonder if I would ever see all the lads at Pittodrie again. When the war was over you felt so glad just to be alive and I was really looking forward to coming back.'

The moment of return for George Hamilton is one of the precious memories of schoolboys like me who had known him only as a name, revered by those older men who had bemoaned his loss. Well, Hammy was back and we stood on the terracing that day in 1945 when he was due to reappear and kept our eyes on the players' door for our very first glimpse of this pre-war wonder boy. Out of the ruck of dull civilian clothing around the doorway, the bright red shirt emerged in that splendid moment which sets football hearts beating faster. They had appointed George captain for the day and out he came, waving to those fans he had wondered if he would ever see again. We stood there swallowing hard in one of football's highly charged moments. Hammy was back and all was well at Pittodrie. What the crowd did not know was that his arrival in this country had been hastened by the tragedy of his sister's death. He was back for the creation of a team which was to be one of the finest ever seen at Pittodrie and would make history before the end of that first post-war season. As much as anyone, George Hamilton embodied the spirit and enthusiasm of that post-war period in football, when a wearied world renewed its old acquaintances, felt glad that it didn't have to mind the black-out any more and came up with a determination to enjoy itself, despite the impoverished state of the country and the austerity which the politicians decided should remain in vogue. As we breathed the fresh air of peace again, a normal crowd at Pittodrie ranged from 18,000 to 22,000, rising to 28,000 for Hearts or Hibs, 35,000 for Celtic and 40,000 for Rangers. Boom-time was here for Scottish football in general and for Aberdeen not least.

George Hamilton's sheer enthusiasm for the game at that time and until the end of his career is something which continued to raise a gleam in his eye when he had long since untied his last lace. Like many another ex-player, he doesn't go to matches any more, regarding the watching of it as an unbearably poor substitute for being involved in it. But he will talk with a glow and tell you: 'I lived for my football and I would follow exactly the same career again. Do you know, I used to enjoy it so much that I would ask the referee how long there was to go. If he said there was only ten minutes left, I felt genuinely disappointed that it was nearly over.'

Hamilton's obvious love of the game and determination to play it skilfully and fairly earned him the name of 'Gentleman George', which tended, like most of these appellations, to be more of a newspaper label than a phrase you would hear on the terracing. In all truth, George was perfectly capable of looking after himself if the occasion arose, gentleman or no gentleman! In eighteen years at the top, however, he collected only a single booking. That arose in a League Cup tie with Hibs when the Dons had drawn 5–5 and the game went into extra time. George dared to say to referee Jackson: 'I don't think that was a foul, ref!' and down went his name. Compare that with some of the Anglo-Saxon expletives which referees have to cope with today!

So George was back at inside-right after the war but what had become of people like Stan Williams and Archie Baird to complete the inside-forward trio? Alfred Stanley Williams was the diminutive South African who had been playing for the railway team in Cape Town that day in 1937 when the Dons went along as spectators in the aftermath of Jackie Beynon's death. He hadn't required a second invitation from Paddy Travers and had arrived in Scotland in 1938, thrilled to be rubbing shoulders with men such as Mills and Armstrong and his own fellow countryman, Billy Strauss. But the war soon had him scurrying off to help build Sunderland flying-boats at the Blackburn factory in Dumbarton. He guested with Dumbarton and Clyde, at that time managed by Travers, but also travelled back to play for Aberdeen. Called up and stationed in England, he played for Stoke City, Reading and Millwall – and was actually chosen to play for Scotland against England at Wembley in a wartime international when rules about nationality were not so strict. Stan still proudly remembers shaking hands with Winston Churchill when the Prime Minister stepped out on the sacred turf to meet the teams. Scotland lost 2–0 in a match which included such names as Jerry Dawson of Rangers and Tommy Walker of Hearts. Even after the war, however, he was still stationed in the London area and used to travel up to Aberdeen from Woolwich to play for the Dons on a Saturday. He was doing so right up to the Scottish League Cup Final of 1946, by which time he was established as a dashing centre-forward of only five feet four.

There was no lack of height with his partner at inside-left, Archie Baird, who had also come to Aberdeen in 1938, in the same season that his team-mate at Strathclyde Juniors, Willie Waddell, went to Rangers. When Archie arrived at Pittodrie he found himself recruited on the very same day as another Willie Waddell, who had come from Renfrew Juniors. As the two boys settled into the same digs, both unknowns in the city of Aberdeen, they had no inkling of the part they would play in a historic moment for Aberdeen Football Club nine years later. Nor could they have foreseen the interruption of the war. They were just fresh-faced boys with a lifetime ahead of them. Archie had been an apprentice architect in Glasgow and continued his training with the Aberdeen firm of Jenkins and Marr, which seemed like a sensible precaution, especially since his first season at Pittodrie left him with some doubts as to whether he was really going to make it as a professional footballer after all.

By 1940 he was en route to a wartime adventure which would

turn him and many other young boys into men overnight. Archie was earmarked for the field ambulance of the Eighth Army, as it battled through the ferocity of the North African campaign, and his only change from that encounter was to find himself ensnared as a prisoner-of-war with the Germans at Tobruk. But that was not at all to the liking of the young man from Rutherglen. (Archie was later to become the brother-in-law of television's Magnus Magnusson, who might well have found a mastermind of escape in 1943 as the imprisoned Aberdeen player sat down to work out a flight to freedom.) With a characteristic body-swerve, Baird made a daring escape from German captivity and spent a year behind enemy lines on the Adriatic coast, with the assistance of an Italian peasant family for whom he ploughed, sowed grain and made wine and to whom he writes to this day. When the Germans came, the family would hide him. Then he tried to break through to the British side of the battle-line but finally had to contain himself until the British troops pushed the Germans up the leg of Italy and he was free to join his own side.

It was a more mature and confident Archie Baird who returned to Pittodrie after the war; and who could blame him for thinking that, with that kind of escapade behind him, there could be few terrors to be faced in the less complicated machinations of football? Indeed, he was to continue his experience of breaking through enemy lines and eluding tight situations on the football field to the point that he was chosen to play for Scotland against Belgium. He was also chosen for that famous Victory International at Hampden Park in 1946 but had to withdraw with cartilage trouble, his place going instead to George Hamilton who shared the glory in one of Scotland's finest hours. Baird's form, however, encouraged 'Rex' of the *Sunday Mail* to forecast that the new partnership of Gordon Smith and Archie Baird would turn out to be the best right wing that Scotland had ever seen. Unfortunately, his forecast was never to be properly tested. The cartilage was the most serious part of a catalogue of troubles, extending to a broken leg, broken jaw, broken nose and a variety of broken ribs in a career which Archie Baird still maintains he thoroughly enjoyed!

As a postscript to the Italian connection, he developed an interest in the language and, at the age of fifty, took an honours degree in Italian, giving further credence to that old cliché about an ill wind. On returning after the war he became a gym teacher, while displaying what a fine footballer he really was – tall and distinctive in style with forearms and fingers pointing rigidly from the elbows in the manner of a toy soldier.

So David Halliday had his three inside men – Hamilton, Williams and Baird – and the three survivors of the 1937 Cup Final team, Johnstone, Cooper and Dunlop, as well as Andy Cowie and George Taylor from before the war and an outside-left who had come on the scene in 1944 and whose name was Billy McCall. There were not too many places left to fill. In a game against Dunfermline he fielded a junior from Blantyre Celtic at right-half and gave him the prompting of the veteran Willie Cooper from behind. The youngster caught the eye by blotting out Dunfermline's left-winger, who was to become better known as Liverpool and Scotland outside-left Billy Liddell. And the junior who overshadowed him? None other than Pat McKenna, whose signature was secured by David Halliday at half-time. With a stripling of a lad from the Dundee area, Alec Kiddie, he had the personnel for one of the great Aberdeen teams, though the reality of it had yet to be proved.

He signed up others. That all-powerful St Clements team of the 1940s would surely have something to offer the Dons and Halliday signed three of them: goalkeeper Ian Black, left-half Johnny Cruickshank and inside-forward Martin Buchan. Ian Black was to become Scotland's goalie but by then he had been called up for military service, guested with Southampton and decided to stay at The Dell. Martin Buchan was as good a ball-player as Aberdeen junior football had produced in many a year, though he never did command the place which his earlier form seemed to merit. But if the beautifully balanced Buchan did not realise his full potential at Pittodrie (he later gave twelve distinguished years to Buckie Thistle), he was to make a contribution to the fortunes of Aberdeen Football Club which he could scarcely have imagined in those immediate post-war days. Within a few years he was to father another Martin Buchan who would grow up with all his father's instincts, follow his route to Pittodrie and become captain of a Scottish Cup-winning team, making him, at the age of twenty-one, the youngest-ever skipper to achieve that distinction. All that, however, lay twenty-five years ahead.

David Halliday was looking for a blend of players who would bring some kind of prize to Pittodrie after forty years and more of Scottish League football. The public was grasping at anything which looked like the reality of peace and Scottish football made a brave attempt at restoring a pre-war face when it launched an A and B

Division of a League programme on 11 August 1945, just five days after the atomic bomb had been dropped on Hiroshima and the Japanese capitulated.

The Dons team which ran out that Saturday afternoon to a very special cheer of joy, relief and welcome-home was: Johnstone; Cooper, Dyer; Bremner, Dunlop, Taylor; Miller, Driver, Pattillo, Baird and Williams. Against visiting Third Lanark, the Dons won 3–0 with two goals from Johnny Pattillo and one from Miller.

Before the season was out, a limited version of the Scottish League Cup had been instituted and Aberdeen found themselves beating Ayr United with a team which had already altered to: Johnstone; Cooper, McKenna; Pattillo, Dunlop, Taylor; Wallbanks, Hamilton, Williams, McCall, Strauss. The semi-final tie took Aberdeen to meet Airdrie at Ibrox Park, Glasgow, but that event was rather overshadowed by the fact that on the same day, Saturday 27 April 1946, Aberdonians were lining Union Street by the tens of thousands to give a hero's welcome to Winston Churchill, who had led the country through the war and was now on his way to the Music Hall to receive the Freedom of Aberdeen. I remember running alongside his car to cheer in gratitude for the man who had seemed to the wartime child to be all that stood between us and disaster.

Meanwhile the Dons needed a replay and more extra time to dispose of Airdrie but suddenly they found themselves with a date to appear at Hampden Park, Glasgow, on 11 May 1946 for the final of the League Cup. It was the first opportunity for a whole new generation of football supporters to visit the national stadium and when the Aberdeen party arrived in Glasgow for the match, after three very refreshing days at the Marine Hotel, Largs, they found the city seething with red and white.

In heatwave conditions, the Dons were given a tremendous welcome outside the stadium, while inside the terracings were already packed. The opponents, if I have forgotten to mention it, were Glasgow Rangers and the Lords Provost of the two cities, Sir Thomas Mitchell of Aberdeen and Hector McNeill of Glasgow, shook hands with the teams before the start. Sir Thomas, or Tammy Mitchell as he was affectionately known, turned with characteristic pawkiness before he left the field and gave the Dons players the Churchill V-for-Victory sign. He had hardly reached his seat when the long-striding Andy Cowie sent one of his equally long throw-ins to Stan Williams, who headed it on to Archie Baird. The big inside-left completed the heading act by scoring Aberdeen's first goal. This was the day when a slightly built lad from Dundee, who was generally referred to as A. A. Kiddie, played the game of his life, turning his own dream-like performance into a nightmare for Rangers' left-back stalwart, Tiger Shaw, who was not accustomed to chasing shadows. In yet another successful joust, Alec Kiddie gained possession, raced ahead and crossed to George Hamilton, who guided the ball on to Stan Williams for the little centre to score a second goal. Rangers hit back with two second-half goals to draw level and, in the nature of things, they might have been expected to snatch a typical Ibrox victory.

But that man Kiddie put a different complexion on things. The game had entered its very last minute and the atmosphere was felt not only on the slopes of Hampden Park but in places like the common-room of Gordon's College boarding house at Queen's Cross, where a group of us were clustered round the wireless set, hanging on every word from BBC commentator Peter Thomson. He had just checked his watch for the number of dying seconds when suddenly Aberdeen were on the attack, the ball had been crossed by Kiddie . . . Cowie was going for it . . . Hamilton was going for it . . . George Taylor was going for it. . . .

Peter Thomson, who had a fine voice for football commentary, was sometimes accused of a Rangers bias and when his voice eventually confirmed what the roar had already told us — 'Aberdeen have scored' – it seemed suspiciously like a wail. But Aberdeen had, indeed, and there was time only for a re-start before a final whistle which brought to the sideboard of Pittodrie its first national trophy, albeit a slightly limited honour because the competition had been organised on a makeshift basis and did not include all the teams which would compete in subsequent years. The victory, in fact, does not appear in the official list of League Cup wins but that did not inhibit the joyous celebrations, while the fact that it had been achieved against the might of Ibrox made it a worthy success by any standards.

The Dons had other fixtures in the south during the following week so they returned to the Marine Hotel at Largs, where congratulations came pouring in. It was nine days later before the cup was finally borne north by train but that did little to dampen the reception. A huge crowd waited at the Joint Station and Frank Dunlop just managed a hug from his wife before he was hoisted high on shoulders and carried to the waiting open-topped bus. Shop and office workers rushed to their doors and windows as the bus came up Market Street and Union Street to give as many people as possible a chance to see the victorious team on its way to the Caledonian Hotel. They were all there except Stan Williams, who had to return to his army base in the south, and George Hamilton, who still had military commitments at Maryhill Barracks, Glasgow.

On the following day the Scottish League Cup went on display in the window of the *Evening Express* branch office at the top of Union Street, near Bon Accord Terrace, along with the boot of George Taylor with which he had scored the winning goal. The team sat down in that same office to sign autographs and the picture which appeared in the *Evening Express* showed a queue of autograph-hunters headed by a shiny-faced schoolboy who never dreamed that one day he would be writing a book about it all. Such is the beautiful uncertainty of life.

20
SCOTTISH CUP AT LAST!

The dust of the Second World War had settled on a jaded Britain and people were anxiously searching for a return of some colour to their lives. Everything that was good seemed to have happened 'before the war', which elevated the 1930s to a golden memory beyond its rights. Now, there was the strange anti-climax of peace and a bursting desire to shout. That opportunity was to come in abundance on an April day of 1947, in the first full season after the war, when the grey-granite hordes of Aberdeen set out to cheer the Dons at Hampden Park.

For only the second time in its history, the club had reached the final of the Scottish Cup and that northern army of football loyalty was sweeping south by every known form of transport, determined to fortify an attack on the Hibernian of Edinburgh which would surely, at last, bring the national trophy to Pittodrie.

In the austerity of the time, most folk settled for the decent modesty of a rosette pinned to their utility coats but in the effervescence of youth there were those of us who were determined to make more of the occasion. I can still recall my dear mother converting an old red jumper into a tammy, with the aid of some knicker elastic and a tassel on top, and waving me off in my dark blue trenchcoat to the unknown wilds of darkest Glasgow.

The seething mob at the Joint Station was funnelled out of chaos into train-loads of orderly enthusiasm which rumbled southwards in a gay chatter of anticipation, excitement mounting by the mile but sometimes muted in a scanning of the morning papers in the hope of finding a sports writer who would confirm our own high hopes. Then we would recall that this Scottish Cup journey had begun, not at the Joint Station that morning but three months earlier, on Burns' Day of 1947.

It was then that Partick Thistle had come north for the first round of the Cup with a formidable reputation, having beaten Aberdeen 4–0 in a League game at Firhill a few weeks earlier. It was vital that Aberdeen should take advantage of the home ground to see them into the second round. With the final minutes of that match running out, the score stood at 1–1, with Partick happily contemplating a replay on their own territory and Aberdonians dreading that very prospect. To make matters worse, skipper Frank Dunlop had been hurt and was limping on the wing when the Dons were awarded a corner kick on the left. The ball was cleared from the visitors' goalmouth and seemed to be going to Willie Sharp of Partick. Aberdeen right-back Willie Cooper had moved upfield, however, suddenly realising that he could reach it first – and he hit a first-time, soaring shot from forty yards out. What happened next is part of the folklore of Pittodrie. There are still plenty of witnesses to tell you that the ball seemed to be heading for the upper reaches of the terracing at the Beach end, at a time when there was no thought of an enclosure there. Jimmy Steadward in the Partick goal seemed to share that opinion. Now, whether it was a gust of wind, or a skeely Cooper spin, or a downright act of God we shall never know, but we do know that the ball seemed to halt in its upward tracks and drop nonchalantly down behind the Partick keeper. Willie Cooper denies that it was a fluke and gives you a broad, cheery grin when he reminds you that, in hitting a shot like that, a player has every intention of scoring. Even Willie was too far away to confirm the truth of the situation, however, and it was a jubilant Tony Harris who turned to give him the first news. 'You've scored, auld yin!' roared the former Queen's Parker. Two–one. The referee was looking at his watch. And as he raised his hand to blow that final whistle, 34,000 people – yes, think of that for a first-round tie with Partick Thistle! – rose to acclaim the thirty-six-year-old full-back who had given the Dons the right to prove that they could make it all the way to Hampden this time. But if that winning shot owed anything to luck, that fickle lady was bent on deserting poor Willie before the contest was over.

In the worst winter of living memory, which left snow behind many a dyke into June, the Dons battled through a play-to-the-finish fourth round against Dundee at Dens Park and returned to that same ground for the semi-final with Arbroath which was played just one week before the final. In that game Willie pulled a muscle which had no time to recover before the big day.

So the journey south was more than tinged with regret that the old warrior himself, without whom there would have been no journey at all, had lost his very last chance of a Cup medal in twenty-one years of magnificent service to Aberdeen Football Club and to the game as a whole. The team which we contemplated that April morning looked strangely unfamiliar in defence. Pat McKenna had moved from left- to right-back; George Taylor had dropped back from left-half and the wing-half positions would be taken by Joe McLaughlin and Willie Waddell. The teams would therefore appear as: Aberdeen – Johnstone; McKenna, Taylor; McLaughlin, Dunlop, Waddell; Harris, Hamilton, Williams, Baird, McCall. Hibernian – Kerr; Govan, Shaw; Howie, Aird, Kean; Smith, Finnegan, Cuthbertson, Turnbull, Ormond.

Outside Buchanan Street Station, Glasgow, toothless beer-barrels with bow-legs and gravel voices stood ready for the business of selling red rosettes to the foreign invaders, offering free advice on how to get to Hampden Park. So we negotiated alien-sounding streets, across the Clyde, through the Gorbals and out along Cathcart Road to the spiritual home of Scottish football. In the gathering momentum of people and atmosphere, it would have taken an insensitive creature to resist the excitement. Meanwhile, the Dons party was travelling up by bus from Largs, where they had gone to prepare for the Cup Final. On the night before the match they had attended a whist drive at the invitation of Largs Thistle and skipper Frank Dunlop won the miniature trophy; a good omen? Willie Cooper can still recall the sense of emptiness in not being an active part of it, sitting on the trainer's bench with Bob McDermid. But Willie was just emerging from the dressing-room as the game got under way and he had not reached his seat when disaster struck Aberdeen's bid to land the Cup.

Within thirty seconds of the starting whistle, George Taylor was passing back to goalkeeper George Johnstone, who had stood between those same posts exactly ten years earlier in the final against Celtic. It seemed like a safe and simple ball which the ever-dependable George, who made goalkeeping look easy, would collect as he had done a thousand times before. For some unaccountable reason he seemed to take his eye off the ball or develop butterfingers and it slipped through his arms and legs and presented itself on a plate for any willing forward. Without pausing to consider his luck, John Cuthbertson was round him like a man in a hurry and accepting as generous a gift as Hampden Park had ever seen. Pat McKenna raced across to avert disaster but it was all in vain.

Within the opening minute, the great army of Aberdonians was silenced into disbelief. This was not what they had come all this way to see. At least the game was young and there would be time to make amends, as long as the Dons could prevent a second goal from a Hibernian team which was driven on by a man who would yet play a significant role as an Aberdeen manager: Eddie Turnbull.

They weathered the storm all right and in thirty-six minutes Tony Harris started a clever move. The ball went to Stan Williams, who put a side-flick into the path of George Hamilton. Hammy, who was as good a header of a ball as Pittodrie had known, darted forward and headed a fine equaliser. The Dons were back in business and what happened six minutes later was a feat which will be talked about for as long as there are still witnesses. If Stan Williams had done nothing else in his career, he would have earned his Pittodrie pedestal for his achievement as he bore in on that goalmouth at the east end of Hampden Park. But I leave it to the man himself to recall what happened:

I liked the way we were fighting back after that early goal. We were clearly the better team and were confident, despite the setback, that we would get that cup. After the equaliser by George Hamilton, Tony Harris, who was playing at outside-right, hit the ball downfield but it was too fast and seemed to be going for a goal-kick. However, I chased it just in case there was a chance and managed to catch the ball before it went over the by-line to the right of the Hibs goal. As I cut in along the line, everyone expected me to cross the ball to either Archie Baird or George Hamilton, who were better placed. One of them was shouting for it. Suddenly I spotted a small space between Jimmy Kerr in the Hibs goal and the near post. There was no time for careful aiming and no margin for error. I just remember saying to myself 'Here goes!'

The rest of the story is lost in a red riot of jubilation. The consequence of fluffing that shot instead of making the obvious pass to Baird would have been a howl of disapproval from the fans, who will tolerate brilliance only when it comes off! But brilliant it was, full of the cheeky confidence which characterised the style of the South African's game. Press pictures of the day show what those of us there did not have the time to analyse – the sheer disbelief on the faces of goalkeeper Kerr and full-back Jock Govan, and even on the face of Archie Baird, who had expected that cross. It was a golden goal-in-a-million. But the match was not over yet. After thirteen minutes of the second half the same Stanley Williams was cleverly eluding the Hibernian defence when he was brought down in the penalty box by Jimmy Kerr, who no doubt felt that he had had enough of the little man's nonsense for one day. Referee Bobby Calder, who later played a major role in the fortunes of Aberdeen Football Club, had no hesitation in awarding a penalty. As George Hamilton came up to take the kick, the Pittodrie supporters were warming themselves with the thought that this would surely settle the issue and take the Scottish Cup safely to Pittodrie. Placing the ball on the penalty spot, Hamilton was having some different thoughts, as he recalled to me later: 'When Stan was brought down, he was injured and had to be taken behind the goal for attention. All this meant a delay, which gave me too much time to think. I remember looking round the crowd and saying to myself, "If I miss this and we happen to lose, I'll be held responsible." At last I was able to take the kick. I sent it to Jimmy Kerr's left-hand side – and he saved it. After that, I can tell you, I was never so glad in all my life to hear the final whistle!' Stan Williams, too, has agonising memories of being torn between his physical injury and an anxiety about the penalty kick. Behind the goal he kept asking trainer Bob McDermid if George had scored.

In the event, the Hamilton penalty kick merely added to the volume of bitten nails. At 4.45 p.m. on Saturday 19 April 1947, the Right Honourable Joseph Westwood, His Majesty's Secretary of State for Scotland, stepped across the hallowed turf of Hampden Park and handed the trophy to Frank Dunlop, centre-half and captain of the first Aberdeen team to win the Scottish Cup. The presentation took place where presentations should always take place – out there on the field in full view of every man, woman and child who had come to see the game. Alas, it is doubtful if the rowdier spirits of today could be trusted to stay behind the boundary wall and give everybody a proper view. So they have been forced to take the ceremony up into the south grandstand, where the culminating point of all the glory is reserved for the privileged eyes of those who are clustered around the directors' box. Back in 1947, when the unruly would not have dared interfere with the rights of the majority, it was the democratic privilege and delight of all to share in the joyous moment. And so it was that April day, which is written in large red letters across the history of the Dons.

Photographs show the crowd of 82,140, including 10,000 from Aberdeen, dressed in sober raincoats, soft hats or bonnets, well-dressed, well-behaved people intent on absorbing a memorable moment in their own personal history.

But the best was yet to come. Amid the scenes of jubilation out there on Hampden's turf, with Frank Dunlop holding the cup for all to see, the crowd set up a chant of 'We want Cooper. We want Cooper!' From his place in the shadows of the south stand, the square-cut figure was coaxed out to that same pitch where he had suffered the disappointment of Cup Final defeat from Celtic ten years earlier. Out he went to a thunderous cheer which told him of the gratitude and affection of every living soul who called himself an Aberdeen supporter. They handed the cup to Willie, for to him it truly belonged, and there were grown men with red rosettes who blew their noses and pretended that a sudden cold had come on, for the solid folk of the North-east do not readily display their tears.

This was one of football's finest moments. Willie Cooper himself remembers it like this: 'It had been my day of greatest disappointment in a long career. Yet, when I heard the shout from the crowd, it also became my greatest day. I'll tell you this: I was nearly greetin'!'

Willie played on for another year before retiring from big-time football in 1948 after twenty-one years' service. He went to work for Stewart's Cream o' the Barley whisky, later part of Allied Breweries, and in his retirement became liquor storeman with the Cooperative at Berryden. Looking back on his career, Willie told me how he had never even considered playing anywhere other than Pittodrie. He just played on, season after season for twenty-one of them, delighted when the manager would ask him to sign on for another year. It was another year's work, as Willie recalls it, a guarantee which meant something in the 1930s when men were scrambling for jobs and were glad of anything they could find.

Willie was happy in his work, with a loyalty which belonged exclusively to Aberdeen Football Club, and the appropriate post-script to that 1947 Cup Final was that, while there was no medal for a non-participant in those days, the SFA displayed a commendable humanity when it allowed the club to strike a special medal for a very special man. Willie Cooper, whom many will nominate as a better footballer than his predecessor, Jock Hutton, stands out as the archetypal Aberdeen man – frank, honest, industrious and loyal. No player in history has ever served a club more faithfully. That special medal was, in fact, all he had to show for his services to football. There had been no runners-up medal in the 1937 Scottish Cup Final, nothing for the League Cup winners of 1946, because football had not then resumed a peacetime footing, and now he had missed the 1947 final. But if football had offered him little silver, he at least had enriched the game.

Willie was there two days later when the players arrived back at the Joint Station. Not even torrential rain could dampen the spirits of the 15,000 who waited in the station forecourts to endorse a high moment of the club's history. This time the open-topped bus made a longer detour, by Guild Street, Regent Quay, Marischal Street and Union Street to the Caledonian Hotel, where the players were entertained to an early-evening dinner.

Chairman William Mitchell thanked the players and Frank Dunlop replied that 'the boys could travel far and wide and still not find a club like Aberdeen FC. Personally, I consider it a great honour to be a member of the club.' Afterwards, officials, players and friends were guests of Mr James Donald at His Majesty's Theatre, where Dave Willis was doubling them up with laughter.

The fact that the Dons had been at Hampden just two weeks before the Scottish Cup victory, being beaten 4–0 by Rangers in the League Cup Final, is something which few Aberdeen supporters can even recall today! The Light Blues may have avenged the defeat of the previous year but the game was played in a hurricane which had already blown away the memory. The Dons had now won the Scottish Cup after forty-four years in existence and that was enough to put a spring in the northern step and to sustain for many a day the buoyancy of a patient Aberdeen support.

21
HAMMY SPOTS A STAR

The team which brought the Scottish Cup to Aberdeen for the very first time had been sadly robbed of a proper lifespan by the war, coming together only in the year before that triumph and beginning to disintegrate very soon afterwards. After all, it was not a young team. Apart from the veteran Willie Cooper who had missed the final, George Johnstone and Frank Dunlop had been in the Dons' Cup Final team of 1937, while others like Willie Waddell, George Taylor, George Hamilton, Stan Williams and Archie Baird had all been on the books before the outbreak of war in 1939. Stan Williams, who had bounced in as an enthusiastic twenty-year-old in 1938, was approaching his thirtieth year before that moment of Hampden glory. By the following year he had been given a transfer to Plymouth Argyle, though he didn't settle and returned to play for George Anderson's Dundee. He finally left Scotland in 1951 and spent two years in Malta before settling back in his native South Africa, this time in Johannesburg. It took twenty-five years for Stan to set foot on Scottish soil again. He came back to bring in the New Year of 1977 with his old friend and team-mate of 1947, Billy McCall in Bishopbriggs, Glasgow.

Billy had been another great favourite at Pittodrie, a small, stocky left-winger; but he too departed during the year which followed the Scottish Cup victory. He claimed that his departure all began with a row over a cigarette. On a match day, he was heading for the dressing room with an unlit cigarette in his hand when chairman Mitchell stopped him and accused him of smoking before a game. McCall said he displayed the unlit fag but the chairman did not accept his explanation and reported him to manager Halliday. Some bad blood was generated out of a rather trivial incident and one thing led to another until Billy McCall was transferred to Newcastle United in an exchange deal involving Tommy Pearson. Despite the unfortunate circumstances of his departure, however, McCall still upheld Aberdeen as a place of great happiness, to which the people who leave are eventually anxious to return.

I had arranged to meet Williams and McCall in the Central Hotel, Glasgow, during the New Year visit of 1977 and there I sat in the foyer, rekindling memories of the fair-haired Stan and the dark-haired Billy and wondering what the years had done to them. I kept watch on the revolving doors of the hotel when suddenly two small men with grey-white hair and the lines of age about their faces swung into the foyer. The years may have left their mark but at least they had more hair than the schoolboy of 1947 who was now there to meet them. Stan had had one of those warning heart attacks and Billy had suffered a thrombosis but that did not prevent us from engaging in a good old blether about happy days in Aberdeen. Football apart, Stan Williams remembered dancing at the Palais, for which Mr Bromberg used to issue complimentary tickets to the Dons players; there was snooker with Tony Harris, Andy Cowie and Billy McCall and golf at Stonehaven, followed by a swim in the open-air pool.

For the Dons players, as for many more people in Aberdeen, the social centre of the city at that time was the Caledonian Hotel. Visiting teams from the south stayed there and the Caley became the place where you went to see and be seen, a social crossroads with a palm court trio in the lounge and a staff of personalities who are still remembered – Charlie Bultitude the head waiter, big Arthur at the door, Andy the cocktail king of the American Bar upstairs, the little Greek chap in the dining-room and, of course, the inimitable Jean in the back bar, who kept everybody in order. Stan remembered it all with warm affection: 'Back home, they don't believe me when I tell them that we were treated like film stars when I played for Aberdeen. People used to stop you in the street or on the tramcars to ask for your autograph.'

By then, he was making parts for the rock drills which cut diamonds in the South African mines, working at Benoni, twenty miles outside Johannesburg. Every Sunday morning he would look in the paper for the Aberdeen result and give a thought to other Sunday mornings when he would wake up in his digs at 9 Forest Avenue, the home of Mrs Ella Large, who later moved to Cults. Stan had come to Aberdeen on a wage of £5 a week in the reserve team but by 1946 that had risen to £10 with a £2 bonus for a win. Inflation makes a mockery of such figures but out of that seemingly modest sum Stan Williams saved enough for a deposit account which rested in a South African bank awaiting his retirement.

Williams talked with much respect for manager David Halliday and confessed that he had to cope with a high-spirited bunch of players, some of whom gave rise to rumours about drinking, dancing and outrageous hours. He reckoned that Mr Halliday was too inclined to believe the rumours, when in fact half of them were not true. In fairness to the manager, however, it must be said that if even half of them were true, he was probably well justified in taking the firm line he did!

Meanwhile, back at Pittodrie, George Hamilton was overcome by a restlessness in the aftermath of the Cup Final and put in a request for a transfer. It was granted and an exchange deal was arranged with Hearts which took Hamilton to Tynecastle and Archie Kelly to Pittodrie. But Hammy had reached no further than the train which would take him to Edinburgh for the signing formality when he realised that he had made a mistake. His natural instinct was to turn about and run straight back to Pittodrie but he had given his word and that was binding on a man of honour. At Tynecastle he teamed up with another famous newcomer, Bobby Flavell of Airdrie, but he never did settle in Edinburgh and was feeling miserable about the whole business. He was still playing well enough to be chosen for the Scottish team to meet Eire, however, and on the boat crossing to Dublin was leaning over the rail, gazing into space, when there was a voice behind him: 'Are you happy, George?' John D. Robbie, the Aberdeen director travelling with the Scottish party, did not have to wait for a reply. 'If I make the effort, would you come back?' George broke into a broad smile. 'You go ahead, Mr Robbie, and I'll be delighted to come back to Pittodrie.' Thus a great servant of football returned to the place where he belonged and continued in a red shirt for another eight or nine years.

But the wheels of change were still turning, grinding out the old and in the new. Indeed, George Hamilton himself had already played a major part in laying the foundation of the next generation of players who would add lustre to the Pittodrie story. It happened in that euphoric period after the 1947 Cup Final when he went down to visit his parents in Irvine, where local folk were glad to shake his hand and share a pride in his achievements. Little did he think, as he wandered along to Kilwinning to watch a local junior cup final, that he was about to find a future captain for Aberdeen

Football Club. In the Annbank United team that evening he spotted a player whose performance sent him scurrying to the telephone to contact David Halliday (just as Billy Halliday had made a similar phone call when he spotted the young Hamilton at Dumfries). Meanwhile, George's father had made contact with the lad and confirmed that his name was Archie Glen from Mauchline. Mr Halliday went hot-foot to Ayrshire and there he encountered young Archie's father who, true to his solid, mining background, laid down the condition that his son could sign for Aberdeen only if he continued with his plans for a university degree in chemistry. Mr Halliday agreed, and Archie Glen was heading north. He recalls:

The club were even better than their word, because they paid my fees for a B.Sc degree course at Aberdeen University and for that I am eternally grateful.

I remember arriving in Aberdeen in July 1947, looking at Willie Cooper and thinking that he had been playing for the Dons three years before I was even born. I was soon to play with him in the reserve team and found him a tremendous competitor as well as a good teacher. He had basic rules which were very sound and which he felt you should learn.

So the young Glen settled into his digs with Mrs Petrie in Burnett Place, just round the corner from Willie Cooper's house in Leslie Road, and willingly paid his landlady £2 out of his wage-packet of £5. His first-team debut came along in February 1949, against Falkirk at Brockville when he had the joy of playing on the same pitch as one of his childhood heroes – former Rangers keeper Jerry Dawson. By then he was also being inspired by that supreme artist Tommy Pearson, who crusaded for the belief that football had to be skilful and entertaining as a first priority and that, hopefully, the rewards of winning would follow. Glen would listen with rapt attention to the philosophies of Pearson, who was playing out his veteran days at Pittodrie, having given his prime to Newcastle United. It was all a matter of assessing your own strengths against those of your opponents, said Pearson, and he would give a practical demonstration. Archie Glen recalls a lesson from an afternoon session at Pittodrie. Pearson's gift for putting a ball through an opponent's legs was almost as legendary as his famous double-shuffle and young Glen was about to experience the torment of many a defender. 'I'll come up to you with the ball three times,' said Pearson, 'with the intention of putting it through your legs twice.' So, with at least some forewarning of events, the exercise began, and when it was over the bewildered Glen found that the ball had been put through his legs on all three occasions! Such was the magic of Pearson, who was not only a juggler but an expert at taking up position as well.

It all helped Archie Glen to develop a special technique of tackling. As an opponent came towards him with the ball, he picked up the rhythm of the man's step, which sounded in his head like the beat of a metronome; then he tackled on the half-beat – and the success of it is part of the memory which Dons fans retain of one of the most effective wing-halves Pittodrie has seen. Glen attended university by day and trained at nights, graduating in 1950. With National Service, he was off to join the army in 1951, at a time when he still had reservations about his ability to play at top level.

He soon found himself playing in the British Army team alongside the great Welsh internationalist John Charles and that other superb footballer, Tommy Taylor, who was later killed in the Manchester United air crash of 1958. Inspired by that kind of company, Archie began to believe that he had it in him after all, until one day when his world collapsed. A bad injury had caused a bone to press on the Achilles tendon and the verdict of a serious-faced doctor at the hospital was that he would have to find another occupation. Glen came out stunned, unwilling to believe that his career was over before it had properly begun.

When his army service was over, he returned to Pittodrie without saying a word to anyone. He started training and was experiencing no ill effects; so he went quietly to a doctor friend to have his ankle X-rayed. The report confirmed the previous diagnosis but added that the bone had now slipped back into position – and to this day no one at Pittodrie has ever been told about it! So Glen returned to the fold at an interesting time of reconstruction in which the Dons were coming close to having another good team. Jimmy Mitchell, the former Queen's Park and Morton full-back, had come north to be captain. Alec Young came late to senior football from Blantyre Victoria but turned out to be one of the finest centre-halves of them all, out-jumping the best despite his lack of inches, and gaining fame for his sliding tackle in which he not only did the splits but gave a heaven-sent opportunity for 'Chrys', the cartoonist of the *Evening Express*, to caricature him. A stubby-haired Edinburgh lad called Jack Allister, who had gone to Chelsea after his army service, took over at right-half and Archie Glen completed a very competent half-line of Allister, Young and Glen. Before that, however,there were surprises in store for the Dons fans – and for Mr Halliday in particular.

22
PEARSON'S MAGIC

One morning in the late 1940s, a telegram dropped on the Pittodrie desk of manager David Halliday. He opened it and read 'Request permission to play goalkeeper Martin, who is on your books – Sgd Manager of Crystal Palace FC London.' Halliday scratched his head, considered that there had been some mistake and despatched a reply which said: 'Sorry, we have no goalkeeper called Martin.'

Thus arose one of those curious football stories. David Halliday was, of course, technically correct. He had only one Martin on his books and that was the big inside-forward he had signed from Carnoustie Panmure in 1946, a lad with height, strength and fine ball control who had played in the reserve team for nine months before going off to National Service training, which continued to take young men into the services for many years after the war. Two months before his departure in June 1947 he had sat at Hampden with the entire Pittodrie staff watching that first-ever Scottish Cup win. But it was during National Service that fate took a hand in the astonishing career of big Fred Martin. Playing for the British Army in the south of England, as a forward of course, he was drafted into goal one day when the keeper was injured. The regular man was out for several weeks and in that time his deputy was performing with distinction, so much so that he was spotted by Crystal Palace – and off went that telegram to Aberdeen.

How could manager Halliday ever have imagined that the mysterious message was bringing him the first hint of a fairy-tale; that the man he had signed for his outfield skill would, within a very few years, be chosen as Scotland's first-ever World Cup goalkeeper! It is the very stuff of schoolboy adventure stories, except that this time it had nothing to do with fiction.

All that, however, was still in the future when big Fred found himself as an Army goalkeeper, having committed himself to a professional career as a footballing forward. Recalling the dilemma, he says: 'Everyone has an idea of his own capabilities and when I went into the Army goal I sensed that I had a certain aptitude for this part of the game. I was given permission to play for Crystal Palace, then came that day in 1949 when my National Service was over and it was time to return to Pittodrie.'

During pre-season training, Mr Halliday called him in and said: 'Well Fred, what are you going to do? Are you going to be a forward or a goalkeeper?' He left the choice entirely to Fred, who decided to take a chance on the latter. George Johnstone was coming to the end of his career, though there were others around, such as Pat Kelly, John Curran and Frank Watson. Out of that transitional period, however, it was Fred Martin who was to emerge as the goalkeeper of the 1950s, playing through three Scottish Cup Finals, a League Cup Final and a League Championship season, as well as keeping goal for Scotland in the World Cup adventures of 1954. But more of that later.

Pittodrie was gathering up some remarkable personalities, some of whom would last through the historic days of the mid 1950s. Others would be best remembered by people who like to absorb the essence of a distinctive player, to store it away in the crevices of the mind and bring it out for an airing whenever those of us with the football disease succumb to our periodic bouts of nostalgia.

Two names spring readily to mind because they stirred the public imagination in totally different ways: Tommy Pearson and Don Emery. If I were asked to nominate the players who had brought me the greatest amount of pleasure during close on fifty years of watching the Dons, I would turn out favourites like Johnny Pattillo, Ernie Waldron, Archie Baird, George Hamilton and come through the century to classical ball-players like Charlie Cooke, Jimmy Smith, Zoltan Varga and Gordon Strachan. But if I were forced to name one man above all others who satisfied the highest aspirations of football grace, intelligence and excitement, that man would have to be Tommy Pearson. He had spent his prime years with Newcastle United, before and after the Second World War, but we caught the tail-end of his genius at Pittodrie and were grateful for the privilege, because Pearson was one of the supreme artists of this maddening game, a barrel-chested dream of a player with the balance of perfection in his body and the sheer power of poetry in his movement. With the deftness of a conjurer, he practised a kind of sleight-of-feet which produced his famous double-shuffle. There are other players who have done a double-shuffle but I have never seen one to match it. Knowing that he would turn it on perhaps half a dozen times in a game, there were those of us who would set out to watch precisely what happened. Each time he gained possession, we would keep our eyes riveted on his feet to await the moment. That moment would arrive, he would weave his magical deception and it would be all over before we had time to chart the details. Then, like a conjurer who assures his audience that the trick is really quite simple and that he will let them into the secret, he was capable of taking on the same man again – or any other who cared to be demoralised – and beating him in precisely the same manner, leaving us still as mystified as ever about how it was done. Oh, for the benefit of an action replay!

There are people today who will tell you that Pearson would not survive in the modern game and they may well be right. But if that means that he would be a natural target for some of the thuggery that passes for defensive play, then we are coming close to the root of the malaise which persuades countless thousands to stay at home these days. It is well worth remembering that Pittodrie could draw crowds of 8000 for a reserve game in the early 1950s and a large proportion of those people would tell you they were there for the sole purpose of savouring the magic of Tommy Pearson, aiding and abetting his lanky protégé Hughie Hay. That kind of genius comes but rarely in a lifetime and lingers like a perfume when so much else that seemed important at the time has been forgotten.

If Pittodrie remembers Tommy Pearson for his silken talents, the affection for Don Emery is based on a somewhat different premise. For Don was one of the personalities of the game, a colourful character with a cannonball kick whom one writer of the day described as being built on the lines of a small rhinoceros. Older men likened him to the build and shooting power of Jock Hutton. Neither of them used their chunky frames to unfair advantage but anyone who sought to precipitate a collision with either of them was liable to rebound like an arrow from a bow. The point was illustrated with fine dry humour by the late John Fairgrieve, writing in the *Scottish Daily Mail* and setting the scene for a collision between Emery and Bobby Parker of Hearts, a man whose robustness encouraged him to believe that any left-winger who had the temerity to go near the ball deserved all he got. It was uncommon in those days for left-backs to come in direct contact with right-backs but the Almighty, we were told, had decreed that the question should be settled. Fairgrieve described the encounter as Parker and Emery went for a fifty-fifty ball one day:

Tynecastle was hushed, the kind of silence often decreed in memory of some respected official. The ball bounced awkwardly but the ball was no longer of any importance. Parker and Emery were on their way and could not be called back. The impact itself was not particularly noisy; more of a thud than a crunch. Emery had ground to a halt a fraction of a second before, the better to brace himself no doubt. That, of course, was not Bobby Parker's way and possibly his tactics were basically unsound. Parker stotted backwards and fell flat on his back. Emery stared down at him, expressionless, hands on hips. Parker rose, grinned, waved and loped away!

Pittodrie people who are grateful for the Emery memory should thank a lady called Maude Cheyne for the fact that they ever saw Don at all. Maude, whose father was George Cheyne of the motor firm, joined the WAAF during the war and was stationed at Newport, Monmouthshire, when she met the solid Welshman, at that time a Swindon Town player. During his RAF service he was playing for the works team of Lovell's, the confectionery people, by whom he was literally paid in sweets! Don and Maude were married and when he resumed at Swindon Town he ran quickly into an exciting time in the FA Cup. As a Third Division team, Swindon found themselves drawn against First Division leaders Burnley. With a courage which would not be tolerated today, the manager decided that they did not have a snowball's chance of beating Burnley so he took them off to Southport for a week's holiday and told them to relax, enjoy themselves and forget all about football. That is exactly what they did and on the following Saturday they knocked table-topping Burnley right out of the FA Cup by 2–0! Ten thousand people welcomed them back to Swindon. In the next round the opponents were Notts County and this time that splendid manager decided that Weston-super-Mare was as good a place as any to forget all about football. Once again, as Don recalls, the players had a magnificent week of indulging – and came back to knock Notts County out of the Cup. The recipe ran to the sixth round when Swindon were running short of seaside resorts and Southampton managed to stop the fun. I cannot help feeling that such a civilised approach to a game which has become far too serious deserved a better fate.

Don might never have left the south but for the home-sickness of his Aberdonian wife, which was a lucky break for manager David Halliday, who heard about the situation. Andy Cowie, that splendid wing-half who had come from Dundee in 1938 for £2500 and played in the League Cup Final team of 1946, was out of favour at Pittodrie. He was on the transfer list at £5000 but Halliday arranged instead an exchange with Swindon's Emery, who came to Aberdeen and took over the right-back position of Willie Cooper. The Pittodrie crowd took him straight to their hearts, this solid chunk of a man who seemed to embody those traditional local emblems of granite rock and prime Aberdeen Angus. The power of an Emery free kick became absolutely legendary, the post-war generation having seen nothing to compare with it.

Percy Dickie, who was coaching at Pittodrie at the time, got in the way of an Emery ball at training one day and sound men who are not given to exaggeration will swear that the manufacturer's name was imprinted on Percy's backside for weeks afterwards! Fred Martin still carries a badly bent finger, the result of an Emery practice shot – and the apologetic Don will tell you that he was only wearing plimsolls.

The statistics show that, in four seasons at Pittodrie, he scored thirty-three goals, nineteen of them from penalties, while most of the others were free-kick balls which keepers tended to see for the first time as they retrieved them from the back of a shattered net. In a game with Rangers, goalkeeper Bobby Brown called for a 'shield' at an Emery free kick. At the last minute, however, his defence all ducked and left poor Brown to take the sting on his fingertips as the ball streaked into the net. Some Rangers defenders turned to criticise the keeper and Don, always a gentle and kindly man, felt that that was most unfair. On another occasion a young Celtic goalkeeper moved away from the middle of the goalmouth to seek the protection of the upright. Tommy Gallagher of Dundee, who later became a sports writer with the *Dundee Courier*, often reminded Don that his head had never been quite the same since the day it got in the way of one of his blockbusters. So the stories go on.

For certain, a penalty kick was a matter of very special excitement at Pittodrie when Emery was there. There was no ceremony. The routine was that Harry Yorston would place the ball on the spot as the bulky figure came ambling down from his own penalty area. He did not stop to handle the ball or take special aim. Instead, he simply did what a penalty-taker should never fail to do and blasted it with total ferocity to the back of the net. Goalkeepers who failed to touch those Emery specials were generally regarded as lucky (or particularly agile!). It was better than the infirmary. Just after the famous 'Jimmy Cowan' international at Wembley in 1949, Morton came to Pittodrie and that heroic goalkeeper who had defied the English was given a standing ovation as he ran on to the field. But he was soon brought back to the harsh realities when the Dons were awarded a free kick thirty-five yards from the Morton goal. Cowan thought he could cope at that distance and signed to his defence to keep clear. But a Wembley reputation counted for nothing when a Don Emery free kick went past him like a blur, rebounded from a stanchion and was back at the eighteen-yard line while Cowan was still searching vainly in the net!

His huge thighs and high instep gave him a natural advantage in power, but it was not all brute strength. He used to practise direction with great diligence against the Pittodrie boundary wall, arousing concern in manager Halliday because of the number of balls he used to burst. At 5 ft 8 in tall, he admits to a weight of thirteen stone during his playing days, though in all honesty it looked more. He had a stout heart to match his bulk and, once again, John Fairgrieve used his wit to throw light on the Emery character when he alleged that he once played a game with a broken leg and might never have noticed if someone had not said in the dressing room: 'Excuse me, but isn't that a broken leg you've got there?'

Don went to East Fife, won a Scottish League Cup medal in the same team as a future Aberdeen manager, Jimmy Bonthrone, then broadened out to a square-cut eighteen stone. He became sales manager of the Webster Tyre Company, driving a Mercedes with the registration DON. What better insignia for one of the most colourful Dons of them all?

But Pearson and Emery were not alone among the fascinating figures at Pittodrie in that era. Like Pearson, Jimmy Delaney, who was one of Celtic's greatest-ever names, came to spend part of his twilight with Aberdeen, a balding figure from Manchester United who could still turn on some of those right-wing forays. He was followed to Pittodrie by another Manchester United Scot, Tommy Lowrie, who idolised the great Delaney.

Aberdeen went on tour to Norway in 1950 and Don Emery was out sunbathing in a little boat with Delaney and Lowrie when the latter began larking about. One undergarment was thrown overboard and, in a tit-for-tat caper which went from bad to worse,

Delaney and Lowrie ended up with nothing on but their trunks and had to walk up the main street in a state of undress to buy themselves a new set of clothing, at a time when clothes were still rationed.

Staying at the same hotel in Norway was the future President of the United States, General Dwight Eisenhower, who was at that time Supreme Commander of the Nato forces but had no command at all over the high-spirited Dons. It was the irrepressible Lowrie again who happened to be investigating the layout of the hotel when he spotted smoke through a glass panel in a door. The story goes that he immediately raised the fire alarm, extended the hoses and sparked off a full-scale emergency, only to discover that the room with the glass panel was none other than the hotel's steam laundry!

In the event, Pearson, Emery, Delaney and Lowrie were members of transitional teams and were not to figure in the exciting period ahead. But they were there at a time when the Dons could field the oldest and one of the most talented forward-lines in the land, in which only Harry Yorston was on the under-side of thirty. Just contemplate the market value of this quintet at the height of their fame: Delaney, Yorston, Hamilton, Baird and Pearson. It was a period, too, when the distinctive styles of individuals gave tremendous scope to George Chrystal, who became one of the best cartoonists of his day under the contracted name of 'Chrys'. As an art student in Aberdeen he had submitted his early efforts to the *Evening Express* and later joined the staff, producing a regular Monday caricature of the Saturday action and establishing that well-loved North-east character, Wee Alickie. The popular belief was that he modelled Wee Alickie on Alick Murray, the fair-haired, pink-cheeked odd-job man at Pittodrie, who always danced about with excitement at the players' door and became a familiar face to every Dons supporter. Alick was an innocent soul who was first engaged at Pittodrie by Paddy Travers. He stayed at 11 Linksfield Place with his mother, who turned flour bags into pants for the Dons players in the wartime scarcity. He later moved in with his brother Ernest when he retired to Carden Terrace from his antique shop in Ballater and is now in his late seventies, living at Fergus House residential home at Dyce. Chrys played down the idea that he had based his character on one man and claimed that Alickie was an amalgam of the young Dons fans of the time. But Alick Murray was one of many in no doubt about the identity.

The up-and-coming players of the day included Frank Watson, the Peebles Rovers goalkeeper who not only joined up at Pittodrie but enrolled as a student at Aberdeen University. Frank had played for the young Dons against St Johnstone at Pittodrie on 6 September 1952 but was then taken to hospital suffering from poliomyelitis and was placed in an iron lung. Public concern for a highly popular young fellow eased with reports that he was improving and that there were high hopes of a full recovery. Frank was already married with one child and had completed the third year of his studies for an Honours MA in geography. It came as all the more of a shock, therefore, when his death was announced on 5 November. The Pittodrie flag flew at half-mast and on the following Saturday the Dons, playing Raith Rovers at Kirkcaldy, wore mourning bands as a genuine token of sorrow for a man and his family who had so much to look forward to.

George Chrystal also died in his early years but his twinkling humour and soft voice come alive every time I set eyes on Wee Alickie. How splendid that the character of the wee man lives on.

23
COURAGE OF HATHER

The 1950s were bursting with a new vitality at Pittodrie. David Halliday had worked quietly at creating the framework of a new team and felt that he was coming close to the blend he wanted. Sometimes the required player would crop up on his own doorstep, as in the case of the breezy boy who grew up just round the corner in Park Street and came bounding into Pittodrie to become one of the most controversial players in the history of the club. His name, of course, was Harry Yorston.

Harry had stood on the terracing as a little boy before the war, idolising George Hamilton, whom he still regards as the greatest Aberdeen player he has ever seen. Ten years later, he could hardly believe his luck when he found himself playing alongside his idol and forming a partnership which was to assist him in becoming the Dons' leading goal-scorer, a record which lasted through a whole generation until it was overtaken by Joe Harper in 1977.

Harry was the cheery-faced, good-looking golden boy of the 1950s, a player with a busy movement who could raise both ecstasy and exasperation in close succession, hitting glorious goals and missing glorious opportunities with an equal amount of the spectacular. 'Maybe I didn't work at it as a career like some people,' says Harry reflectively, 'but I did enjoy my football.'

There was a section of the Pittodrie crowd, however, which fixed upon Harry Yorston as a target of abuse, a fate not unknown to local lads. This caused anger among his fellow players who will tell you to this day that Harry's work-rate took the burden off every man in the team. Mr Halliday had signed him from St Clements A as early as 1946 and called him back from National Service in Portsmouth to make his first-team debut during the Christmas games of 1948. Over the festive period he scored four goals which were to prove vital in a season when the Dons were struggling to avoid relegation.

But the manager had not been so fortunate as to find all his players in convenient corners like Park Street. Indeed, it must be said in retrospect that David Halliday showed great diligence in pursuing the players he wanted. The fact that a promising lad from the coalfields of north-east England had turned down a chance to join Queen's Park Rangers did not deter the Aberdeen manager from making the journey to watch him play for Annfield Plain at Horden. Annfield lost but Mr Halliday had set his mind on signing their outside-left, a human flying-machine called Jackie Hather. The player was in the bath when the club secretary came with the news that there was a man from Aberdeen who wanted to see him. Hather sent back word that he was not interested and later left for home, which was not far from the Horden ground. When he got there, who should be waiting for him but the same gentleman from Aberdeen who was not to be put off by a message from a bathtub. Jackie, who had had a spell with Newcastle United as a youngster before returning to the semi-professional Annfield Plain, still refused to have anything to do with signing. Then his father stepped in and said he would like a private word with him and within a short time Jackie had changed his mind and he became an Aberdeen player in December 1948. An injury to Tommy Pearson, whose talents he knew well from the Newcastle connection, gave him his first-team debut on New Year's Day 1949 and that was the start of a career which lasted for twelve years and is imprinted indelibly on the memories of all who saw him. What fan could resist a nostalgic thought of the flying winger, probably the fastest man Pittodrie has seen, as he would take off down the wing or through the middle, lean and slightly hunched, his frail body suddenly accelerating into a sprint which would leave defenders floundering on a variety of wrong feet?

Jackie Hather, who is now back living in Peterlee, County Durham, still talks with great warmth about his days in Aberdeen and is so glad he took his father's advice. He speaks enthusiastically about the lasting impression which was made upon him by George Hamilton and he raves about Aberdonians being the salt of the earth. After all, he married one and their son John returned to Aberdeen to be a player like his father, before moving on to Blackpool. Jackie remembers well the day when John was born. Aberdeen were playing Queen of the South, whose goalkeeper was

Roy Henderson, one of football's characters who had had a brief but memorable spell with Aberdeen at the end of the war. Hather was a left-footer who used his right leg for balancing only but on that particular day he was driven along the eighteen-yard line to an angle where he had no chance of using his left foot. For once he decided to give an airing to his spare leg – and the ball which flew past Roy Henderson was one of Hather's greatest goals! It was a novel way to celebrate fatherhood and when the two teams were chatting over a cup of tea afterwards, the rumbustious Roy fished him out and said: 'Hey! Who the **** taught you to use your right foot? I never expected that!'

Hather, who is still a regular visitor to Aberdeen, was playing non-league football in the north of England until 1966. There is one postscript to his career which must be mentioned, if only to illustrate the courage of the man. All that speed and effort was achieved on only one kidney. The other had had to be removed when Jackie was eleven and he had been told that he would not be able to take part in any sport. His colleagues at Pittodrie were sometimes anxious about the risks involved and big Fred Martin can still wince at the memory of the screams which reached him at the other end of the field one day when the boot of a well-known Scottish defender lunged dangerously at Hather's only kidney while he was lying on the ground.

But if the flying Englishman, who was known to his team-mates as the Hare, was the fastest Don over thirty yards or more, there was one player who could beat him on the ten-yard burst and that was Paddy Buckley, the dashing centre-forward who came from St Johnstone to become a firm favourite at Pittodrie. It was a happy coincidence that two of the fastest men the game has ever seen played in the same team, a fact which cannot be overlooked when you consider the events which followed. Six years had passed since Aberdeen had won anything but now the team which Halliday had struggled to create as a successor to the heroic eleven of 1947 was showing signs of emerging.

In the Scottish Cup competition of 1952–53, the Dons had disposed of St Mirren, Motherwell and Hibs before making heavy weather of beating Third Lanark in a replay of the semi-final. Now they were set to meet Rangers in what was still only their third appearance in a Scottish Cup Final after fifty years in existence. In the Aberdeen team that day were three men who had appeared in the 1947 final: George Hamilton, who was still at inside-forward;

Tony Harris, who had played his prime years at outside-right but was by then converted into a useful right-half; and David Shaw, the Hibs' left-back of 1947 who was now occupying the same position for Aberdeen six years later. The line-up was: Aberdeen – Martin; Mitchell, Shaw; Harris, Young, Allister; Rodger, Yorston, Buckley, Hamilton, Hather; Rangers – Niven; Young, Little; McColl, Stanners, Pryde; Waddell, Grierson, Paton, Prentice, Hubbard.

The full limit of 135,000 people packing the slopes of Hampden saw big John Prentice put Rangers ahead in eight minutes. It seemed as if that might be enough to see the Light Blues through, despite the fact that their goalkeeper, George Niven, had been off for a spell with injury and big George Young had taken over in goal. But with time running out, Harry Yorston swung a fine pass out to Jackie Hather, who returned the compliment with an equally fine cross which was tailor-made for Harry. He ran in to meet it with his head and that glorious equaliser gave the Dons a second chance.

In the customary imbalance of Scottish football, Rangers had an even greater crowd advantage for the Wednesday replay which took place, as always, on their own doorstep. As many of us as possible made the long round trip from Aberdeen but the crowd of 113,700 showed clearly the drop in the number of Dons fans from the first game.

There was a popular belief that you were never given a second chance against the Old Firm and so it proved on that Wednesday evening in 1953. Billy Simpson scored the only goal of the night and we carried our misery into the darkness of a long drive home, leaving the celebrations to the broad blue sea of Rangers supporters.

But the Pittodrie players had by now developed a taste for the big occasion at Hampden and in the Scottish Cup of the following season they beat Hibs and Hearts with two first-rate performances to reach the semi-final. The mighty Rangers stood between them and a place in the Cup Final but that at least gave the opportunity to avenge the defeat of 1953. A lanky lad called Joe O'Neil was turning in some useful performances at that time but his chances of figuring in the Scottish Cup seemed to have vanished when he took a serious head knock and sustained a depressed fracture of the skull just three weeks before the semi-final. But Joe was built of hardy material and he made a miraculous recovery, running on to the Hampden pitch with a close-shaven head to take his place against Rangers on Saturday 10 April 1954. Harry Yorston was suffering from one of his rare injuries and the Aberdeen team that day read: Martin; Mitchell, Caldwell; Allister, Young, Glen; Leggat, Hamilton, Buckley, O'Neil, Hather.

A crowd of 110,939 could hardly have bargained for the spectacle which was to unfold before their disbelieving eyes that afternoon. It all began with a typical cross from Jack Hather, which was headed on by George Hamilton to the path of Joe O'Neil. Big Joe took it in his stride to put Aberdeen one goal ahead. But the fun had only started. Another cross from Hather on the left sent goalkeeper Bobby Brown and centre-half Willie Woodburn rising together for the ball. In stepped O'Neil and headed home a second goal with that skull which had so recently been depressed into fracture. The example of big Joe was infectious and Rangers could make nothing of this Aberdeen team as Hamilton laid on the perfect pass for Graham Leggat to make it three. With eight minutes to go, O'Neil scored his own third and Aberdeen's fourth goal and was going through again when he was brought down in the penalty box. Jack Allister had the privilege of making it five. Meanwhile, Aberdeen's hero had been taken off the field, causing some concern about that head injury, but he was soon returning to savour the final glory of his greatest day. That day reached its incredible climax when Paddy Buckley scored a last-minute goal to make the final score Aberdeen 6 Rangers 0. Six goals against Rangers and every one a beauty!

Before the final whistle, however, the blue brigades of Ibrox fans had drained from the Hampden bowl like water down a sink, leaving the red glow of success to the northern visitors who had wrought their sweet revenge. Aberdonians were unwilling to leave the scene of their triumph that night and many of them hung around Glasgow. One of the happiest supporters was John Cooper, of 8 Kidd Street, Aberdeen, whose memories stretched back to that first appearance of Jock Hutton in 1919 when he had played for Aberdeen wearing a blue scarf. On the night of the 6–0 win over Rangers, John and some friends landed at the Carntyne dog-racing track in Glasgow and crowned a wonderful day by backing five of the winning greyhounds. That success was the result of some excellent tips passed on to the red-scarved Aberdonians by appreciative Celtic supporters!

Before the team left Hampden Park that day, frustration reached such a point with at least one member of the Rangers team that a boot through the dressing-room window! By then the Aberdonians were making the most of their big moment in the knowledge that the peak of pleasure might be short-lived. After all, it was not the final. That ultimate encounter would bring them back to Hampden to meet Celtic, as it had done in 1937, when Britain's biggest-ever crowd had looked on.

On Friday 23 April 1954 the Aberdeen party slipped quietly off to their Glasgow headquarters, with the handshakes of station workers and students out on their Charities' Week collection. On that same day Rangers announced that they had given a free transfer to their famous centre-forward, Willie Thornton.

Demand was so high that a 2s 6d ticket was being bought on the black market for 15s as 20,000 Aberdonians headed south in their red and white scarves and tammies. Both Celtic and Aberdeen were being quoted by the bookies at 2 to 1 but the news which depressed Dons fans was that Joe O'Neil, heroic figure in the rout of Rangers, had received an ankle injury in a League game with the Ibrox club the previous week and would not appear in the final. His hour of glory had come in his first-ever appearance at Hampden Park but now he was to be denied the chance to follow through that success. Joe was openly broken-hearted and declared that he 'could hae a good greet'. What is more, Darkie, the Pittodrie cat, had to be destroyed that week after being involved in a fight and some people shook their heads and said the omens were not good.

O'Neil's absence was the only change in the team and his place was taken by big Jim Clunie, a maintenance man from the Fifeshire coalmines whose real position was centre-half but who found himself drafted in at inside-left for the day. By now the outside-right position was firmly in the grip of Graham Leggat, a product of Banks o'Dee who drew well-founded forecasts from admiring fans that he would turn out to be a truly great player. Indeed, James Forbes of the *Evening Express* bracketed him with Willie Mills as the two best Dons he had seen. At nineteen, he was now playing in a Scottish Cup Final alongside George Hamilton, the sole survivor of the 1947 team, who was nearly twice his age. Hammy and Fred Martin were in Scotland's World Cup party in Switzerland that same year and Leggat's turn for World Cup duty was to come four years later.

But the business on hand on 24 April 1954 was the Scottish Cup Final, and the teams which took the field were: Aberdeen – Martin; Mitchell, Caldwell; Allister, Young, Glen; Leggat, Hamilton,

Buckley, Clunie, Hather; Celtic – Bonnar; Haughney, Meechan; Evans, Stein, Peacock; Higgins, Fernie, Fallon, Tully, Mochan. This, of course, was the Celtic team which had been revitalised under the captaincy of Jock Stein, the Lanarkshire miner whose years in the obscurity of Albion Rovers and the Welsh non-league club Llanelli suddenly turned into a belated burst of glory at Parkhead.

Alas for Aberdeen, the game turned out to be a repeat of the previous encounter in 1937 – Celtic scoring first, Aberdeen equalising from the re-start and the Celts making the final score 2–1. The only difference was that Celtic's first goal was scored by Alec Young of Aberdeen. Poor Alec! It was cruel luck for such a big-hearted player. He tried to clear a Mochan shot which was well covered by Fred Martin, and sent it reeling past the keeper. From the re-start, Paddy Buckley took a pass from Leggat, rounded Jock Stein, drew Bonnar and flicked home a magnificent equaliser. Sean Fallon, normally a full-back but playing at centre-forward that day, scored the winner. So the Cup went to Parkhead and the 20,000 followers from the North-east went quietly back to their trains and buses to reflect on how easily the ecstasy of one week can become the dejection of another. It was now fifty years since the present Aberdeen Football Club had entered Scottish League football and in all that time they had won the Scottish Cup once and the League Championship not at all. But there would be another day . . .

24
SCOTTISH CHAMPIONS!

The Dons had now been defeated in two successive Scottish Cup Finals but there was surely some substance in a team which was getting that far. In season 1954–55 they were heading for yet another Hampden appearance when they were unexpectedly stopped by Clyde, whose penalty goal in the semi-final replay at Easter Road, Edinburgh, was enough to see them through.

By then, however, the Aberdeen players were caught up in the exciting prospect that the Scottish League Championship was within their grasp. Was this, at last, to be their greatest year?

The team had struck a new consistency in the early stages of season 1954–55, with everyone playing for each other and no one resorting to backbiting if a goal was lost. The sixteen-team League of that period meant a programme of thirty games and as they coasted towards Christmas the players themselves had begun to sense that this could well be their year. After all, it was the greatest achievement in football to win the League Championship and in half a century of the club's existence it had never been done by an Aberdeen team. The instant glamour may belong to the Cup but that could be won over five or six games in which good fortune was liable to play an outrageous part. The League called for the sheer grind of consistency against the best and the worst of opposition, in all their upsetting variations, home and away, in sunshine, wind or driving snow. This would be the real test of their mettle and these Dons were anxious to write their names into the Pittodrie history book by being the first to do it. Harry Yorston recalled it like this: 'We played to a pattern as a workmanlike side, with confidence in each other, and we just knew we were going places.' Throughout the season they lost five games with only one drawn result and it all boiled up to a day of decision in the rather undramatic setting of Shawfield Park, Glasgow, where football has a habit of looking like an intruder upon that other activity of Shawfield, greyhound racing.

The Dons needed to beat Clyde that day to clinch their first-ever title and, in what turned out to be a scrappy and otherwise forgettable game, the opportunity came with a penalty kick. Jack Allister and Archie Glen used to take the penalties time about and it happened to be Archie's turn. The photographic evidence shows that he shot it high into the Shawfield net, past the left-hand shoulder of South African goalkeeper Ken Hewkins. Thus, without the noise and excitement of a big crowd and in a setting which was totally bereft of glamour, the Dons won the greatest honour that could come to a club. On that historic day – 9 April 1955 – the *Green Final* was rolling off the printing presses of Broad Street and spilling into the streets by 5.30 p.m. with a deliriously happy Wee Alickie declaring: 'Cocks o' the North and Scottish Champs – Fa's like us?' Back in the Shawfield dressing room the champagne corks were popping, David Halliday quietly surveying the joy of the lads who had given shape to his most ambitious dream. More than twenty years later, Jackie Hather told me that he still retained a vivid memory of Halliday's face when the players came off the Shawfield pitch. Pride was written all over it.

It was a carefree Aberdeen party which boarded the train at Buchanan Street Station that evening. The fact that big Fred Martin occupied the luggage rack on the journey north is a fair indication of the mood of the occasion, as well as a tribute to the endurance of British Railways' luggage racks! When the train drew into the Joint Station at 11.30 that night there were ten supporters waiting to welcome them home. So there were no crowds, no cheers, no sense of occasion; just home to a champagne sleep and up next morning to read the final confirmation that the Dons of 1955 had done what no other Aberdeen team had managed to achieve. The Champions of Scotland had won twenty-four of their thirty games, scored seventy-three goals and equalled the record by conceding only twenty-six. That record would have been broken if Fred Martin had not been injured one day. His deputy, Archie Glen, lost a goal which only an outfield man would have missed.

Those of us with longer memories would hesitate to say that the championship team was the most entertaining we had ever seen at Pittodrie. It was more effective than attractive, failing to imprint its style on the public mind in the way that the more colourful combination of 1947 had done. But how can you argue with its success? Archie Glen, who was later to become captain, gave me his assessment of the ingredients which produced the winning formula:

Basically, the plan was to retreat as a team when under pressure, keeping the opposing wingers wide but always ready for a quick break, with long balls from Jack Allister and myself setting off those lightning darts of the front men, who could beat the best of defences for speed. It was that tendency to retreat which looked rather negative at times. When we did fall back to the penalty area I always knew, if I forced a player to shoot from two or three yards in front of me, that Fred Martin would get it. His reliability in goal had a tremendous influence on the rest of the defence who could then get on with their own jobs. Fred was one of the best readers of a game I have ever known and I would put him right in the top grade of goalkeepers I have seen. We had a fair pair of full-backs in Jimmy Mitchell and Davie Caldwell, Mitchell in particular being extremely fast. Caldwell replaced Billy Smith, who had broken his leg. The half-back line was good in the air and the wing-halves could give accuracy to passes of more than ten yards. Jack Allister was a tremendous player but without doubt the most under-rated man in the Aberdeen team was Alec Young at centre-half, who covered for everyone and did it so willingly. People still speak about his famous sliding tackle but he could do more than that. The fans were not in a position to know that Alec was an extremely thoughtful person, always concerned for the people around him. Up front we had those three fast men, Leggat, Buckley and Hather, with Harry Yorston and Bobby Wishart slotting in between.

The Dons had found a blend of contrasting talents which produced a pattern of success – a conforming blend which had to allow for a single exception, because genius does not readily fit into patterns. That football genius of the mid 1950s was Graham Leggat, a thoroughbred from local junior football who was training to be a teacher of physical education at Jordanhill College, Glasgow. Leggat was a clean-cut figure with the college-boy look, fast, cunning, alert and instinctive and capable of surprising even his fellow-professionals with the skill of his movement. He had the ability, for example, to bring a difficult cross under control and convert it into his next movement when most players would still have been struggling with the awkward cross. The full range of Leggat's talents was displayed in a game with Airdrie. By coincidence, this was also the first appearance of another great Pittodrie favourite, the skilful Billy Little from Dumfries, who gathered many admirers from the 1950s to the mid 1960s and who later became a schoolmaster and manager of Falkirk FC. Aberdeen beat Airdrie 6–0 that day and Graham Leggat scored five, each with a distinctive character of its own. Billy Little had provided much of the ammunition and, in the rivalry of Glasgow's evening newspapers for clever puns in their headlines, one of them declared: 'Leggat goals come Little by Little!'

If there was a criticism of Leggat it was that he was better at taking the team from 1–0 to 3–0 than helping it out of a goalless rut, but that was an aspect of his performance which was more evident to his fellow players than to the spectator. On the terracing they still talk about one particular Leggat goal, the background of which is filled in by Archie Glen.

At training one day, Leggat wanted to consult Glen about the way defences lined up to face a free kick near the penalty area. He had noticed that goalkeepers, having placed a wall of players to cover the goal area nearest to the ball, then seemed to take their attention off that area and concentrate on the other part. So the most vulnerable spot lay behind that wall, if only you could chip the ball over it unexpectedly. Glen agreed and Fred Martin was called into the discussion to confirm that there was such a tendency among goalkeepers. But the free kick had to be just outside the penalty area – and there would need to be that element of surprise. There was a game against St Mirren at Pittodrie on the Saturday, so when better to try it, they said. All week they practised. On the Saturday the Dons were attacking the King Street end when the Buddies gave away a free kick, exactly where it was needed. Leggat looked at Glen to confirm that their moment had come. Archie stood back and watched as Jim Lornie, St Mirren's Aberdonian goalkeeper, went through his routine. By then Leggat was bending down to place the ball. He did not move from that position until the whistle blew, then, drawing back his leg from the knee, he released the perfect chip-shot which sailed over the 'wall' and into the net before anyone had moved a muscle. It was a goal in a million which became a talking point, rather like the Willie Carr free-kick incident at Coventry in more recent times when he flicked the ball up with two feet. But, like all such feats of cunning, it could not be attempted too often.

Graham Leggat's capabilities extended far outside football and many remember him as a singer and impersonator, much in demand aboard the *Empress of France* when the Dons went on tour to Canada the following year. That tour must have sown some thoughts in his mind for after he had left Aberdeen and played for Fulham he eventually landed back in Canada where he became general manager of the O'Keefe Sports Foundation. Apart from Leggat the entertainer, there is much about the football stars that the average supporter seldom gets to know. Who would have guessed that the solemn, unrelenting Jack Allister was also the life and soul of any social occasion? Harry Yorston seemed like a confident extrovert – some mistook his manner for big-headedness – yet Don Emery remembers him as a shy young man, so diffident that he would hardly venture into Lewis's store in Glasgow unless someone like Don went with him.

Paddy Buckley, on the other hand, was the happy-go-lucky chap he always seemed to be, a proper joker in the Pittodrie pack – and if we are talking about a pack of cards, he was also one of the best solo players in Aberdeen. With all the travelling that has to be undertaken by the Dons, there has always been a card school and in the 1950s it consisted mainly of David Shaw, Alec Young, Archie Glen and Paddy Buckley. If Paddy was not exactly an academic, he did have that special memory of the card-player which enabled him to chastise the more scholarly Glen for not remembering all the cards already played. Archie could only shrug and plead that he didn't have Paddy's brain-power! Last time I met Buckley in Edinburgh, those legs which had made him the fastest man in football were scarcely able to take him for a short walk – and he was still only in his forties.

In pinpointing the contrasting skills of that championship team, it is easy to overlook the contribution of Bobby Wishart, a clever manipulator of a ball whose ability to slide past an opponent with individual guile cleared the way for so many of those final runs by other forwards. The grace and prompting of Wishart stand out in many a mind as one of the richest memories from that championship era.

25
SOUR TASTE OF SUCCESS

The Dons were Champions of Scotland for the first time and the public front was one of joy and celebration for players, directors and supporters alike. Behind the scenes, however, it was a very different story. The Pittodrie dressing room was seething with bitterness and discontent after a head-on collision between players and the board over the question of financial rewards for their historic achievement.

It had all boiled up during the final approach to the championship title when the team began to turn their thoughts to incentives. From contact with other teams which had won the title, they had heard the talk, and perhaps the boasts, of what was offered for a winning spurt. The League programme was within weeks of completion and, with no move by the directors, the players decided it was time to do something about it. A deputation consisting of captain Jimmy Mitchell, Archie Glen and Fred Martin asked for a hearing at the regular directors' meeting in the Caledonian Hotel and that was granted. They had a proposition to put. Archie Glen had reasoned that a team intent on winning the League Championship should win its home games anyway, otherwise it had no right to regard itself as a title contender. The key factor was the away games and the proposition was that there should be a special incentive bonus to collect these vital points. The case was put and was followed by a pause. Then one director is said to have leaned across and repeated the proposition to make sure his ears were working, before turning to relay it to the chairman, Mr Mitchell, who was still wearing an incredulous look. As far as the directors were concerned, the Scottish League would be paying out the customary £1000 to be divided among the winning players and enough was enough. Well, there may have been a day when players would have sought the heights for honour alone but that day did not extend into the second half of the twentieth century. The Dons were looking for hard cash, though all they got from that confrontation at the Caley was a cool reception. There was to be no incentive bonus for the final run-in, said the directors.

What is more, when the championship was finally clinched and the players had brought home the greatest honour in the history of Aberdeen Football Club, they did not receive a single extra penny from club funds. All they got was the £1000 from the Scottish League, divided into eleven parts – £91 for each position – which had to be further divided among the players who had occupied these positions. For example, Fred Martin, as fine a goalkeeper as Pittodrie had ever known, missed three games in the course of the season and was therefore subject to a deduction of three-thirtieths of £91. Big Fred contemplated a sum of just over £81 which was surely, by any standard, a pretty niggardly reward for his services. Other Scottish players could hardly believe the story when they heard it and who could blame them? For men like William Mitchell who had done so much to bring football glory to the city of Aberdeen, it was, to say the least, an exercise in poor psychology which did them no credit at all.

It gave rise to a resentment which left a sour taste for the start of the new season and who can say what part that had to play in the subsequent decline in the fortunes of the Dons? There were other factors, too, which undermined any prospect of a sustained success. The Dons' record under David Halliday had not gone unnoticed elsewhere. In that difficult period after the war, he had guided them to three major prizes and three more Cup Finals inside nine years. That was good enough for Leicester City, who needed a manager, and before they had time to gather thoughts for the new season, Aberdeen were without the man who had transformed them from a club without a single national honour into one which had won everything that was available at the time.

In the tradition of giving a man a chance to prove himself, the Aberdeen board decided to give Halliday's job to the club trainer, Davie Shaw. Davie had been a clever left-back for Hibs, opposing Aberdeen in that 1947 Scottish Cup Final and partnering his brother Jock, of Rangers, in the Scottish team which beat England in the Victory International of 1946. He had been transferred to Aberdeen and later took over as trainer, in which capacity he had done a splendid job. He was a man who would have done anything for his players and could make them, in turn, feel important. His appointment as manager does not seem to have been a unanimous one, however, and James Forbes of the *Evening Express* told a story which was frightening in its frankness. The story had it that, as David Shaw entered the room to receive the good news, he was greeted by Mr Mitchell, the chairman, in the following terms: 'Well, David, they have appointed you the new manager of Aberdeen Football Club – but you might as well know, it is against my wishes!'

Davie celebrated by taking his players off to Ballater for a day's golf. The players who had pulled on a jersey to play their part in that championship year lined up for a photograph and their names are interesting to recall: F. Martin, J. Mitchell, D. Caldwell, J. Allister, A. Young, A. Glen, G. Leggat, G. Hamilton, H. Yorston, P. Buckley, R. Wishart, J. Hather, W. Smith, J. O'Neil, R. Morrison, J. Wallace, J. Brown, R. Paterson and J. Clunie.

It was virtually the end of the line for that great Pittodrie servant, George Hamilton. His colleagues from that post-war team had now finally disappeared. Archie Baird was playing for St Johnstone, then managed by his former team-mate Johnny Pattillo, before concentrating on a teaching career which took him to Rosemount Secondary, Summerhill Academy and Hilton Academy, where he was assistant head teacher. Tony Harris, another of the game's colourful characters, was now well established as a dentist. Only Hammy remained as a remnant of the pre-war days, then well through his thirties and feeling it was time to retreat to his news-agent's shop in Rosemount, a career which was succeeded by years as a traveller for Bell's whisky.

As he mulled over it all in his home in Hosefield Avenue, Aberdeen, George picked out the name of Billy Strauss as the one which first sprung to mind when he considered the great talents he had seen at Pittodrie. He remembered Strauss as fast and graceful and with such a powerful shot that he was altogether a fantastic player. But he followed that up with the names of Archie Baird, Stan Williams, Frank Dunlop, George Taylor, Andy Cowie, Graham Leggat, Charlie Cooke, Zoltan Varga, Willie Miller and Gordon Strachan. Not least, he mentioned Jackie Hather, who was not dissimilar in talent to Billy Strauss. He remembered the deep scar on Hather's back, which told of that serious kidney operation. He remembered Harry Yorston as a great-hearted player who was totally under-rated. ('People tend to forget that, when we were bogged down, it took only a couple of flashes of Harry and we could win a game.') He remembered the jokers in the pack –

goalkeeper Reggie Morrison, who was not averse to spreading itching powder in the players' clothes, and the formidable Don Emery, whose talent for planting stink-bombs once created a chaos of accusing looks among guests in Glasgow's North British Hotel! Morrison, incidentally, transferred his talents as a custodian from the Pittodrie goalmouth to the confines of Peterhead Prison where he became an officer – keeping them in instead of keeping them out, as it were.

So George Hamilton bowed out at the end of a distinguished career which had earned him the deep affection of the Pittodrie faithful. It is a measure of his frankness that he does not hide the one occasion when he fell foul of the board-room. It happened during the recall of able-bodied men as Z-Reservists during the early 1950s. Hamilton was posted to Aldershot and had been engaged in heavy manoeuvres when a message arrived from Mr Halliday asking him to travel to Glasgow to play for the Dons. On the same train that day was Roy Henderson of Queen of the South, whose club had sent for him in similar circumstances, except that they had booked him in a sleeper compartment on the train. Hamilton had to curl up in a corner seat and that, on top of army manoeuvres, rendered him in pretty poor shape for a game of football when he arrived in Glasgow. To crown it all, Mr Halliday explained that he wanted him to play at right-half, a position he had never occupied before, and that was not well received. When the manager reported the player's mood to the directors, they took the view that he was shirking and Halliday relayed that opinion back to the player. Hamilton was furious. Pointing to a badly broken nose (it has not recovered to this day) he said: 'I did not get that for shirking so just go back and tell the directors that, if that's the case, I am not playing today and I'm prepared to take whatever punishment is coming.' Back at Pittodrie on the Monday, the directors held a meeting and decided to suspend George Hamilton for one month. There was no bitterness from Hammy. He asked for an interview with the chairman and said: 'As far as I am concerned, Mr Mitchell, this will make no difference to me. I'll still give my best for Aberdeen.' They shook hands. Wasn't that so typical of George Hamilton?

In the troubled aftermath of that championship season, with some dressing-room discontent and the manager gone, there was yet another factor which rankled at Pittodrie. Scotland had been talking about taking part in the European Cup but it needed the pioneering initiative of Hibernian chairman Harry Swan to bring about the final decision to enter the mainstream of continental football. The European Cup is, of course, aimed at producing the best club team in Europe and is contested by the teams which have won the league championships in their respective countries. So fate had brought about a glorious coincidence, as Scotland would make its entry into Europe in 1955 – and the champions of that year were Aberdeen Football Club, having just celebrated their half-century in top-grade football by winning the League title for the first time. But fate did not stand much of a chance when confronted by the Scottish Football Association. That august body decided that, in gratitude to the man who had advocated the move, Hibernian FC should be given the honour of representing Scotland in its very first venture. It was a noble gesture no doubt, but don't ask an Aberdonian to understand why it had to happen when Aberdeen had won the right of entry in the place where it is supposed to matter – the field of play. So Hibernian FC became the first Scottish club to compete in Europe's premier competition and Aberdeen, denied its place, had to wait another twenty-five years for the opportunity.

David Shaw did not have his sorrows to seek as he embarked on his first season as manager but he did succeed in rescuing some of the championship euphoria for the Scottish League Cup, which came early in the season. The Dons defeated Rangers in the semi-final and by 22 October 1955 they were heading for another League Cup Final, feeling that Hampden Park was by no means as unfamiliar a place as it used to be. The opponents were St Mirren and the fact that that was not exactly a final to fire public imagination was reflected in the attendance of 44,104, which was more than 100,000 below the numbers which had turned out when the Dons made their first appearance at Hampden Park in 1937. In the event, it was not a game to be remembered. Mallan breasted the ball into his own net to give the Dons the lead before Holmes equalised for the Saints. Then Graham Leggat released a harmless-looking shot which Lornie seemed to misjudge and Aberdeen were winners of the Scottish League Cup by two goals to one. The Aberdeen team that day was: Martin; Mitchell, Caldwell; Wilson, Clunie, Glen; Leggat, Yorston, Buckley, Wishart, Hather.

But if the game was lacking in distinction, the hour of success is seldom regarded as a time for analysing merit. In any case, it was a way of offering a belated salute to the Scottish Champions, who had clinched the title in rather undramatic circumstances a few months earlier. When the Dons arrived back at the Joint Station with the League Cup that night there were 15,000 there to greet them. It was nearly midnight, but who cared?

As late-duty reporter on the *Press and Journal* that Saturday night, I went down to write about the welcome as well as to join in. Several thousand fans had arrived back in earlier train-loads, each one greeted by loud cheers, and most of them waited on to swell the throng of people who had had to follow it on the radio and had started to turn up at the station two hours before the train was due. When it finally drew in, as I reported on the Monday morning, the canny Aberdonians erupted like excited Continentals:

A miniature Hampden Roar nearly lifted the roof off the station as the team captain, Jimmy Mitchell, stepped from the train and was lifted shoulder-high, carrying the cup. A large cordon of police had to clear a way as the players were chaired, with great difficulty, through the seething mob to the bus waiting inside the station building to take them to their homes.

There were repeated chants of 'We want Leggat' but the popular outside-right was not with the party. Along with Jim Clunie, he had stayed on in the south. At snail-pace, the bus managed to leave the station but the crowd heaved forward and at one time there was a serious threat of people being crushed against the vehicle.

I was speaking from personal experience, having been pinned against a wheel of the team bus as it started its manoeuvre out of the station.

A smiling Jimmy Mitchell pleased everyone by holding the cup high and acknowledging the cries of 'Well done the Dons!' The players drove in triumph along Guild Street, Market Street and Union Street on their way home.

It turned out to be the greatest moment of manager Davie Shaw's career. He had little to cheer about during the rest of his time as boss at Pittodrie but on that night at least he could savour the success and say: 'I played for Hibs when they won trophies but never have I seen such enthusiasm as that displayed by the Dons' supporters.' Jimmy Mitchell, who had been swallowed up by the menacing affection of the station crowd, arrived home with his blazer torn but that was a small price to pay for such a night of undiluted joy.

When the Dons returned to the bread-and-butter business of the League programme in season 1955–56, the whole rhythm of success began to elude them. Alec Young, who had come late to senior football, was one of the first to go out of the side and the effect of his departure was the clearest indication of how the champions had depended on the shepherding influence of that great servant. Just as it takes time to grow a tree and no time at all to cut it down, so can a football team arise with careful nursing over a number of years and disappear without warning. Players of that era will tell you that they seemed unable to recover the comradeship which had existed in the previous few years and the disintegration set in fairly quickly.

Some semblance of the old comradeship was still evident, however, when the Dons went off on a tour of North America in the close season of 1956. Scrapbooks show Jack Hather playing piggy-back with Harry Yorston on the decks of the *Empress of France*; Archie Glen about to throw Paddy Buckley overboard; Fred Martin and Graham Leggat, sporting the straw hat, with a background of Idlewilde Airport, New York; families in the well-known Scots community of Kearney, New Jersey, welcoming the Dons; and Harry Yorston, in a magnificent red bow-tie, enjoying a glass of beer with Jack Hather, Bobby Wilson, Fred Martin and Bobby Wishart. There are pictures of the Rockefeller Center and Times Square and the skyscrapers of New York, Niagara Falls and the racecourse at Winnipeg; Alec Young reloading his camera; and director Dick Donald carrying crates of Coke for the boys. Davie Shaw, Ian Macfarlane and Jim Clunie were enjoying the sunshine and there were the farewells and the last looks at Montreal and the St Lawrence River.

The *Empress of France* had to make a two-hundred-mile detour on the outward journey because the normal route through Belle Isle Strait was blocked with ice and the Dons landed at Quebec instead of Montreal. They were due to play their opening match against Everton in New York, under former Aberdeen referee Jim McLean, but when the bus-loads of Scots arrived down from Boston, they discovered that the match had been washed out by rain. Graham Leggat, acting part-time journalist for the occasion, reported that the Dons party was absolutely mesmerised by the size of everything. Television had only recently reached Aberdeen at that stage and Graham wrote, as a matter worthy of special note, that they actually had TV sets in their hotel bedrooms. Paddy

Buckley, also playing part-time journalist, sent a despatch about Alec Young and captain Jimmy Mitchell having taken New York by storm, turning out in their kilts and eliciting calls of 'Gee, aren't they real cute!' from wide-eyed Americans.

The Dons had a series of draws with Everton, who were also on tour, but they chalked up victories like 8–0 over Montreal All Stars and 8–3 over Ontario All Stars. That included a brilliant hat-trick by that stylish ball-player Hugh Hay and an amazing overhead goal from the inimitable Harry Yorston.

One columnist observing an Aberdeen–Everton game in Vancouver divided his attention between the actual game and the enthusiasm of another Vancouver journalist in the press box by the name of Jack Webster. My namesake, I should explain, is an exiled Glaswegian who is notorious for his outspoken broadcasts in British Columbia. Enthusing over a splendid game, he was reported as straining his voice through a bowl of porridge and uttering remarks like, 'If I could see a game like this ever-r-r-y week, I'd never-r leave the par-r-r-k.'

On the *Empress of France*, trainer Charlie McCaig was discovering that he was never very far from home. The second officer who took them on a tour of the bridge was Jimmy Walker from Collieston and the male nurse in the ship's hospital was George Garden from Portgordon.

26
GOLDEN HARRY

In the superstitious ways of footballers, Archie Glen liked to be last out of the dressing room and Harry Yorston was just in front of him. On the way to the exit door, Harry would say to Archie: 'I bet that wee chap who always shouts at me will start before I even reach the track.' Sure enough, as soon as Harry appeared this wizened little creature would begin his torrent of abuse. Lamentably, he was merely a symbol of a wider section of the support which picked on Yorston as the outlet for their frustrations, which had perhaps as much to do with a nagging wife as it had with any imperfections of the Dons' inside-right.

Why did it happen? Local boys have often received rough justice from football supporters, on the principle that people feel entitled to be harder on their own. In Harry's case, there was the additional hazard that he had acquired the 'golden boy' label and that left him open to a North-east talent for pulling people down a peg if they are in danger of getting 'bigsy'. But there was no question of Yorston getting above himself. He was the golden boy of Pittodrie for the simple reason that he was the most prolific goal-scorer Aberdeen had seen in more than fifty years of football.

Well, the much-maligned Harry Yorston gave them something else to speak about one day in 1957 when the *Evening Express* came out with a sensational story: Harry was giving up football at the age of twenty-eight. Basically, the story was that Harry's father was a fish-market porter, a well-paid and much-prized job in Aberdeen and one in which there was a tradition of sons having the privilege of following their fathers. But the son could not leave it too late and the deadline had come for Harry's decision. It was a difficult one, as he recalled himself: 'I didn't know if I was doing the right thing. I had so enjoyed playing football that I was reluctant to give it up.' Harry was at the peak of his career as a top-class professional footballer who might have expected to play through to his mid-thirties.

But deep in the privacy of his heart there was that other element which helped to swing the balance. Harry is such a thoroughly nice fellow that he does not want to be critical but he did admit to me that the barracking from the crowd played its part in driving him out of the game. There must be many people in Aberdeen today who long for the exciting dashes of Harry Yorston while at the same time suffering a pang of conscience about the way they treated him when they had him.

Throughout the week he would be subjected to uncomplimentary calls about some missed opportunity of the previous Saturday and he admits that it did not improve his confidence. So Harry made his big decision and exchanged his £16 a week as an Aberdeen player for the same £16 a week as a fish-market porter, with a security which would far outlast the career of a footballer. Harry was finished with football but, in the manner of a fairy story, football was far from finished with Harry.

Over the Spring Holiday weekend of 1972, his attractive wife Joey, a former nurse at Foresterhill, added her 25p permutation to his Littlewoods coupon and thought no more about it. That Saturday evening, Harry cast a casual eye over his wife's effort but was not impressed by the first part of it and passed on to something else. It was later that evening that he gave it a second glance and realised that there was more to it than he had thought. There were six draws and two non-scoring draws but it would still depend on how many millions of other people had placed their lines. Having sent off a claim, Harry and Joey went away for the Monday holiday and when they returned that evening there was a phone call from Littlewoods. Their man was at the Joint Station and would be up by taxi. The Yorstons waited excitedly and, when he arrived, Joey went to fetch the man a whisky. When she returned with the tray, she was more in need of the stuff herself, for the gentleman from Littlewoods, while unable to confirm the actual amount until next morning, was breaking the news that it would be running somewhere into six figures. When all was revealed next morning, the sum which Joey and Harry Yorston had won on their Littlewoods coupon was a resounding £175,000.

Harry gave up his job but he and Joey saw no reason for leaving the house in Burnieboozle Crescent for which they had saved in his days at the fish market. They bought Harry's parents a house nearby and strove to strike the balance of generosity which neither embarrasses with too much nor offends with too little. The main capital sum is managed by Littlewoods' experts and provides an annual income which obviates the need to work for a living. But idleness was no life at all for the bustling Harry, who was built for activity, whether down the Pittodrie arena or across the fish-market floor, so he compromised in a job as a van driver for Baker's the china people. He is now with George Jolly, the printers.

In the late 1970s he was back at Pittodrie, helping to coach the cream of Aberdeen schoolboys and plug that escape route through which great talents like Denis Law had vanished to England before Pittodrie had even heard their names. To the youngsters coming under his supervision, the name of Harry Yorston was one they had heard from their fathers. He was the great goal-scorer of his day, indeed of any day, and his only rival has been Joe Harper who was credited with overtaking his total of 171 in 1977. The truth of it is that there is no accurate tally of Yorston's goals in existence; there are no official records at Pittodrie. So the fans are left with the memory of a player who, in some of his ten seasons at Pittodrie, had scored twenty goals before Christmas. They remember a great-hearted player who deserved all the luck that was coming to him – and a good deal more gratitude than he received.

But Harry's good fortune did not make him the wealthiest of former Dons. That privilege almost certainly falls to chairman Dick Donald, followed by Willie Waddell, who arrived on the same day as Archie Baird and who played in the Scottish Cup Final team of 1947. When Willie was released in 1950 he found his way to lowly Kettering Town, near Northampton, to play out his career. He had married Betty Barlow, a nurse at Foresterhill. Kettering Town was run by people in the ball-bearing business and Willie gained a knowledge of that industry and started his own small enterprise. From modest beginnings he built it up until there were sixty employees and a prosperous turnover. Then he sold out for £500,000 and was asked to stay on as managing director. Thus Willie Waddell, the lad from Renfrew Juniors who shared Scottish Cup glory with the Dons, became an extremely wealthy man – thanks to a course of action which began with a free transfer from Pittodrie.

With Yorston gone, the disintegration had taken another step forward. The downward curve can be gauged from the League positions in the five years which followed the title success. When the Dons were champions in 1954–55, this is how the top of the table read at the end of the season:

	P	W	L	D	F	A	Pts
Aberdeen	30	24	5	1	73	26	49
Celtic	30	19	3	8	76	37	46
Rangers	30	19	8	3	67	33	41

In season 1955–56, the Dons took second place in the League.

	P	W	L	D	F	A	Pts
Rangers	34	22	4	8	85	27	52
Aberdeen	34	18	6	10	87	50	46
Hearts	34	19	8	7	99	47	45

In 1956–57, they dropped to fifth place, sandwiched between Raith Rovers and Celtic.

	P	W	L	D	F	A	Pts
Aberdeen	34	18	14	2	79	59	38

By 1957–58, the drop continued to 11th place, between Dundee and St Mirren.

	P	W	L	D	F	A	Pts
Aberdeen	34	14	18	2	68	76	30

The slide had become even worse in season 1958–59, when the Dons finished in 13th place, with Stirling Albion just above them and Raith Rovers just below.

	P	W	L	D	F	A	Pts
Aberdeen	34	12	17	5	63	66	29

The fall from grace was complete in season 1959–60 when they ended up in 15th position, just three off the bottom. This is how they fared:

	P	W	L	D	F	A	Pts
Aberdeen	34	11	17	6	54	72	28

A steady drop from champions in 1955 to the bottom regions inside five years was not exactly a recipe for managerial survival. In three of those seasons, in fact, the Dons of Davie Shaw's management would not have been in the Premier Division setting of today. So it became clear that, with all his talents as player and trainer, the one thing he was not cut out to be was a manager. In the harsh world of football realities, he had to go.

Earlier that year, however, there had been a chance for reprieve when the Dons managed to fight their way through to the Scottish Cup Final of 1959. Archie Glen had taken over as captain in those troubled times and he faced the paradox of heading for the glamour of Hampden Park on the one hand and struggling to avoid relegation on the other. Just before the Hampden date, Aberdeen had to face Rangers at Ibrox in a League game which they desperately needed to win for survival, while Rangers needed the points to clinch the title. At the toss of the coin, captain Bobby Shearer joked with Archie Glen that they couldn't expect any favours from Rangers. But no favours were needed for the Dons won 2–1, stayed in the top division – and Rangers still managed to win the title.

The prospects of winning the Scottish Cup must have seemed much brighter since the other finalists, St Mirren, were at the wrong end of the League table too. Altogether it was not regarded as a major attraction, though the plight of the pair in the League programme lent a certain poignancy to the occasion, which may explain the perfectly respectable attendance of 108,591 at Hampden on 25 April 1959. Aberdeen's team was: Martin; Caldwell, Hogg; Brownlee, Clunie, Glen; Ewen, Davidson, Baird, Wishart, Hather.

The Dons noticed that St Mirren had always managed to score in the first twenty minutes of their previous rounds so they set out to prevent a repetition, believing that that would diminish the Paisley confidence. But you cannot bargain for everything. Early in the game Aberdeen's David Caldwell, who had been converted from a forward with Duntocher Hibs into a left-back at Pittodrie, was badly hurt. There was no substitution in those days so the Dons played out the rest of the game with ten men. In the emergency, Archie Glen called Jack Hather from his raiding beat on the left wing to fill the Caldwell vacancy and he reckons that that was a tactical error which left the Dons short of power up front and for which he accepts responsibility. The game ran well for St Mirren, with Tommy Bryceland scoring before half-time, Miller and Baker increasing the total and Hugh Baird retrieving a consolation for the

Dons in the last minute. By three goals to one, the Scottish Cup went to Paisley and the red-tammied brigade beat the northward track with precious little to brighten their horizons.

Earlier that season, the waning fortunes of Aberdeen Football Club had not prevented a take-over bid by that rumbustious city businessman, Mr T. Scott Sutherland. It was his second attempt. In March 1958 he had abandoned a bid to gain control when he discovered that the reigning power lay with five directors who, with their families, held 6000 of the 10,000 shares, worth ten shillings each.

Sutherland, who had made a lot of money, was a hardy character, short and stocky and with a stubble of red hair, not exactly a candidate for a beauty contest but as dynamic a figure as Aberdeen has ever produced. He ran an architect's practice among his various enterprises – he gave generously for the school of architecture which bears his name – and found time to write a book called *Life on One Leg*, which was all he had. Despite his handicap, however, he could play tennis with such agility as to demoralise many a player with two legs.

Sutherland said he had offered £4 per ten-shilling share and that he did not want to buy the whole club but only to hold fifty per cent of the shares. He said he would abolish the right of the directors to ban the sale of shares by individual shareholders.

Said Scott Sutherland at the time:

My whole action has been altruistic, hence my willingness to plonk down a small fortune for little or no return. I want to see the Dons a happy and successful team always at or near the top. A successful Pittodrie Park is a valuable asset to the city of Aberdeen, not only to the sporting fraternity but to the business community. Big gates and the influx of fans fae a' the airts bring extra shekels to the city transport department, country bus owners, taxi firms, shops, restaurants, cinemas and pubs. Furthermore, consider the morale of the spectators who brave all weathers to watch their favourites.

I consider the directors' power to veto share transfer unsound, bad for the club and minority shareholders. By exercising such a veto, they can gobble up shares coming on the market at prices around thirty to thirty-five shillings each. They have complete financial control, leaving outside shareholders with little or no say in the club's affairs.

But Sutherland's law was not to prevail at Pittodrie, as the bid came to nothing and William Mitchell and his colleagues continued to hold sway.

The only change to be made was that of manager, with David Shaw reverting to his former job as club trainer. His career as a manager came to an end on 17 November 1959 and the pictures in the newspapers on the following morning showed the new man shaking hands all round. The sight of his familiar face and the news of his appointment were enough to quicken the heartbeat of those who had long admired his very special talents. The new boss was Tommy Pearson.

27
CHANGES AT THE TOP

With the Dons struggling in the late 1950s, the devoted thousands who had seen them through from 1946 to the end of a golden decade and then down the slippery slope were deserting in large numbers. The car-loads which had come faithfully from Foggieloan and farther afield were now just as likely to head for a Highland League ground on a Saturday afternoon, whether it was at the Broch, Buckie, Banff or Elgin. But a fresh gaze of expectancy was turned on Pittodrie that November day of 1959 when the headlines told us that Thomas Usher Pearson, legendary footballer, was returning as manager to the scene of his twilight glory.

Since hanging up his boots, Pearson had not been far away. Those intervening years had been spent as northern sports writer for the *Scottish Daily Mail* and a large part of his week was devoted to reporting on the affairs of Aberdeen Football Club. Now it was time to put his pen aside and show what he could do in the reshaping of a team in the doldrums. His very presence raised a hope among the supporters that the magical talent of his playing days would somehow reproduce itself in managerial form, charming skill from mediocrity and moulding a team in his own distinctive image. That was, of course, a large and irrational expectation.

In the season of his arrival some key names were either gone or going. Time was drawing to a close for that flying winger from the north of England, Jack Hather, and for centre-half Jim Clunie who, in more recent times, coached the Southampton team to their FA Cup Final victory at Wembley. As the Dons embarked on that season 1959–60, skipper Archie Glen was only fifteen seconds into a match at Kilmarnock when a collision with centre-half Willie Toner put him out of the game for nineteen weeks and virtually ended his career at the age of thirty-one. For three seasons before that, however, Archie had been taking care of his future in a way which is not always open to footballers. With a B.Sc behind him he had taken up the offer of a job as a quality control chemist with the paint firm of Isaac Spencer and, while still a young man, rose to be managing director, with sixty-eight employees, a turnover of £1 million and a very comfortable living to replace his football career.

Time was also catching up a little prematurely with goalkeeper Fred Martin. In a match with Dundee, he rose to a ball with Andy Waddell and the outcome of a collision was a broken jaw for the Dons goalie. In hospital he was freely photographed, sporting a face which had swollen to the size of a football. That injury, as in the case of Archie Glen, more or less put an end to the remarkable career of one of the finest goalkeepers ever seen at Pittodrie. Transforming himself from a professional forward to a World Cup goalkeeper had been a feat in itself. Fred Martin's international record does poor justice to the talents of a man who could be massively commanding in a manner which was strongly reminiscent of England's Frank Swift. There were days when his large frame seemed to fill every one of those 192 square feet which make up the goalpost area. He would clutch and palm and rise to cut out crosses in a way which demoralised opponents and gave his own team the kind of confidence which won the League Championship. Like many another footballer, Fred went to work for the whisky blenders and rose to be a senior executive with Dewar's of Perth.

So faces which had been fixtures since the 1940s were gone with the 1960s and some folk thought that things would never be the same again. But life never fails to turn up new talents and opportunities, high points and surprises as well as disappointments. Local lads like Douglas Coutts and Dave Bennett were coming through. A bright young lad called Charlie Cooke had arrived from Greenock to come under the influence of Tommy Pearson, who could not have been long in detecting that here was someone who, like himself, could yet be remembered as one of Pittodrie's purest talents.

Meanwhile, Tommy Pearson was declared to be in charge of the team and that had not always been the case with football managers in the post-war era. The dominant figures like Bill Struth of Rangers, Willie Maley of Celtic and Paddy Travers of Aberdeen, men who were never seen out of business dress, had all but disappeared and the age of the track-suit manager was not quite established. But the 1960s were to produce a new breed of powerful manager, of whom Jock Stein was eminently the most successful example. His sojourn with Dunfermline and Hibernian between 1960 and 1965 was merely a prelude to an incomparable career with Celtic. Willie Waddell was soon to guide Kilmarnock to a Scottish League Championship and later to be invited back to the Rangers camp of his playing days to balance the weight of Stein at Parkhead and help counter the Celtic domination of the domestic front and their spectacular achievements in Europe.

Pittodrie, too, was to benefit from the strength of one of the toughest and shrewdest men in team management, the aggressively dedicated Eddie Turnbull, who came from his coaching job with Queen's Park and was still remembered as the driving force behind the Famous Five of Easter Road in the middle of the century.

But first there should have been that golden era under the command of Tommy Pearson, whose own skills would surely germinate similar talent and produce for Pittodrie a team of football artists to warm our hearts on cold, winter days. Such dreams did not materialise and, while it is true that he did improve the League positions of the following five seasons, his performance as a manager was lacking in both lustre and silverware.

The novelty of floodlights installed in 1959 was the brightest topic of conversation, while the balance sheet of 1960 showed a loss of £13,000 and a bank overdraft of £21,000.

In the pubs of King Street or Netherkirkgate they would turn to argument or reminiscence and one observant journalist with an ear for the contemporary situation managed to convey the reigning mood. Over their pints, folk were divided on the merits or inadequacies of a certain Norman Davidson, a tousle-haired loon from Kintore who followed the irregular route from Donside to Chelsea to Fraserburgh – and from Bellslea Park to Pittodrie. Norman came into the saint-or-sinner category and was a ready target for those who feel the better for a bawl. Then conversation would go back to Matt Armstrong and Paddy Moore.

'And whit aboot wee Benny Yorston?' asked a nostalgic man who knew he had struck upon the indisputable. 'Noo there wis a personality for ye. Five feet fower o' dynamite and bloody impidence.'

'And Willie Mills,' said another. 'Ah, there was an inside-forward. Legs like Andy Cunningham and what footwork! This new boy Charlie Cooke reminds me o' him. Weaves through half a dozen opponents wi' the ba' tied tae his feet.'

'Ach, they played Willie Mills intae the ground afore he was eighteen because he was sae good box-office. Hope they dinna dae the same wi' Cooke.'

'This is different,' said another man. 'Notice how Tommy Pearson drops him occasionally or shifts him to other positions? Tommy has the right idea and it's paying dividends. Let the kid hang on to the ball while he's young. It'll wear off.'

The talk would turn to defenders as the barman joined the conversation: 'Naething wrang wi' the backs or half-backs. I can see a gran' half-line takin' shape oot o' Ian Burns, George Kinnell, Doug Coutts and Ken Brownlee, ay, even Hugh Baird. They could settle doon tae being as good as Black, McLaren and Hill.'

'Ay, those were the days!'

Inevitably someone raised the name of Jock Hutton, who had been sold to Blackburn Rovers for £4,000 when money was money and £4,000 was a fortune. Up piped a fairmer chiel through a cloud of pipe-reek and said: 'Fower thoosan'? Damn't tae hell min, ye'd get a gweed Shorthorn bull for 'at.'

So they would return to the thorny problem of Norman Davidson and concede that, whatever his deficiencies, he had scored twenty-seven goals in the 1957–58 season, which put him into the company of Graham Leggat, with twenty-nine in 1956–57, and Paddy Buckley, who scored twenty-eight goals in 1955–56.

Such talk in the hostelries of Aberdeen and the North-east was a suitable diversion from the fact that there was very little to shout about at Pittodrie. There was not even a glimmer of relief from the Scottish Cup adventures which can still work wonders on the football spirits even when all else is despair. In 1963 the Dons were dismissed from the Cup by Raith Rovers, despite a penalty save by John Ogston. In 1964, Ayr United may have been third from the bottom of the Second Division but they were still good enough to put the Dons out of the Scottish Cup at Pittodrie. As if such humiliation were not enough, the unthinkable became the intolerable in 1965 when East Fife held the Dons to a draw at Pittodrie and beat them in the replay at Bayview Park.

In the midst of all that, there had been a Summer Cup competition during 1964, in which the Dons managed to reach the final against Hibs. After two games the teams were still level, so it went to a third and deciding tie. But before that could take place, Aberdeen had been thrust into the international headlines by an outbreak of typhoid. When the scare had finally cleared and the

Summer Cup Final went ahead, Hibs came to Pittodrie and won by 3–1.

By the dawning of 1965, Aberdeen supporters had been forced to thole an entire decade in which nothing at all had been won, a fact which was all the more unpalatable since it came hard on the heels of that golden decade in which every possible prize had come to the Pittodrie sideboard.

Time had run out for Tommy Pearson, whose achievements as a manager had not measured up to what was required by an ambitious club in an age when patience was not the virtue it had once been. His resignation was announced on 13 February 1965 and there were sixteen days of speculation before his successor was named. Eddie Turnbull needed no introduction to anyone who had been in touch with football in the previous twenty years. Back from a war in which he had served as a sailor with the famous Murmansk convoys, he had played for Hibs in the Scottish Cup Final of 1947. Then followed that memorable forward-line of Smith, Johnstone, Reilly, Turnbull and Ormond, one of the best in the history of the game, in which the inside-left was the dynamic instigator of events. So often it is that type of player who turns out to be a good manager when the time comes, having already learned about shouldering responsibility and motivating others. These were basic qualities he brought to Pittodrie in 1965, complemented by other features like dour determination, hard work and an ability to be more than blunt when the mood took him. He may not have been an easy man to know but he was respected for his knowledge and his enthusiasm for imparting it.

His arrival was to herald a whole new era for Aberdeen Football Club, in keeping with the changes which were taking place elsewhere in the game. The style and mood of football at that time had been influenced by an extraordinary South American called Helenio Herrera, who became manager of Inter Milan and took them to three European Cup Finals in the mid 1960s. The crinkly-haired Latin was already a legend in Italy, the full truth of which I verified for myself when I flew to interview him at his home in Appiano Gentile. Jock Stein, who was then with Dunfermline, and Willie Waddell of Kilmarnock had also flown out to study the methods of the great Herrera and there may be more than coincidence in the fact that Waddell returned to lead Killie to that Scottish League Championship in 1965 and Stein was soon to embark on his fabulous career with Celtic, taking them on an unparalleled run of nine successive League titles. At least their Italian visit did no harm. Turnbull came to Aberdeen in the same month as Stein went to Celtic Park, a new breed of manager with a streak of steel which would both enhance their chances of success in a competitive world and fortify them in the event of failure. There may have been a day when Jimmy Philip and Paddy Travers could have survived as Dons managers for a total of thirty-five years without winning anything but that day was gone. Davie Shaw had been given four years and Tommy Pearson just over five, and now it was the turn of the former Hibs player whose coaching at Hampden had brought Queen's Park more success than they had known for some time.

The leathery Turnbull breezed in that March day of 1965 and by the end of April had handed out seventeen free transfers. Two years later, when the dust had settled, he was far enough removed from the event to be quoted as saying: 'I had had doubts about the wisdom of my move but it was such a shambles – and the lack of ability in many of the players was an eye-opener to me. I decided there and then I just had to weed them out. An immediate reorganisation of the scouting staff was imperative. I got men of my own and retained only Bobby Calder, the club's chief scout, for whom I have great admiration.'

By the time these quotes had appeared, Turnbull had taken Aberdeen to fourth position in the Scottish League and into the final of the Scottish Cup. At any other stage in football history his new-look Dons would have been good enough to win that Cup in 1967. Unfortunately for Aberdeen, it coincided with Celtic reaching their all-time peak of performance. On 25 May 1967, Billy McNeill captained the very first British team to win the European Cup, a team which lined up as: Simpson; Craig, Gemmell; Murdoch, McNeill, Clark; Johnstone, Wallace, Chalmers, Auld, Lennox. Precisely that same formation had lined up just twenty-six days earlier in the Cup Final at Hampden Park, Glasgow, to meet an Aberdeen team which read: Clark; Whyte, Shewan; Munro, McMillan, Petersen; Wilson, Smith, Storrie, Melrose, Johnston.

For skipper Harry Melrose it was a third encounter with Celtic in a Scottish Cup Final. He had been in Jock Stein's Dunfermline team which won in 1961 and on the losing side with the Fifers four years later, when his former boss had just taken over at Celtic Park. Alas, there was to be no luck in his third attempt for Harry or anyone else in the Aberdeen camp. Bobby Lennox scored three minutes before the interval and Willie Wallace added a second just after it, ensuring defeat for the team which their own captain would be managing within ten years.

As if it were not enough to be meeting the best club team in Europe, the Dons had other problems to cope with that day. Manager Eddie Turnbull had been ill all week and missed training. He started out from Aberdeen, however, intending to accompany his men to Hampden and they all stayed overnight at Gleneagles Hotel. But he was too ill to start out on the Saturday morning and it was a pretty headless party which boarded the bus without him for a journey to Glasgow which was further upset when the Dons' vehicle was involved in an accident. The party arrived late, with time only to change and take the field and without a moment to gather their thoughts. It was a disastrous day altogether and the sole consolation for the Aberdeen team was that, by virtue of Celtic qualifying for the following year's European Cup contest, they were able to make their debut in European football as Scotland's representatives in the Cup Winners' Cup.

So Eddie Turnbull had at least restored a contact with success, and the kind of influence he had on the team deserves some examination. That story really begins back at Hampden Park, when he was still coaching Queen's Park and keeping an eye on a very young goalkeeper who, he knew for certain, was going to the top.

28
TAKE-OVER BATTLE

Before the arrival of Eddie Turnbull as coach to Queen's Park, the training routine of the Hampden players had been four laps of 880 yards and one ball among the lot of them. It all changed with the new boss, who gave them a ball each and transformed it from an athletic exercise to an exciting football experience.

Among the youngsters whose imagination was fired by the new man's methods was a Glasgow teenager who had been keeping goal for the first team since he was sixteen. Bobby Clark, whose father was a director of Clyde FC and a well-to-do businessman, revelled in the fact that he was under the direction of a real coach for the first time. Turnbull taught him simple things, like the intelligent throwing of a ball, and inspired him to think about football. Needless to say, the coach's talents were being appreciated elsewhere and, with Queen's Park riding high in the Second Division, it was no surprise that he was invited to fill the vacancy at Pittodrie left by the departure of Tommy Pearson. Turnbull's influence was sorely missed by the Queen's players and young Clark, for whom big things were being predicted, realised that his career had reached a point of decision. If Queen's gained promotion, as had seemed likely under Turnbull, he would stay at Hampden. Instead, they lost their momentum and drifted back down the League table.

I well remember making my way out to the Clark family villa in the Sandyhills district of Glasgow to interview the boy who was being hotly pursued by many of Britain's top clubs. Having just completed a year of his physical education course at Jordanhill College, he knew that the time to move had arrived, and it only remained for him to contemplate the line-up of clubs like Rangers, Chelsea and Tottenham Hotspur and decide which one it was to be. The boy talked idealistically about wanting to give whatever talents he had to Scottish football, despite the lure of fame and fortune in England, and that seemed to settle it for Rangers. Suddenly I realised that my Aberdeenshire accent was of more than passing interest and I spared Bobby Clark the embarrassment of prematurely spelling out what I now knew – that he was going to follow his old boss to Pittodrie. Turnbull took both Clark and left-half David Millar to the Granite City and if he had done nothing else for the club he would still have deserved high gratitude for signing and moulding the man who was to become the most-capped player in the first seventy-five years of Aberdeen Football Club. Little did I imagine, as I interviewed that boy in 1965, that I was talking to one who would so carve his name in the Pittodrie history – or that I would be here to write it!

Clark took over in goal from the larger frame of John Ogston, who was known as Tubby and whose career might have been a great deal more distinguished had he landed at a better time. Turnbull's team was beginning to take shape, running twelve games without defeat. Aberdeen had followed a fashion of the 1960s, begun by that colourful innovator from Greenock Morton, Hal Stewart, and imported some Scandinavian players, notably Jens Petersen, Lief Mortensen and Jorgen Ravn. In Turnbull's first season proper, 1965–66, he gave warning of things to come by taking the Dons to the semi-final of the Scottish Cup, losing after a replay with Rangers. The new broom was sweeping away what he did not want and paving the way for the players who would reflect his own distinctive personality. Tommy McMillan and Chalky Whyte were coming into their own, alongside players like Dave Smith, Ally Shewan, Harry Melrose, Jimmy Wilson and Billy Little. By season 1966–67 the players were conscious of the fact that they had been poured into a Turnbull mould and were now part of a busy set-up in which something was almost bound to happen. It has to do with vibrations, which had been switched on through the years by men like Stein, Shankly and Revie.

Pittodrie was buzzing and among the new excitements on the horizon was eighteen-year-old Jimmy Smith, who had come from Glasgow Benburb, the junior club within shouting distance of Ibrox Park, which had already produced men such as George Johnstone and Frank Dunlop. The fact that he earned the nickname of Jinky tells of his very special talent as a ball-player, a tall lad with a deceptive movement who would seem to work himself into trouble one moment as if to demonstrate how simply he could get himself out of it the next.

Turnbull was fielding a team which was emerging as: Clark; Whyte, Shewan; Petersen, McMillan, Millar; Little, Smith, Winchester, Melrose, Wilson.

Dave Smith, who had blossomed as a fine young player from local junior circles, was seeking a move and his opportunity came when Rangers went on a spree of buying up their opponents' best players. They denuded Dundee of Penman, Dundee United of Persson, Hibernian of Stein, St Johnstone of MacDonald, Dunfermline of Ferguson and Smith, and Aberdeen of Dave Smith – and still failed in their objective of lowering the Celtic supremacy. So nothing was gained and half a dozen clubs lost a personality, another example of the damaging imbalance of power in Scottish football.

So Dave Smith was off to Ibrox and Jens Petersen became 'sweeper', in the modern jargon, while Harry Melrose was classed a midfield man along with Francis Munro, who had been signed from Dundee United. It was a young formation, five of whom were contenders for Scotland's Under-23 team: Francis Munro, Jimmy Smith, Tommy McMillan, Jimmy Whyte and Bobby Clark. In fact, all except Munro found themselves chosen. By Christmas 1966 the Dons were challenging in second position in the League but the Scottish Cup began to dominate events and the League form shaded off. In the first round of the Cup, Aberdeen went to Dens Park and beat Dundee 5–0, a game best remembered for a scintillating display by Jimmy Smith. St Johnstone were the next victims before the Dons met Hibs in the quarter-finals at Easter Road. Hibs were in the lead when the silken Smith scored the equalizer with the last move of the match.

The replay at Pittodrie on the following Wednesday presented special problems for Bobby Clark, who was still a student at Jordanhill College, Glasgow, and had an important examination due that day. After he had put his case to the college, he was allowed to sit the examination an hour earlier, supervised by Roy Small, lecturer and occasional radio commentator. Bobby was put on his word of honour that he would not divulge the questions to anyone and he remembers that he had never been so popular with the college students! But the college knew that he would not let them down. Mr Clark senior was sitting outside the gate with the car engine ticking over, ready to speed his son northwards for an evening replay which had aroused a fire of enthusiasm, particularly after that last-gasp equalizer on the Saturday. There might well have been a record crowd inside Pittodrie that night but they decided to close the gates when it had reached more than 40,000. Jimmy Smith had been injured on the Saturday but Turnbull brought off one of the master strokes which characterised his managership. He remembered that Ernie Winchester, the bustling centre-forward who first made his name as an Aberdeen schoolboy, had been highly successful against centre-half Madsden when the Dons played Morton. Madsden had since been transferred to Hibs and Turnbull saw no reason why it shouldn't work again. It did. Ernie had a tremendous game and the Dons won 3–0.

People queued all night at Pittodrie for tickets to see the semi-final against Dundee United at Dens Park and their wait was well worth it, for the match turned out to be an exciting cliffhanger, with the Dons hanging on to a one-goal lead. Aberdonians thought the referee had lost his watch and there are those who will tell you that, in the last ten minutes, Chalky Whyte kicked the ball high into the stand on half a dozen occasions! On top of that, Jim Storrie missed a penalty.

The Dons had played Celtic twice that season and beaten them both times, so there was no lack of confidence in the Aberdeen camp about the outcome of the final, despite the Parkhead team's triumphs in Europe. But the reality was very different. Celtic won 2–0, as already described, and the Dons supporters consoled themselves with the fact that Eddie Turnbull had at last brought them to the brink of success. His day would surely come.

At the end of that season the Dons went off to America to take part in a novel experiment. The Americans, whose football is played by men with monstrous shoulders, decided that they should at least try to introduce the other variety. So they invited a number of overseas sides, including Aberdeen, Hibs, Stoke City and Wolves, to become the adopted teams of American cities, playing out a contest in two sections with the winners meeting in a sudden-death finale. The Dons became the Washington Whips for the occasion and gathered up a new set of supporters for their stay in the capital. Even President Lyndon B. Johnson was caught up in the event and gave the President's Cup as the winning trophy. Aberdeen did the US capital proud, winning the Eastern Section and qualifying to meet Wolves, the Western Section winners, in the final in Los Angeles.

Jimmy Smith was sent off for a foul on Dave Wagstaffe and a ten-man Dons team survived for a 4–4 draw at full-time. The game went to extra time which ended at 5–5 and during a further period of extra time it was Ally Shewan, the lad from Cuminestown, who put through an own goal to give Wolves the American President's Cup.

In a memorable experience, the Dons had played in such places as Los Angeles Coliseum and the Houston Astrodrome, with its synthetic astroturf. Even more important, however, was the fact that the tour had seen the introduction of that local lad who had followed his father to Pittodrie and bore the same name – Martin Buchan. He had been brought in as a midfield marker and had shown that, in a one-against-one situation, he could mark a man out of the game. A lad of that talent would soon be here to stay.

Having taken over the European Cup Winners' Cup place from Celtic, the Dons launched themselves into their first experience of competitive European football, exactly twelve years later than they should have done when they were Scotland's League Champions. In the preliminary round they were drawn against KR Reykjavik, whom they beat 10–0 at Pittodrie and 4–1 in Iceland. A better test of continental opposition, however, was to come in the next round, against Standard Liège of Belgium, when the Dons managed to win 2–0 at home but went down on an aggregate of 3–2.

In the following season the Dons' League position gave them a place in the Inter-Cities Fairs Cup, forerunner of the UEFA Cup, and it was in the first round of that competition that Martin Buchan came truly into his own. Aberdeen were drawn against the highly rated Bulgarian team Slavia Sofia, which followed a familiar communist pattern in that the players were all soldiers. As part of the new-fangled numbers game, Eddie Turnbull listed young Buchan at outside-left, but as soon as the game started he went straight into defence and took up the role of a double-centre-half, alongside Tommy McMillan. His outstanding performance helped the Dons to hold the Bulgarians to a non-scoring draw and to beat them 2–0 at Pittodrie in the second leg. Thus Martin Buchan became the man at the back who cleaned up whatever danger came through the defensive net, a role he was to play with distinction not only for Aberdeen but also for Manchester United and Scotland. Unfortunately, the success against the Bulgarians was not maintained against Real Zaragoza of Spain and the Dons went out of the competition on an aggregate of 4–2.

Meanwhile, Eddie Turnbull was all but lured away to Rangers

to take on a team-coaching role but the deal fell through and the North-east breathed again.

In season 1968–69 the Dons found themselves in an extraordinary position over goalkeepers. Bobby Clark had fulfilled all his early promise and was not only the undisputed choice for Aberdeen but had also collected his first few caps with Scotland. An injury gave a first-team opportunity to Ernie McGarr, however, and the reserve man performed with such distinction that he not only kept Clark out of the Aberdeen team but went on to become Scotland's World Cup goalkeeper against Austria in 1969! It was during his absence on that particular engagement that Bobby Clark was given a chance to show that he was still a top-class keeper and Aberdeen were reminded of their unusual dilemma of having Scotland's two best men on their staff at the same time. In the intervening period, Clark had not only contented himself with reserve-team football but developed an earlier talent as a centre-half and actually had a brief spell in the first team as an outfield player in season 1969–70. It was Fred Martin in reverse, except that Clark was clearly better suited to his former role. Turnbull told him so, allowed the situation to resolve itself and after a year in the wilderness the former Queen's Parker was re-established as the first choice and began to build up his record as the Don with the most caps. Ernie McGarr was nevertheless an exciting goalkeeper and it seemed rough justice that his career headed down the echelons of Scottish football instead of outwards to some of the more fashionable clubs in Scotland or England, where he might well have become a major personality.

Eddie Turnbull had experienced mixed health and the players felt he had lost his edge, a fact which may have been reflected in the mediocre performance of 1968–69 when the Dons finished in fifteenth position in the League.

But whatever dramas were being enacted on the field of play, a greater drama was mounting behind the scenes where the board found themselves fighting off a take-over bid. The group which had designs on running Pittodrie consisted of well-known names in the Aberdeen business world. Gordon McIver was a Turriff man who had been the Dons' secretary in 1948 before expanding as a businessman to become boss of Lawson Turnbull, the plumbing people. Sandy Mutch was prominent in local politics and was to become the first convener of the Grampian Region. John Leiper was an insurance broker, Henry Robertson a fish merchant, and Don Emery and Tony Harris were two former Aberdeen players of note whose shadows had grown no less in retirement. These were the men who signed the letter to shareholders indicating an offer of £8 for each ten-shilling share, but there were indications that there was someone else behind them, a Mr Big who was keeping out of the way. Rumour said it was Mr Peter Cameron, the wealthy builder and racehorse owner, but he flatly denied it. Several years later Gordon McIver assured me that he personally had had the backing of £500,000 and that Peter Cameron was no part of that. 'I don't know if he was behind some of the others but he was not behind me,' he said.

One of those others believed that Mr Cameron was involved, out of a genuine desire to see the Dons at the top, and that he not only planned a super-stadium at Pittodrie but intended to offer the job of manager to Jock Stein, with whom he was well acquainted. Mr Cameron has since repeated his denial to me. Gordon McIver weighed in at the time with some criticism of Pittodrie's public relations and felt there was something wrong with local scouting arrangements which enabled players like Denis Law to escape the net before their names were even noted. There was some truth in what he said.

Chairman Charles B. Forbes led the board's resistance to the take-over bid and not least of his weapons was the fact that the reigning directors held 3157 of the 10,000 shares. Richard Spain, boss of Henderson's, the King Street engineers, was soon to join the board with his 754 shares, but, most important of all, there were three powerful ladies holding the balance somewhere in the shadows. Who were they?

Mrs Mabel Callander, daughter of former Dons director John D. Robbie, was said to have 268 shares. A regular attender at Pittodrie, she declared that she had been brought up with the club since she was knee-high to a kipper and was perfectly happy with the present board. Miss Moyra Mitchell, daughter of former chairman William Mitchell, had 602 shares and she, too, saw no need for a change. The third and most powerful of those ladies was Mrs Flora Duncan, widow of former director John Duncan, who held 838 shares and was also on the side of the ruling board. So petticoat power sealed the fate of the 1969 take-over bid and not even the great Don Emery, who seldom failed to score when he set his sights, could do a thing about it.

Mr Forbes, the chairman, said very little about this matter, then or later, but in an interview with Ronald Main of the *Scottish Daily Express* he did open up as much as to say:

The bid was doomed from the start. But, if by some chance it had succeeded, it could have been the worst thing that ever happened to this fine old club. What most people don't know is that, in this game, football know-how is just as important as football knowledge. There is far more to running a club than picking a team. There are national contacts to be made, transfers to be negotiated and all sorts of things which members of the public don't realize.

The 1960s were now departing with a mixture of memories but still nothing tangible to show for them. Was it too much to hope that the luck would change in 1970?

29
'CUP-TIE' MCKAY

When Bobby Clark regained his place in goal from Ernie McGarr after a year in the cold, he could not have returned at a more inopportune moment. It was early in 1970 and the Dons were meeting Clydebank in the second round of the Scottish Cup. The Bankies were then a very modest side, far short of the respect they were to gain in the mid 1970s, but despite the calibre of opposition the Dons just managed to scrape through by two goals to one. The occasion is still remembered as the day when Aberdeen supporters lost patience with their team and started booing and slow hand-clapping. Round three produced further problems, which raised the question of whether a jinx had descended on the Pittodrie scene. As that third-round tie with Falkirk approached, a virulent flu bug put so many Aberdeen players in bed that manager Eddie Turnbull, himself a victim, had to seek a postponement. As that minor epidemic swept on, however, it played its own ironic part in the subsequent fortunes of the Dons that season. Directly because of it, a man from Gellymill Street, Macduff, will have a strange tale to tell his grandchildren about how he gained a fleeting piece of glory in the history of Pittodrie.

After playing for Deveronvale, Derek McKay went on to Dundee and was given a free transfer before landing with Aberdeen. Sporting a George Best haircut, this North-east lad appeared from obscurity to play at outside-right against Falkirk and to have a splendid game against George Miller. Bobby Clark, wishing to encourage the boy, called out to him: 'Keep going, Derek, you can win the game for us.' The words were prophetic, as the rest of the story will show. For Derek McKay scored the only goal of the game and thus put Aberdeen into the semi-final of the Scottish Cup.

He had more than earned his place at Muirton Park, Perth, when the Dons went to meet the Kilmarnock side which now stood between them and another Cup Final. Once again the boy from Macduff turned up trumps and scored the only goal of the match. No wonder they were calling him 'Cup-Tie' McKay, the lad who came from nowhere and carried Aberdeen through to a memorable occasion at Hampden Park.

Once again the opposition was Celtic, the club which had thwarted Aberdeen ambitions in 1937, 1954 and 1967 and was still the dominant force in the land. The signs were not encouraging for the Aberdeen team. Just as Celtic had been on the point of becoming Champions of Europe when they had met in the Scottish Cup Final three years earlier, the Parkhead men were due to play in that European Cup Final again in 1970, this time against Feyenoord of Holland. But a crate of champagne gave Aberdeen a psychological boost – and not a drop of it was drunk! The incident happened at Celtic Park, where Aberdeen were due to play a League game before the Cup Final, a game which would clinch yet another League Championship for Celtic if Aberdeen were suitably defeated. It was just as the Dons party arrived at the ground that they happened to see the bottles of champagne being carried in for the celebration. The Celtic management would have been wiser to have kept their preparations private, because the sight of that champagne was like a red rag to an Aberdeen Angus bull as far as Eddie Turnbull was concerned. In no uncertain terms, he made it plain that there was going to be no celebration at Aberdeen's immediate expense. Out went the Dons with their dander up – they fielded a seventeen-year-old boy from the Castlemilk housing scheme in Glasgow called Arthur Graham – and defeated Celtic by two goals to one. The fact that the celebration champagne had to be quietly stored away that night proved a tremendous boost to the Aberdeen morale. They had learned that they were capable of absorbing everything that Celtic could throw at them and coming out on top. Nevertheless, the public view was that Aberdeen had little chance of beating Celtic in Glasgow twice within ten days.

It was left to the superstitious to hope that the gods might have sent young Cup-Tie McKay from Macduff to play some fateful part in the destiny of the club. He was not the greatest of footballers but the extraordinary role he had played in the Scottish Cup of that season meant that he was at least certain of keeping his place in the Cup Final team. Two players who would not be in the team were the injured Alec Willoughby, whose partnership with his cousin Jim Forrest had been transferred from Rangers to Aberdeen, and former Dundee captain Steve Murray, recently signed for £50,000 but who was ineligible for the Cup.

Whatever the outcome of the match, it was certain to be a historic day for Martin Buchan, at twenty-one the youngest player to captain a team in the Scottish Cup Final. Little of that excitement could have been foreseen by young Buchan when he left Cummings Park School for Gordon's College and found himself in a running battle as to whether he should be playing rugby for Gordon's or football for the Boys' Brigade. He was signed by the Dons while still at school but harboured a doubt about whether he was good enough to make the grade and vowed that he would give himself until twenty-one to decide what to do with his life. At twenty-one, he surely had his answer. Football was his talent, even though his immediate prospects of Cup success were rated at about 5 to 1 against, compared with an odds-on Celtic quotation of 2 to 5. The bookmakers' reasoning was based on the solid evidence that Celtic had now clinched their fifth successive League title and were heading for the European Cup Final, whereas Aberdeen's inconsistency had left them half-way down the table, with only twelve wins in thirty-two games. But every game is a new beginning. Past defeats and disappointments melt away in the heat of fresh enthusiasm, as a sure sign that the good Lord fashioned the human spirit out of Rubislaw Quarry. The red scarves were washed and ironed, tickets bought and buses booked as the North-east made ready to invade Mount Florida with optimism.

Spare a thought, if you will, for a humble scribe whose Dons-daft days began in a wartime childhood and who vowed that he would never miss a major event in the life of Aberdeen Football Club. Can you picture this Buchan loon, whose blood pressure and general well-being go up and down with the Pittodrie fortunes, as he found himself on a journalistic assignment in distant Athens on the very day when his team was liable to win the Scottish Cup for the first time in twenty-three years? With the architectural splendour of ancient Greece all around me, I should have been absorbing the wondrous spirit of a glorious civilisation. But I might as well have been in Foggieloan on a wet Sunday. Never have heart and body been in two such distant places at the same time. On that early afternoon of Saturday 11 April 1970, I stood all the caviar and champagne and abominable luxury of the Hilton Hotel till I could stand it no longer. Out I went into the streets of Athens, walking off the nerves and checking my watch every two minutes, picturing the dressing-room scene at Hampden and the mounting excitement of the stands and terracings, where my ten-year-old son Geoffrey was playing proxy for his father to make sure that the Dons would not be short of a voice, albeit a more restrained one.

Before me stood the arena which had seen the first of the modern Olympic Games in 1896, just seven years before the Dons were founded. I wandered inside and up its stone terraces and sat myself down. Here at least was a stadium, in Greece perhaps but in Glasgow for all imaginary purposes, and from 3 p.m. until 4.40 p.m. I sat in the blazing Athenian heat, a lone figure in a historic but near-deserted stadium, kicking an imaginary ball, swaying, swerving, double-shuffling, talking to myself, punching the innocent air with determined fists and urging the Dons to victory. Our book is not about telepathic power but let me say that the outcome of my imaginary game was that Celtic scored once and Aberdeen three times. I rose with my final whistle, well satisfied with the performance and feeling that, if the Dons had done half as well in Glasgow, the Scottish Cup was surely on its way to Pittodrie.

When I learned the score next morning in the hotel foyer, my leaps of joy and shouts of 'Up the Dons!' sent startled Greeks in search of first-aid books to find the cure for sudden insanity. There it was in a British newspaper – Celtic 1, Aberdeen 3 – just as I had played it. The words revolved in my mouth again and again, 'Celtic one . . . Aberdeen three', with all the purr of poetry.

The dream had indeed come true. Inside Hampden's bowl, 108,434 spectators had watched as Celtic stormed into the early attacks, only to see Aberdeen awarded a penalty in twenty-seven minutes because of a handling offence by Bobby Murdoch. The cross which preceded the penalty had come from none other than Derek McKay, whose name was already written all over the Pittodrie progress that year. Before the penalty kick could be taken, left-back Tommy Gemmell landed his name in the black book by uplifting the ball from the spot and throwing it towards the referee. That caused a delay but Joe Harper, the little man whose golden boots were already building him a reputation, replaced the ball on the spot and coolly scored. When Bobby Lennox had the ball in the Dons' net and the whistle blew for a foul on Bobby Clark, Jimmy Johnstone had his name taken for the vehemence of his protests.

The Dons were still a goal ahead at the start of the second half but Celtic were once again storming the Aberdeen goal, bringing on Bertie Auld as substitute for big John Hughes. With only seven minutes to go, Joe Harper sent Jim Forrest away on the left wing and Celtic keeper Evan Williams could only partly stop his scoring attempt. Who turned up to side-foot the ball into the net from a difficult angle but the Cup-tie specialist himself, Derek McKay. Two–nil. But the drama was not yet over. Bobby Lennox scored for Celtic, a team which is never down until the final whistle. Could they still equalise? That doubt was settled almost immediately when Joe Harper laid on a ball for Derek McKay and the winger ran in to make the score three–one. The teams that day were: Aberdeen – Clark; Boel, G. Murray; Hermiston, McMillan, M. Buchan; McKay, Robb, Forrest, Harper, Graham; Substitute – G. Buchan. Celtic – Williams; Hay, Gemmell; Murdoch, McNeill, Brogan; Johnstone, Wallace, Connelly, Lennox, Hughes. Substitute – Auld.

Jock Stein and his players were quick to express their appreciation of the Aberdeen performance, though the manager did not restrain himself from an outburst against the referee, Bobby Davidson of Airdrie.

Amid the jubilation of that Hampden scene there was not a happier man than Aberdeen chairman Charles B. Forbes, former headmaster of Middlefield School, who was celebrating his three score years and ten in the finest possible manner. Academic discipline had taught him to control his emotions but there he stood in the south stand at Hampden with moisture on his cheeks which told its own story. He was to admit later:

Put it like this – my tear ducts were not functioning properly. I have had my moments in the sixty-odd years I have been associated with the game, but this was the biggest thrill I have ever had. As I stood at the final whistle and realised exactly what had happened, I knew that this was the proudest moment of my life.

The Dons players were still trying to accept the reality that they had been through a great Cup Final and had won it. The Danish right-back, Henning Boel, had been magnificent in the way he bottled up Celtic's clever ball-player John Hughes. Jim Hermiston had been a tower of strength in midfield, and every other player emerged with distinction. But the greatest glory lay with the man from Macduff, Derek McKay, who came from nowhere, earned his brief moment of glory and disappeared again into the night, as if accepting that it couldn't last. His story came straight from the realms of Hans Christian Andersen.

The crowds who had shared the euphoria of that April day in 1970 were reluctant to let it go and those who had stayed behind in Aberdeen were anxious to catch its tail before it subsided for ever. The weather was the final encouragement for the massive crowd which turned out next day to welcome home its Hampden heroes. The players were completely taken by surprise at the size and warmth of the reception as half the population of Aberdeen, or so it seemed, filled Union Street and bulged out to a sea of faces up by the Castlegate.

That talented journalist John Dunbar, who had seen most things in a lifetime with *Aberdeen Journal*, was moved to write that the city had probably never seen the like of it. Describing it as a five-star day, he wrote:

The climax came with the team bus inching its way to a position opposite the Town House door so that Lord Provost Robert Lennox, from the balcony immediately above, could say on behalf of the community: 'Welcome and many congratulations.' Although his remarks were brief and apt, it took him some time to make himself heard above the clamour. The Lord Provost began: 'Today the sun is shining, the long winter is over. This is Eddie Turnbull's birthday and we have won the cup. What a perfect weekend!'

It was the sort of preface that suited the mood of the thousands. They screamed their acclaim. They cheered and cheered and cheered. They roared 'Happy birthday!' as Mr Turnbull, a broad smile lighting his normally rugged face, held the cup aloft. They shrieked as it was passed to two-goal scorer Derek McKay, and then to the youthful captain, Martin Buchan, who had just come of age. As the noise subsided for a moment, the Lord Provost went on: 'In conception and in execution of the game, the Dons were far superior. The victory was not only a triumph for Aberdeen but, perhaps of greater significance, it was a victory for football in Scotland!'

'It was, it was,' yelled those who could hear. And those who didn't took up the chant. It changed to 'E-A-S-Y' and then 'Hail the Dons!' It was nearly incredible – an occasion that those who shared in it will relive for generations to come. Perhaps manager Turnbull assessed it best of all when, in the familiar setting of Pittodrie in the comparative quiet after the din of the home-coming, he said: 'This is the sort of thing that makes it all worthwhile.'

Eddie Turnbull, mastermind of the victory, had been brief in his instructions to the Dons players: 'Play it on the carpet – and beat Celtic to the ball.' How well it had paid off.

As the bus edged its way along Union Street, bringing the players such an emotional welcome as they had not imagined in their wildest dreams, Bobby Clark permitted himself a backward glance along the route they had just travelled – and a backward thought to the route they had travelled in that cup contest. Above the din, he shouted to Eddie Turnbull, the man who had brought him from Queen's Park: 'I wonder how many of these people were giving us the slow handclap in that game against Clydebank.' Turnbull shook his head philosophically and shouted back: 'Ay, son, that's football.'

What mattered was that Aberdeen, to whom so many others look for a lead in stemming the domination of the Old Firm, had won an award for the first time in nearly fifteen years. The Scottish Cup was here again. Not since 1947 had that handsome piece of silverware graced Pittodrie and inevitably there were arguments in comparing the two teams. One man who put down his thoughts in lucid fashion was Archie Baird, popular inside-left in that first victory. This is what Archie wrote in 1970.

To have been part of that 1947 team is a status symbol which has grown with the years. Now, thank goodness, twelve vibrant youngsters have joined the exclusive club. But how *do* the teams compare? First we must be sure that we are comparing like with like and that a comparison is really possible. Twenty-three years is a long time and in that period the character and conception of football have radically changed. Indeed, the whole scope of sports and games has been revolutionized. Men and women are running faster, jumping and throwing further than they have ever done. Is it not reasonable to suppose that present footballers are fitter, faster and more skilful than their counterparts of twenty years ago?

In some ways, yes. European and South American influence has given us great technical advancement and improved training and fitness methods. But it is in the tactical field that the greatest change has come. In 1947, we were still hide-bound by the old traditions. Now football has a new freedom of movement, a new dimension, with the manager more and more pulling the strings. The Dons player who is quoted as saying 'I don't have to think on the field; all our thinking is done off the field, by the manager' unconsciously puts his finger on a crucial point. We had to do all our own thinking, playing football that was almost entirely improvised and spontaneous. We were just as much a product of our age and environment as the present Dons are. Our play reflected the maturity of a team all in their mid-twenties or returning from a war to a public starved of football.

The present youthful Pittodrie squad show many of the excellent qualities and much of the brashness of a computer age – a swinging, affluent society. Perhaps then in trying to judge merit in two entirely different situations we are doing a disservice to both. In the end we are reduced to comparing personalities and individual ability, those qualities which all the coaching in the world will never increase.

Who, for instance, in the present Aberdeen team comes anywhere near George Hamilton for sheer native football know-how? Gentleman George, the acme of correctness, pin-pointing his passes and shots with deadly accuracy was the best header of a ball Pittodrie has ever seen. Or Stanley Williams, diminutive and tricky, with a needle-sharp football brain, years ahead of his time and doing naturally the things which centre-forwards are coached into doing today. In defence there was Frank Dunlop, one of the best uncapped centre-halves of his time, an inspiring captain and absolutely dominant in the middle.

But who can deny the sheer personality and power of the giant Dane, Henning Boel, the cool efficiency of twenty-one-year-old skipper Martin Buchan and the sure hands and lighting reflexes of Bobby Clark of the present Dons? Nor did we have anything quite so jet-propelled as Jim Forrest and Dave Robb whose twin-striker role, curiously enough, was first being developed by Hamilton and Williams in the latter part of their careers.

Let's say that a select from those two Cup-winning teams would have beaten the best. And we did have quite a lot in common too – victory, jubilant return to HQ, champagne, rejoicing, then the triumphant journey back to Aberdeen with half the football-mad city out to welcome us home. There our glory ended. For us there were no fresh fields to conquer. For those bright young Dons of 1970, this is just the beginning. Europe and the world lies before them in a new era that could see Aberdeen, under the capable guidance of manager Eddie Turnbull, blaze a trail for football greatness. Nineteen-forty-seven wishes them well.

Indeed, the whole football world wished them well. As a post-script to that Scottish Cup victory of 1970, let us return briefly to that deliriously happy Saturday night when the din that rose over Hampden still sang in the eardrums and the Aberdeen party made their way to Gleneagles Hotel, where they stayed the night in readiness for the triumphant return. In the heady celebration of the night, the seventeen-year-old Arthur Graham, the Glasgow youth plucked from the anonymity of Europe's biggest housing scheme and thrust into football glory within a few weeks of joining the team, crossed the grand foyer of Scotland's most famous hotel to greet a lively little gentleman who had good reason to be sharing in the joy of the occasion. 'I want you to have my medal,' said Arthur, pushing the precious prize into his hand. It was the boy's way of expressing gratitude to a man who had played an exceptional role in the post-war success of the Dons. He refused the gift but it nevertheless remained the most touching moment in the lifetime of Bobby Calder.

30
INCREDIBLE CALDER

The making of a professional football team begins far away from the glamour of the big occasions. Like the springs and tributaries which make up a river, it is liable to begin on a range of grubby little pitches in the most unlikely corners of a Glasgow housing scheme or an Ayrshire coalfield. It was there on many a blustery day that you would find a master spy of Scottish football, a man whose record of talent-spotting was unsurpassed.

It was the good fortune of Aberdeen Football Club that for nearly thirty years the heart and soul of Bobby Calder from Rutherglen was totally committed to the discovery of promising young footballers for Pittodrie. Credit for that must go to the chairman of the time, William Mitchell, who invited Calder to become chief scout 'not just for a year or so but for the whole of your life', as he said at the time. It was a remarkable piece of foresight on Mitchell's part, designed to establish a loyalty which would not be broken by the bait of clubs like Rangers or Celtic when they discovered how good the little man really was.

Bobby Calder, who worked as a railway signalman in Glasgow during the week, had rounded off a distinguished career as a top-class referee when the took charge of the Aberdeen–Hibernian Scottish Cup Final in 1947. Thereafter, he had a spell as manager of Dunfermline and as a referee in America before returning to Scotland and the Mitchell invitation. He liked the honesty of the approach and entered into a gentleman's agreement. John Lawrence, the millionaire who was chairman of Rangers for many years, dined little Bobby in the Central Hotel, Glasgow, hoping to persuade him to scout for Ibrox. When it came to the crunch, the Pittodrie scout confronted Lawrence with this thought: 'What would you say, Mr Lawrence, if I had made the promise to you that I made to Mr Mitchell of Aberdeen and then you found that I had broken it?' John Lawrence knew when he was beaten. Taking him by the arm, he said: 'I can see where your allegiance lies, Bobby. I shall never ask you again.'

Bobby Calder built up an impressive network of contacts in the football world, sometimes in the most unlikely places. For example, a policeman stopped him in the streets of Rutherglen one day and advised him to have a look at a lad in Lanark. Calder did not expect much to come of it but he followed up the hint – and that was how Ian Macfarlane, that fine full-back of the 1950s, arrived at Pittodrie before heading for England. It had sometimes been said that Bobby Calder was psychic and the man himself said he did experience a bristling at the back of the neck when something was about to happen. Often he was about to track down another budding star for Pittodrie and, likely as not, would get there half an hour before another scout!

Calder examined young footballers as a jeweller examines diamonds through an eye-glass and could just as certainly pick out the gems. The reputation he built up during the 1950s came to fruition during the 1960s when his collection of boys for Pittodrie ranged from Charlie Cooke and Tommy Craig to Jimmy Smith, Willie Young and Arthur Graham. One thing led to another. On the day he turned up at the Glasgow home of Jimmy Smith to sign the young Benburb star, another boy in the background piped up and said, 'Maybe you'll come back and see me play, Mr Calder?'

'What's your name, son?' asked Calder.

'I'm Joe,' said the boy. 'I play for the school and I'm fifteen.'

'I'll be back next year to see you, son.' And he was – and that was how Joe Smith went straight from school to follow his brother north and to become a key figure in the team of the mid 1970s which carried off the Scottish League Cup.

Across Glasgow, Bobby Calder had pursued another star of the future, a red-headed boy who seemed like one of nature's footballers. But, like many another red-headed Glasgow boy, Tommy Craig's sights were on Celtic Park and he was, in fact, due to meet Jock Stein. Calder wished him well but, as he turned to leave the house, he asked for one promise. 'If, by some chance, you fail to sign for Celtic, will you come to Aberdeen?' he asked. The promise was given. Calder's neck was bristling. A hunch was hovering to the extent that he hung around in the vicinity of Celtic Park as Tommy Craig went for his interview with Mr Stein. When he emerged with his father, there had been no agreement on terms and Tommy was ready to sign for Aberdeen, one of the most talented boys ever seen at Pittodrie.

Supervising his work on the ground staff, Andy Bowie marvelled at how he could saw timber in a dead-straight line without any markings and was not surprised to find that his eye was just as sure when it came to the geometry of football. As in the case of the Smiths, Tommy's brother John followed him north – but not only John. Mr and Mrs Tommy Craig also decided to uproot themselves from Glasgow and settle in the Granite City. As adopted Aberdonians, they lived happily in Ashvale Place and daughter Ellen was married in the city, even though Tommy departed for the richer rewards of English football and John was transferred to Partick Thistle.

A phone call from a contact in Edinburgh sent Bobby Calder scurrying eastwards to pass judgement on the sixteen-year-old Willie Young. He took no time at all to decide that he was a future internationalist. Another phone call from a Rutherglen school teacher brought him in contact with one of the most exciting players of his generation, Arthur Graham. It is a well-known fact that Bobby Calder never arrived empty-handed at a prospective player's house. He went armed with boxes of chocolates for the mother, cigars or cigarettes for the father and a pocketful of loose change for any brothers or sisters who might be dancing about on the fringes. On the night he arrived at the Grahams' home in the Castlemilk housing scheme of Glasgow, he had hardly bargained for the fact that Arthur was one of a very large family. Calder's ready money was soon diminished as a swarm of children buzzed around him like bees. Gradually they buzzed off to bed and, as Mr and Mrs Graham watched young Arthur signing the papers, they heard Bobby Calder saying: 'You are signing for Aberdeen and signing for Scotland at the same time, son.' Stemming the boy's gratitude, he told him: 'I'll tell you what, Arthur, I'll have your first Scottish Cup medal!'

Well, who would have believed it? Within four months, the seventeen-year-old who had gone to Pittodrie, played a few games in the reserve team and gone straight into the first eleven was walking across the grand foyer of Gleneagles Hotel, holding out the medal he had won that afternoon as a member of the 1970 Scottish Cup-winning team. The dream of a lifetime had come true within months. This was the promised medal and Arthur Graham was ready to give it away. Calder controlled the emotion of a great moment and said: 'Just you keep it, son; I'll get the next one.'

The next one came in November 1976, when Graham held out his Scottish League Cup medal and the fatherly figure turned him away for the second time. His own reward had come in the transformation of a boy from the raw environs of Castlemilk to the status of a top-class professional footballer.

But of all the players that Bobby Calder brought to Aberdeen, there was one name above all others which lit up his eyes. Could it be anyone other than that master of football finesse, Charlie Cooke? Calder had no doubt about it. He talked of him in the same breath as great inside-forwards like Alec James. As a boy with Renfrew Juniors, Charlie was the hottest property of his day and the problem was not to spot him but to sign him. Calder won the race and phoned Aberdeen to say: 'I've signed the greatest ball-player you have ever seen.'

Unfortunately, the genius of Cooke did not produce any tangible rewards for the club during his stay from 1959 to 1964, nor did he establish himself with any permanence in the Scottish team. But that did not detract from the very special place he held in the affections of Aberdeen's football public. Cooke was gifted with great talents, which were not all confined to football. He was a deep-thinking introvert, always ready for an intellectual argument and bursting to express himself as a writer. But there were reports of friction between Charlie Cooke and manager Pearson. Calder knew that his greatest catch would soon be on his way. Dundee manager Bob Shankly stepped in and picked up a bargain at £40,000, a transfer which enraged the Pittodrie fans who felt that, if Cooke had to go at all, he should have gone some distance and not been presented as a gift on the doorstep of the nearest rival. Dundee doubled their money within eighteen months when Charlie went to Stamford Bridge, where he was welcomed with the same warmth as Alec Jackson had experienced in an earlier age.

The Charlie Cookes of this world, however, are rare gems in the experience of a football scout and, indeed, not every player despatched to Pittodrie by Bobby Calder even made the grade. But for those who found that the promise of a senior career had collapsed around their ears, the Dons scout had a consoling story to tell as they arrived back at Queen Street Station, Glasgow. It was the story of John Dick from Maryhill, whose performances sparked off a rush of scouting activity in the 1950s. Calder headed the queue at the Dick household and sat late into the night. When the parents asked when he normally went home, the inexhaustible Bobby looked at his watch and said: 'Well, I start work on the railway at 6 a.m. and I would like to sign your son before then.' So John Dick signed for Aberdeen at 2.30 a.m. at the start of what would surely be a distinguished career. At Pittodrie, however, it was decided that he had not come up to standard and within a year he was released to the free market. 'You must be daft!' was Calder's explosion. 'That boy will play for Scotland.' Turning to the lad himself he said: 'Don't worry, son. You're not finished. They will be sorry they let you away.'

For Calder, there was a question of pride and judgement at stake. So he made a phone call to England and the outcome was that John Dick became a West Ham player. Imagine the joy of the Dons' chief scout as he boarded a train for London to see the England–Scotland game of 1959. There, as printed proof on his programme, was the name of John Dick, playing at inside-left for Scotland – the Aberdeen reject whose name could raise a blush at Pittodrie for a long time after that.

The early-morning signing of Dick gave substance to the story that Bobby Calder's technique was simply to sit on so late that exhausted parents would advise a doubting son: 'Ach, you had better sign for Bobby or we'll never get to our beds!' More accurately, it could be said that Bobby Calder gained the confidence of parents, who felt he could be depended upon to look after their sons' best interests. He extolled the virtues of the wide open spaces and fresh air of Aberdeen, a task made all the easier by the long-standing connection with the holiday-makers of Glasgow Fair. So they came north to develop their talents, sometimes to stay, sometimes to follow the rainbow in search of gold; but almost invariably to prove that a remarkable little man called Bobby Calder knew a footballer when he saw one.

Bobby, alas, is no longer with us but his role has passed into the hands of Jim Carswell, a talented successor who is building his own reputation as a judge of the youngsters who will make it to the top one day.

31
TROUBLE AHEAD

That Scottish Cup victory of 1970 was, understandably, a tremendous boost to the morale of the Dons players and they themselves, in their new-found confidence, could sense that they were in the early stages of being a great team.

The night of celebration at Gleneagles had ended with the directors gathering in a corner with manager Eddie Turnbull and chief scout Bobby Calder and talking the whole night through about where the Dons were going from there. The aim would be to project the club over a five-year period; but how should they tackle it? With young Martin Buchan as captain, Turnbull had built a team of high promise, one which looked as if it could develop into as fine a team as Aberdeen had ever known. The first step towards consolidating the success of 1970 was to keep the players together if at all possible. After all, there was a rare blend of skills, starting with the stability of Clark in goal. Surveying it all from his goal-line, Bobby reckoned that Martin Buchan was the best defensive player he had played with. Steve Murray had arrived from Dundee to strengthen the pool and he had turned out to be something more. In Bobby Clark's opinion, Murray was the best all-round performer he had had the privilege of playing with. Whereas others could play to an effectiveness of fifty per cent, Steve did everything to a level of ninety-five per cent. His passing was as accurate as that and in a man-to-man situation he was seldom beaten. He was a truly thinking player with a great awareness of the game, who later went to Celtic and then departed from football prematurely because of injury. Martin Buchan had a splendid understanding with Tommy McMillan at centre-half; Jim Forrest, who had previously become Rangers' greatest goal-scorer, and his cousin Alec Willoughby had developed a maturity of play which they had not attained in their twin-days at Ibrox. With players like Davie Robb and Ian Taylor adding their own contrasting styles, the Dons entered season 1970–71 with great expectations and these became largely fulfilled as the team went to the top of the League and looked as if they were going to halt the Celtic domination which had been unbroken since Jock Stein's first full season in 1965–66. There was a run of thirteen games in which the Dons did not lose a single goal and this sense of being invincible was growing by the week, just the kind of feeling to lead a team on to a championship.

In the curious workings of the world, that is so often when the most unexpected things can happen. Into the early-morning darkness of Saturday 6 February 1971, flames were suddenly rising on the Aberdeen skyline. As the fire engines raced down King Street, it soon became clear that Pittodrie's main grandstand was in the process of being destroyed. The fire, it appeared, had started after an explosion and soon the offices, dressing rooms and equipment were going up in smoke. Consternation! The Scottish Cup was in there! Firemen strove to rescue it as a priority. News of the outbreak reached the first team who had left the previous night for the League game at Dunfermline that day.

The players were in disarray, now without a home and forced into unfamiliar routines like training at Woodside and changing at Linksfield for matches at Pittodrie. It is not an excuse but a fair explanation to say that the fire marked the turning point in the route to the 1971 Championship. The crowds, which had averaged around 18,000 that season, restoring something of the atmosphere of the post-war period, were still willing their team to victory but in the end the Dons were pipped for the title by Celtic. Nor had there been any consolation in the European Cup Winners' Cup contest, which the Dons had entered with the confidence of having beaten the all-conquering Celtic to get there. In the first round they beat Honved of Hungary 3–1 at Pittodrie but lost by the same score in the away game. With a 4–4 tie, the second game went to penalties and out went the Dons on the cruelty of a 5–4 margin. So a season of much promise petered out without reward, other than the satisfaction of having provided the only real challenge to the superiority of Celtic.

Meanwhile, a new and refreshing force was emerging at boardroom level in the person of Chris Anderson, still remembered from his playing days in the 1950s. Mr Anderson was part of a trinity of former Aberdeen players – with chairman Dick Donald and the elder statesman Charles B. Forbes – who could claim to be the only football board in Scotland with the added authority of having played for the club.

Chris Anderson, born in 1925, had grown up on the pathway to Pittodrie, on King Street near the top of Pittodrie Street, where he would stare in childhood wonder at the big names of the 1930s as they went to and from the ground. There were Paddy Moore, Willie Mills, Matt Armstrong and the man with the distinguished air and fine straw basher, Donald Colman. So football was bred into the daily life of boys like Chris Anderson and fostered throughout the city at that time by many a dedicated teacher, none more so than Mr Eddie Ross, headmaster of Linksfield school, to whom Aberdeen owed a deep debt. Young Anderson had been a lad of great promise, chosen as a Scottish schoolboy internationalist but little knowing that his schoolmaster at Sunnybank, Charles B. Forbes, would one day welcome him as a co-director of Aberdeen Football Club. His first step was to the junior Mugiemoss and the second was nearly to Ibrox Park, where manager Bill Struth was so keen to land him that he despatched another former Moss man, Duggie Gray, to try to persuade the boy south. But those ties down Pittodrie Street were strong and Chris Anderson joined the Dons instead. It was 1943 and he was eighteen. As ever in those days, war service intervened and it was not until the famous team of 1947 broke up more than a year later that Chris Anderson made his first-team debut along with Jack Hather.

Chris was soon good enough to be named for the Scottish League team – and he had particular reason to remember a Scottish Cup tie against Celtic at Parkhead in 1951. In the days before that game, a letter arrived at Pittodrie addressed to Don Emery and carrying a threat that if Celtic did not win, the burly Welshman would have his features rearranged by means of a razor. If the poison-pen man had cared to check his statistics he wouldn't have bothered with his threat, because no one could trace an occasion where Aberdeen had beaten Celtic in a Cup tie at Parkhead! But evil has a habit of recoiling upon itself and the Dons went storming through that game at Celtic Park as a glorious goal by Chris Anderson put the Glasgow team out of the Cup.

Looking back over his Pittodrie connection, Chris picked out Frank Dunlop as the finest wing-half he had seen at Pittodrie, though he had been converted to a centre-half by the time he captained that post-war team to Cup-tie glory. He also credited Tommy Pearson with fostering a renaissance in Scottish football

180

when he played out his veteran years in Aberdeen and encouraged a type of thinking which led to the successful Dons team of the mid 1950s. Chris Anderson's playing career suffered from the fact that he landed in that leaner spell of the late 1940s and early 1950s but he was to play his most significant role as a young-at-heart director, not only helping to update the Dons' image in the 1970s but playing a major part in reconstructing Scottish football to give it a Premier League in 1975.

Having joined the board in the late 1960s, his first taste of success had been the Scottish Cup Final in 1970 and there he was at Gleneagles that night, prominent in the discussion about the future and urging that the team be kept together. Departures were strictly to be discouraged. Well, there was one departure which no one had bargained for and it was the very first to happen.

The Dons players were back for their pre-season training in July 1971, still without a proper home after the fire and training at Woodside, when Eddie Turnbull came amongst them and told them that he was leaving to be manager of Hibs. A silence fell over the players. Some, like Davie Robb, were visibly shattered by the news. Turnbull said he was sorry because he had been with some of them for a long time and he was attached to the club. He wished them well. Behind his departure was the fact that a wealthy Edinburgh builder, Tom Hart, had achieved the dream of many a self-made man and gained control of the club for which he had had a lifelong affection. He was not going to settle until his friend Eddie Turnbull was back as manager of the club he had served so well. Chris Anderson took up the story:

So Eddie was going and nothing we could do was going to stop him. There was no point in being bitter about it. But, having been caught in an awkward situation, we had to find a replacement; so what were we to do? Though Turnbull's health had been suspect, he and his coach, Jimmy Bonthrone, had been an excellent team. The calmer approach of Bonthrone balanced the rumbustious, out-going, dominant personality of Turnbull and they seemed to act as catalysts to each other's success. We decided to give Jimmy a chance to prove himself and he got off to an encouraging start.

That start was the Drybrough Cup, a new competition which opened the 1971–72 season and saw the Dons rocketing to the final against Celtic, for which they won the home-ground advantage. It turned out to be a wonderful occasion. Pittodrie had now been renovated after the fire and this return to normality drew out a crowd of 25,000 on Saturday 7 August. Davie Robb scored the first goal, which was one of the greatest ever seen in Aberdeen, and Joe Harper's penalty kick gave the Dons the Drybrough Cup and a measure of consolation for the upheaval of the fire and all that that had meant in terms of losing their grip on the League leadership earlier that year.

In the League programme which followed, it was Celtic once again who were to dominate, with Aberdeen snapping at their heels as the main challengers. Jimmy Bonthrone worked himself in as the new manager, changing the style to suit his own personality. But the fact that the Dons were repeating their success of the previous season merely helped to conceal the fact that a general unrest was spreading through the dressing room. Chris Anderson remembered how players like Martin Buchan and Joe Harper were virtually saying to the club: 'We can collect a lump sum and double our wages by going to England, so you must let us go.' So the cracks appeared in a potentially great team.

Martin Buchan was allowed to pursue his southern ambitions and signed for Manchester United at a fee of £125,000, heading for the kind of fame and fortune which his father, Martin Buchan senior, could only have dreamed about. The son was a thoroughbred in the modern manner, dovetailing effectively into the defensive patterns. Curiously, there are some who will tell you that the grace of the father remains a more distinctive memory, even after all those years. So Buchan was gone (he was followed from Pittodrie to Old Trafford by younger brother George) and when little Joe Harper, who had come from Morton, was sold to Everton for an Aberdeen record price of £180,000 the Dons had lost their star defender and the best striker in the land. When disintegration of that sort begins, it is hard for any club to stop it.

In the midst of it all, Bobby Clark was so conscious of the downward trend that he, too, put in for a transfer. Stoke City were seeking a replacement for Gordon Banks, their international keeper who had received a serious eye injury in a car crash, and it seemed that Clark was their man. He travelled down for talks and manager Tony Waddington was keen to sign him on the spot. The Dons, however, were due to play Celtic on the Saturday and Stoke were told that the keeper was not for sale until after that game. Martin Buchan had driven his former team-mate across from Manchester to Stoke and on the way he told him that manager Frank O'Farrell was interested in taking Clark to Old Trafford, though his hands were tied at that moment. When the Dons played Celtic on the Saturday, a Stoke director came north to cast an eye over the man whom his club was evidently ready to buy for £100,000. When the match ended, the visitor shocked everyone by announcing that the offer for Clark was now only £60,000. Out of an unpleasant atmosphere, the only good that emerged was the fact that Bobby Clark remained at Pittodrie. Privately he would much have preferred Manchester United to Stoke City but within a few weeks Frank O'Farrell had left Old Trafford in the now-familiar pattern of departing managers.

In 1972 the Dons had gone on a tour of North America, best remembered for some remarkable scenes when they met the Montreal Olympics. Trouble flared when the Dons were awarded a penalty and Joe Harper scored. It was a friendly, they said, but you would never have guessed it. The crowd booed Harper's goal and followed up by letting off fireworks and throwing stones, cans, shoes and a dustbin at the Dons players! Davie Robb, who is not known for cowardice, confessed that he had never been so scared in all his life. Luckily, the field was fenced off from the spectators, who were trying to climb over. The referee took the players off the field and for thirty minutes officials tried to calm the crowd but without success; so the game was abandoned. Martin Buchan's brother George had come on as a substitute for Bertie Miller but with the early whistle he did not have a single touch of the ball.

By now, players like Henning Boel and Tommy McMillan were departing. Derek McKay, of Cup-tie fame, was in the Far East, Jim Forrest in South Africa and George Murray had become coach. Drew Jarvie, who was to develop into one of the most stylish and talented of Pittodrie players, had arrived from Airdrie for season 1972–73 and there were young players such as Joe Smith, Willie Young and Billy Williamson coming through from the reserve team. Several of those youngsters found a new maturity during a tour of Australia and New Zealand, benefiting from world travel in more than just a playing sense.

But the situation at Pittodrie had gone into a trough. It was becalmed – and that can be fatal in the football context. The crisis which built up in 1975, however, included incidents which were anything but calm. Big Willie Young, the red-headed boy from Port Seton Athletic who had not only established himself as the

Dons' central defender but in Scotland's team as well, was one of five Scots to land in trouble with the SFA. It arose after an international match between Denmark and Scotland in Copenhagan in September 1975, when players were alleged to have been drinking in a night club and to have been thrown out by the police after a rumpus over a disputed bill. The newspapers were full of it. Back at the hotel there were reports of more trouble and someone was reputed to have felled Billy Bremner, the Scottish captain. Whatever the rights and wrongs of the matter, the upshot was that five Scots were banned from ever appcaring in a national jersey again. Alas, two of them were Dons – Willie Young and Arthur Graham – and the others were Joe Harper, at that time with Hibs, having gone there from Everton, Billy Bremner of Leeds and Pat McCluskey of Celtic. That life ban was lifted in 1977 but at the time it had an upsetting effect on the players concerned.

For Willie Young, the troubled time was not yet over. Back at Pittodrie and playing against Dundee United just two weeks after Copenhagan, he was substituted for the first time in 234 games. The decision to take him off so angered him that he strode gigantically to the touchline, pulled off his shirt, threw it in the direction of manager Bonthrone and walked bare-chested along the track to the dressing room. Before the final whistle sounded he had left the Pittodrie precincts and that, believe it or not, was how Aberdeen's international centre-half literally left the club, never to wear its colours again. Before there was time to think about disciplinary measures, the matter was resolved during the following week when Willie, a large and popular figure, was transferred to Tottenham Hotspur for £100,000. It was a sad end to his Aberdeen career but one which he nevertheless brought upon himself. Whatever the justice of the substitution, the embarrassment of the touchline incident was one which no manager could afford to tolerate.

But if Young was going, the manager who took him off was already sensing that his own days in the job were also numbered. By October 1975 he was telling the Dons board: 'I feel I can get no more from the players and, as Aberdeen deserves a prominent place in the game, I'm getting out.' The directors felt he could soldier on until the end of the season but his mind was made up. It was all very sad because, in the words of Chris Anderson, 'we were losing the most honest man I have ever met in football'. As one of his players told me: 'Jimmy Bonthrone gave Aberdeen everything he had but he tried to be so fair to everyone that he ended up by being unfair to himself.' So Jimmy Bonthrone bowed out with quiet dignity, as befitted his personality, and withdrew to an occupation outside football altogether, back in Fife. His record had not been a bad one. But perhaps, like Davie Shaw fifteen years earlier, his greatest strength had been as a coach and the sterner authority of modern management was not a natural part of his make-up.

If Bonthrone's era went sour on him, it should at least be remembered as the period when he introduced to the Aberdeen team a man whose individual skills were among the greatest that Scottish football had ever seen. Zoltan Varga was a slim-built Hungarian of such exquisite talent that canny Aberdonians wondered by what curious mischance he had suddenly materialised at Pittodrie. His last club had been Hertha Berlin. Mystery was allowed to linger in the background, however, as the Dons' fans concentrated on the soccer specialities of Varga, marvelling at the way he could guide the flight and direction of a ball as if by remote control. He could bend it round a corner with such precision that one felt he needed only to say the word and the obedient creature would return to his masterful feet. The countries of eastern Europe have long provided the best juggling and balancing acts for the circus ring so perhaps it was not surprising that an offshoot of that native talent found its way into football. Zoltan Varga predicted a bright future for the young Arthur Graham. 'Bumper,' he would say in his fractured English, 'when I get the ball, do not look at me. Just run thirty yards and ball will drop in front of you.' Sure enough, it would drop with perfection. Arthur Graham's only problem with such a unique service was that he couldn't always remember to keep running without looking back! In assessing the skills that have graced the Pittodrie turf, from Alec Jackson to Tommy Pearson to Graham Leggat, it might well be the case that Zoltan Varga was the most truly gifted player who ever pulled on an Aberdeen jersey.

If football were a wine, then here was the vintage champagne, a heady experience which was surely too good to last. And so it turned out to be. The newspapers got hold of the background story as to why the Hungarian had left Berlin and landed in Aberdeen. There had been a bribery scandal and Varga had been banned from playing in West Germany. His year in Scottish football had been like an interlude in the wings before returning to the continental stage. The newspaper stories came as no surprise to the Aberdeen directors, who were thoroughly acquainted with the bribery story.

They were convinced that Varga was not the instigator of the corruption and that, having become involved in it, he had been suitably punished and could now seek to restore his reputation in the service of the Dons. Having been tipped off about him by a German contact, Gunter Bachman, they promptly signed him for a fee which was no more than a token of his true worth. Towards the end of 1973, however, Hertha Berlin decided to buy back his contract for a similar sum and he became, technically, their own player once again. But they did not buy him back as a practising footballer. Ajax of Amsterdam had lost that immortal master Johan Cruyff to Barcelona for a compensation of nearly a million pounds and were looking for a replacement. It is the highest possible tribute to the former Don to say that Ajax turned towards Berlin and bought Zoltan Varga, the man who touched Pittodrie like a traveller in the night, playing his Hungarian rhapsody with masterly effect and sweeping on his way while an audience entranced gazed after him in wonder.

1976 League Cup Final – Drew Jarvie heads equalising goal and turns to acknowledge Harper's final pass

Launching party for first edition of this book, Capitol Cinema, 1978. *Front row*: Percy Dickie, W. K. Jackson, Jack Hather. *Back row:* Harry Yorston, Willie Waddell, Matt Armstrong, Archie Baird, Jack Webster (*the author*), Tony Harris, Willie Mills and a new arrival – Alex Ferguson!

Easter Road, Edinburgh, 1980 – McLeish lost in crowd as League Championship is clinched, for first time in twenty-five years

Alex Ferguson's first trophy – League Championship of 1980 – comes home to Union Street

Pittodrie's greatest-ever moment – Hewitt scores the sensational goal against Bayern Munich, which puts the Dons into the semi-final of the European Cup Winners' Cup

European Cup Winners' Cup Final in Gothenburg, 1983 – Eric Black gives Aberdeen the lead

Gothenburg glory – the goal that did it! John Hewitt once more heads the winner which put Aberdeen to the top in Europe

Manager Alex Ferguson and assistant Archie Knox savour their finest moment – victory in Europe!

Union Street, 12th May, 1983 – the European heroes come home to a welcome from 100,000 people, lining the route from the airport to Pittodrie

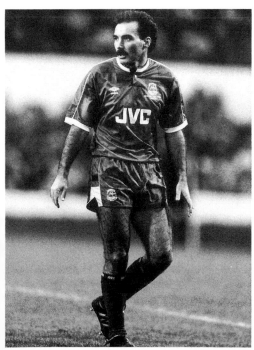

The greatest Don of all – Willie Miller

The play-making genius – Gordon Strachan

Newly signed from Arsenal – the magic talent of Charlie Nicholas, welcomed by vice-chairman Ian Donald and his father, Dick Donald, the chairman

After three lean years, the Dons back in business by winning Skol League Cup in 1989. Manager Smith hails two-goal hero, Paul Mason

New management team of 1988 – Alex Smith, flanked by Drew Jarvie and Jocky Scott

Scottish Cup Final 1990 – climax to the penalty shoot-out, as Brian Irvine scores the winner against Celtic

The 1990 Scottish Cup heroes. *Back row:* McLeish, Gillhaus, Snelders, Connor, Watson, Irvine, McKimmie. *Front row:* Jess, Nicholas, Bett, Mason, Robertson, Grant

32
ALLY'S MAGIC

In the autumn of 1975, when Aberdeen were looking for a manager to replace Jimmy Bonthrone, director Chris Anderson was in Glasgow to appear on a television sports programme. At the TV studios he met a journalist who dropped a hint that, after ten years of solid achievement with Ayr United, Ally MacLeod was ripe for a move to a full-time club. The Dons director raised his eyebrows. Ally MacLeod was indeed the type of man they had in mind for the job. It was time for a bit of razzmatazz in the grey-granite citadel of the north, especially with an oil boom in progress and a latent support which was the biggest in Scotland outside Rangers and Celtic. MacLeod was surely the man to provide it. He was a super-enthusiast, a confident, keen-talking motivator of men who had set a new level of public relations for Scottish managers. Growing up in the shadows of Hampden Park, he had played for the local Third Lanark as a colourful and entertaining winger and was later a member of the Blackburn Rovers side beaten in the FA Cup Final of 1960. MacLeod had returned to Scotland as captain of Hibs before taking over as player–coach, then manager, of Ayr United. His refreshing personality did so much to promote the team and the town that he was once elected local 'Citizen of the Year'. The Dons directors wasted no time in bringing him to Pittodrie but an initial burst of success was followed by a bad run which was all the more noticeable since Scotland had just reorganised its football into a Premier Division of ten teams instead of eighteen. What had formerly been a mid-League position was now a relegation problem and that was where the Dons found themselves in the last days of season 1975–76, along with several others. A death-or-glory game with Hibs at Pittodrie on the last day of the season would decide the fate of an Aberdeen team which had never in its seventy-odd years of existence been relegated.

All seemed black when Mike McDonald saved a Davie Robb penalty kick but the Dons went on to win 3–0 and to remain in the top division. The new set-up had certainly sharpened competition, even if the names involved revealed a curious misunderstanding of the English language. How do you explain to an outsider that Scotland has a 'Premier (meaning First) Division' and a 'First Division'? As a splendid piece of self-deception, it evidently makes the second-grade feel better to be called 'First', so who am I to disturb the illusion!

Starting his first full season as Aberdeen manager, Ally MacLeod was making his red-shirted players feel better, too. The early-season League Cup competition took the Dons into a preliminary section with Kilmarnock, Ayr United and St Mirren. They won it. In the home-and-away quarter-finals, Aberdeen were drawn against Stirling Albion and that turned out to be a nightmarish engagement. Having won 1–0 at Pittodrie, they went to Stirling on a night of gales and lashing rain and were beaten 1–0, just managing to survive a period of extra time. When it went to a third game at Dens Park, Dundee, the Dons won 2–0. So to the semi-final against Rangers at Hampden and by then Ally MacLeod was beginning to establish the kind of confidence he had been looking for. The Dons had taken on the air of Scotland's jet-setters, flying to their more distant fixtures in a charter plane and thus cutting the travelling time which had been such a built-in hazard of Aberdeen teams through the years that Chris Anderson assessed it as a practical disadvantage of eight goals per season.

There were no disadvantages on the night of 27 October 1976, however, as the Dons set about their League Cup semi-final tie with Rangers at Hampden. That was the night when they annihilated the Ibrox challenge in a devastating 5–1 victory in which Jocky Scott set the pattern with a hat-trick, augmented by Joe Harper and Drew Jarvie who volleyed home one of the most spectacular goals seen at Hampden for many years. It was reminiscent of the drubbing which the Dons had given Rangers in the Scottish Cup semi-final of 1954, when the score had been an even more emphatic 6–0. On that occasion, Celtic had had to be faced in the final and the Cup had gone to Parkhead. In 1976 it was Celtic again who would be the opponents but these Dons were not afraid of the prospect. The team had been gaining in depth and experience with the signing of Stuart Kennedy from Falkirk, surely an internationalist in the making, Dom Sullivan from Clyde and Joe Harper, fresh from his travels to Everton and Hibs and proclaiming himself happily back in the place where he felt truly at home. 'King Joe' was re-establishing himself as the goal-scoring hero of the demonstrative Beach-end support which was glad to call itself 'Ally's Army'. Three days after the mid-week defeat of Rangers, the Dons were at home to League leaders Dundee United and Ally MacLeod felt there was little need to elaborate on that fabulous victory. His message in the Saturday programme was printed vertically down the page and simply said: MAGIC! Standing on the Pittodrie terracing that day, incidentally, was a tall man, minding his own business. A breathless latecomer arrived on the scene and turned to verify the score with the tall gentleman. Then, glancing at him in double-take, he caused a thousand heads to turn by exclaiming: 'Christ, it's big Freddie Martin!' And so it was, paying a visit to Aberdeen and dropping in on the scene of his greatest triumphs.

In preparation for the final, the Dons party was staying at the MacDonald Hotel on the south side of Glasgow, where long-serving colleagues Bobby Clark and Davie Robb were sharing a room. Robb, for whom Clark had always had the highest admiration, was to be the substitute in the League Cup Final. Suddenly, on the eve of the big game, Bobby said to his room-mate: 'Davie, you have been a workhorse for Aberdeen all these years and you haven't had much glory. But I have this strange feeling that you are going to come on tomorrow and score the winner. I can just see it.'

Well, the final raged on next day, with Celtic taking the lead through Kenny Dalglish, who took the penalty kick himself after he was said to have been fouled by Drew Jarvie. The highly talented Jarvie soon made amends, however, when Arthur Graham's cross was headed on by Harper to enable him to head the equaliser. Davie Robb had indeed been brought on as substitute, to be greeted with a wave and shout from Clark: 'Remember!' At 1–1 the game went into extra time and only a hundred seconds had been played when Davie duly followed through the pattern of prediction and scored. If that should turn out to be the winner, he would be left wondering if Bobby Clark had perhaps some future in the psychic business! But there were still twenty-eight minutes left for play and, as the fast-raiding Celts came storming into Aberdeen territory like the waves of a Chinese army, northern nails were bitten to the quick and nerves became frayed as a tinker's waistcoat.

In the burning excitement, something significant took place in the relationship between Aberdeen players and supporters. Sensing the plight of their heroes, the 17,000 Aberdonians at Hampden unleashed a vocal support such as I had never heard from the Pittodrie faithful. It rose to the rooftops of Scotland's national stadium and gave notice, perhaps for the first time, that mighty roars of football fervour would no longer be the exclusive preserve of the mob-rule hordes of Ibrox and Parkhead. It was the day when Aberdonians finally cast off their native reticence and, as they galvanised themselves to a deafening chant, while outnumbered three-to-one by the Celtic legions, the referee drew breath for that final blast of the pea – and Davie Robb was hailed as the match-winner indeed.

Exactly a year after taking over as the Dons' manager, Ally MacLeod gazed across towards that Mount Florida street where he grew up and listened to the din of victory rebounding from tenement walls. The man who had given so much to football was gaining his first-ever prize and who but the most blinkered of bigots would have grudged him his moment of glory? The city of Aberdeen, which had held its breath beside transistors and car radios, finally gave vent to the civic feeling as motorists drove the length of Union Street, blaring out the Morse-code call of victory on car horns.

Some Celtic supporters were magnanimous in defeat but there was at least one who had yet to learn about the Aberdonian sense of poetic justice. A young Celt emerged from his little clique at the back of Hampden to throw a brick at a supporters' bus departing for Aberdeen. Without ceremony, four hefty Dons fans (from the Dyce district, I believe) bounded out to isolate the offender, warned off his mates, turned his brick-throwing arm up his back and marched him aboard the bus. 'Drive on!' they said. It was somewhere in the region of Perth, so the story goes, that the young Celt was given a lecture on the folly of throwing bricks at Aberdeen buses and released into the gloom of the night – with sixty-five miles or so between him and home!

The *Scotsport* programme of Grampian STV came live from Pittodrie the next day when the players paraded the League Cup in front of 25,000 people. Ally MacLeod took a brief bow but, for all the jaunty extrovert that he had become, he refused the overtures of the chairman to address the crowd. They had merely wanted to hear the voice of the man who had brought the kind of hope and excitement which Pittodrie had not experienced for a long time. The team at Hampden that day had been: Clark; Kennedy, Williamson;

Smith, Garner, Miller; Sullivan, Scott, Harper, Jarvie, Graham; Substitute Robb.

Looking back on the MacLeod inspiration, Chris Anderson said:

We had needed the buzz and froth and the extravagant and sometimes outrageous comments – and that is what we got from Ally MacLeod. Football is an entertainment and you must have the razzmatazz, while knowing that the back-up is there. Ally was the publicity-minded extrovert we needed so badly and he did the job we thought he could do, projecting the club in an ambitious way, taking it by the scruff of the neck and realising its potential. He cheered us all up, created a touch of the Barnum and Baileys and finally set the adrenalin flowing with the League Cup victory.

Ally MacLeod had done all that – and had proved a tonic to everyone. Something stronger than a tonic, however, was needed for one piece of publicity which MacLeod and his players could well have done without.

It all began when the telephone rang on the editorial floor of the *Press and Journal* on the night of Wednesday 2 March 1977. It was answered by Donald Smith, an experienced reporter, who soon realised that the call was of the type which is well known to late-duty journalists. People phone up to air a grievance or to demand some information which will settle a pub argument. This one came from a Dons supporter who had obviously been drowning his sorrows and for that at least Donald Smith could sympathise with him. For, earlier that evening, Aberdeen had been surprisingly knocked out of the Scottish Cup by Dundee, in a Pittodrie replay which followed a drawn game at Dens Park on the previous Saturday. The man at the end of the line was not alone in his frustration; but he did not leave it at that. He was making the serious allegation that three Aberdeen players – and he found names for them – had each placed a bet of £500 at the quoted odds of 8–1 that Dundee would win the match. Smith challenged him on such an outrageous claim and asked if he had any evidence to back it up. He said he had just come from a golf club and had been told it on good authority. When Smith began to pinpoint that he must be speaking from the telephone kiosk at the bottom of Pittodrie Street and had just come from a certain golf club, the man became irritated, told him to 'piss off' and said that, if he wasn't interested in the story, then someone else would be. Smith left a memo for his news editor, but on that kind of wild and flimsy evidence, the *Press and Journal* ignored the matter.

Two weeks later, viewers of Grampian Television were startled by a Saturday night commercial which implored them to 'read tomorrow's *Sunday Mail*' for a sensational story concerning the Dons players. Understandably, the *Mail* did brisk business that Sunday morning and the front-page headline which greeted the customer read: 'Players in "Soccer Bets" Shock – Cup-tie defeat sparks off police probe.' The story began: 'Detectives are investigating a sensational claim that three Aberdeen FC players bet a large sum of money AGAINST their own team in a Scottish Cup tie.' And on it went, on similar lines to the man on the telephone.

So the matter had now been taken beyond a reckless phone call. The Chief Constable of Grampian Police, Alexander Morrison, explained to me how it had developed:

A responsible member of the public visiting Aberdeen had been at the match that evening. He then went to the telephone box thirty yards from the main grandstand but found it occupied. Through broken panes in the kiosk he overheard a conversation [presumably the call to the *Press and Journal*] and there was no indication that he was listening to a drunk man. It was to the effect that certain players in the Aberdeen team must have 'sold' the game. Players were named. That was what an honest citizen heard. It was still on his mind when he returned to Dundee so he went to the local police, with the result that it landed in the hands of Grampian Police as a written statement. That statement having been made, we had to act. Even if he had said he was listening to a drunk man we would still have acted because drunk men often tell the truth. Our means of investigation was to go to Customs and Excise, who have control over the betting situation, through the taxes, and we established reasonably well that there had been no great payout on the Aberdeen–Dundee match. By the time we had satisfied ourselves of the non-existence of a plot, the whole thing burst upon us in the press. Our investigation had been going for about a week before that. Ally MacLeod made a beeline for my office when the story broke, questioning why we were investigating if it was a drunk man who was involved. But if a citizen makes a written statement like that, you cannot throw it in the waste-paper basket. I had to go through with it for the sake of everyone. If not, the Press would have beaten us round the ears. The lesson which footballers should learn is that, if such allegations are made, it is to their detriment if a police inquiry is *not* held. This case was also a demonstration of the dangers existing in this country when a person who is subject to a police investigation is crucified in print by linking the incident with other terrible things. [He was referring to one newspaper which recalled, in the same breath, the involvement of two former Aberdeen players in a big soccer corruption case in England.]

When the *Sunday Mail* heard about it and asked Grampian Police if they were investigating, the only truthful answer was the confirmation which they got. The *Mail* had a story. If they are to be faulted for not checking the matter with the people of Pittodrie, they are entitled to point to a long-standing and much-criticised pronouncement of Scotland's top judge, Lord Clyde, who had ruled that newspapers were not allowed to interview people who might be witnesses in a subsequent case. Whatever you may think of that kind of journalism, the *Mail* had taken care to stay within the legal limits.

Grampian Police completed their investigation within two days of the newspaper story and found not a shred of evidence to support the allegation. In short, it was a total figment of someone's imagination, a scurrilous piece of work completely without foundation. That day, chairman Dick Donald called a press conference, a dramatic occasion with reporters and television men crowding into the Pittodrie boardroom to be met by Mr Donald, his vice-chairman Chris Anderson, fellow director Charles B. Forbes and manager Ally MacLeod. On the table lay a copy of the *Sunday Mail* alongside the current pride of Pittodrie, the Scottish League Cup, innocently standing there in its red and white colours. It was an occasion for grim faces and words to match. Dick Donald did not mince his language, lashing out at the 'irresponsibility of a sensation-seeking Sunday newspaper' and the gross injustice to the Aberdeen players.

There was talk of legal action but, in fact, the most that Aberdeen FC could perhaps have done was to put the matter of the *Sunday Mail* story into the hands of the Press Council, which is what they did. As for the damage done to Pittodrie reputations, there are times, alas, when injustice has to be borne.

33
McNEILL TAKES OVER

The betting row had scarcely settled in the spring of 1977 when the directors were at Pittodrie one day at lunchtime, having a chat with Ally MacLeod. Willie Ormond had just given up his successful run as Scotland's international manager to return to club football as boss of the ailing Hearts. The question of the moment was: who will get the job of guiding the Scots through the latter stages of qualifying for the World Cup in Argentina – the job already begun by Ormond? The question was all but answered when Dick Donald was called to the telephone. He returned to the room and said: 'Well, Ally, that was Ernie Walker on the phone. They are asking you to be manager of Scotland.'

Dick Donald made it plain that Aberdeen did not want to lose him but, on the other hand, they would not stand in his way. Out of the doubts and confusion and the knowledge that his family had settled so well in Aberdeen, Ally MacLeod accepted the job and carried the Scots through to victories against Czechoslovakia and Wales and on to the World Cup Finals. The loyal battalions of 'Ally's Army' on the terracing of Pittodrie wished him well, sorry to lose him but grateful that, within eighteen months, he had brought new life to the club and given them one of their happiest moments with the League Cup victory. Now the directors had to find a successor. They pencilled in the names of three men who would meet the requirements – Alex Stuart of Ayr United, Billy McNeill, who had recently taken over his first manager's job with Clyde, and Alex Ferguson of St Mirren.

Alex Stuart, an Aberdonian, was the first to be considered but there were problems about his release from Ayr. At first, the choice of Billy McNeill came as a surprise to those who forgot that, despite his shortage of managerial experience, he was a young man of character and stature who was surely a supreme authority on matters like European football. As captain of that greatest-ever Celtic team, he had spent a solid decade not only dominating Scottish football but playing in more top-class European matches than any other player in Britain. In retirement he had become a successful businessman but the lure of football was too strong and he made a quiet return as manager of Clyde. Within weeks of that return, he was driving north in answer to a call from chairman Dick Donald, who was quietly confident that, once again, he and his fellow directors had chosen the man for the moment. The rendezvous point for Dick Donald and Billy McNeill was Perth but the former Celt was soon driving all the way to Aberdeen, delighted to find himself in such an exalted position so soon in his career. In fact, as the board had anticipated, McNeill grew into the stature of the job almost immediately, commanding the respect and admiration of his players and starting off his first season by setting the pace at the top of the Premier League. As League Cup winners, the Dons were competing in the UEFA Cup in season 1977–78, drawn against the formidable Belgian team RWD Molenbeek and travelling to Brussels for the first leg. In a splendid display, the Dons held the Belgians to a goalless draw and brought this tribute from the official UEFA observer:

It was one of the best performances, if not the best, by a British club team playing in Europe that I have seen. So often in the past, it has been a case of teams going to the Continent and achieving success by typical British grit and determination but on this occasion Aberdeen also matched their Belgian opponents in football skill.

High praise, indeed, to set Billy McNeill on his way. The Belgians had a remarkable record in away games, however, and they finally won the tie by two goals to one at Pittodrie.

So concentration returned to the domestic programme and the Dons found themselves with a clear lead at the top of the Premier League, Rangers and Celtic having made poor starts to the season, the Ibrox team landing in bottom position at one stage. While the Parkhead side continued to flounder through a disastrous season by their own high standards, Rangers made a steady recovery and by the first light of 1978, the League had resolved itself into a battle between the Light Blues and the red shirts of Aberdeen, with the others trailing well behind. In one of the most exciting build-ups ever, Rangers pulled clear to a six-point lead, with the Dons keeping up the pursuit and embarking on an undefeated run of twenty-three games.

But the Premier League of 1977–78 was probably decided on 28 February by an incident which had nothing to do with the skills of football at all. On that day Rangers went to play a Motherwell team which had struck an ascendancy under its new manager, Roger Hynd. The Fir Park men went into a 2–0 lead and were playing with the confidence of winners when a chant went up from a section of the Rangers following: 'There's going to be a riot.' It was the lunatic fringe at work again, the horde of hooligans which Rangers' management condemned as a 'troublesome minority' but which turned out to be a very large and ugly 'minority' when you began to analyse it.

These people had already brought disgrace to the Ibrox club in places as far apart as Newcastle and Barcelona and here they were again, in all their lager-laden aggression. 'There's going to be a riot' – and over the boundary wall they came, some perhaps escaping the beer-can ammunition of the main infantry but all on their way to the field of play. Of course, these people could readily be classed as mindless morons, which they were, but whatever the depths of their barren mentality, it did not escape them that a stoppage of play could disturb a winning rhythm.

The rhythm that day had belonged to Motherwell but, with blue scarves swarming around his ears, the referee had no option but to take the players off the field. When play eventually resumed, Motherwell had indeed lost their rhythm and Rangers went on to win the match. The Scottish Football Association felt obliged to take an authoritative stand and recommended to the Scottish League that the match should be played again. But the League Committee took no such action and instead the Ibrox club was fined £2000. It was not only Aberdeen supporters who passed a cynical verdict that the punishment was cheap at the price – £1000 per point. As it turned out, these two points were exactly the number needed to win the Premier League.

With the Fir Park win, Rangers kept their six-point lead at the top, and on the following Saturday the Dons were due at Ibrox for what was now conceded by manager Billy McNeill to be their last chance. If Rangers won and widened the gap to eight points, they would be unstoppable. On a bright and sunny 4 March, Aberdeen attacked from the start and scored a convincing 3–0 victory, with one goal by the irrepressible Joe Harper and two by young Steve

Archibald, only recently signed from Clyde where he had been much admired by McNeill during his brief spell as manager. That win cut back Rangers' lead to four points and indeed the Dons reduced it to level pegging, losing out only on the last day of the season. Rangers had won the Premier League by two points – the margin of their win on the day of the invasion – and the record-books will credit them with one more achievement.

By their decision to take no action, the Scottish League Committee had chalked up a decisive victory for hooliganism.

If Aberdeen had reason to feel aggrieved by the outcome of the League, they had none at all when it came to the Scottish Cup and League Cup. Once again it was the power of Rangers which put them out of both. In the League Cup, the Ibrox men struck their best performance in years to avenge the semi-final defeat of the previous season, with a devastating 6–1 win in the first game of the quarter-final at Ibrox. The Dons won 3–1 in the return game but the cup of 1978 was on its way south and ended up in the marble halls of Ibrox.

In the Scottish Cup, the Dons went through the early rounds against Ayr United, St Johnstone and Morton and beat Partick Thistle 4–2 in the semi-final at Hampden. Having played twenty-three games without defeat to prevent the Premier League becoming a one-horse farce – and having just missed the title – there were high hopes that they would reap some reward for their efforts by lifting the Scottish Cup. Neutral Scotland wished it that way. But it was not to be.

In the Cup Final of 6 May, the team which had played so well so often and had not been beaten since the previous December produced a miserable performance in which they failed to get to grips with the situation at all. Rangers were by far the better team, scoring through MacDonald and Johnstone. A late goal by Steve Ritchie, the full-back recently arrived from Hereford United, merely put a complexion on the final score which was better than Aberdeen deserved.

So Rangers won the treble and the only token of consolation came the following week when the Young Dons beat Rangers in the final of the Second XI Cup, skippered by the popular Chic McLelland who had recently lost his first-team place.

The lack of silverware bit deep into the heart of manager McNeill, whose year of command in the Celtic supremacy had conditioned him to nothing but success. The more objective judgement, however, was that he had done a magnificent job for Aberdeen Football Club within the shortest possible time and in his very first year as a football manager. To finish as honourable runners-up in the League and finalists in the Scottish Cup was no mean feat by any standards. Until the last two weeks of the season, the Dons were still in a position to land the League and Cup double, which would have been a fitting act of celebration for the club's seventy-fifth birthday.

It was not to be; but the new manager had given the club a fresh sense of stature and stability and a feeling that, with such a man around, the moment of success would not be long delayed. He had strengthened the first-team pool by signing Gordon Strachan from Dundee and Ian Scanlon from Notts County, two fine ball-players, as well as Steve Archibald and Steve Ritchie. He had strengthened his own hand by bringing his former colleague, John Clark, from a coaching job at Celtic Park to be assistant manager at Aberdeen. Clark took over the role of George Murray, the coach who had twice cherished the hope of becoming manager. McNeill respected Murray but, finding that their association was lacking in the vital spark, he chose to bring in his own man.

He encouraged local coaches to identify themselves with Pittodrie and he sought to improve his players' financial position through the perquisites of public appearances and so on. In fighting for his players he demanded a respect in return, a fact which was forcibly brought home to Willie Garner and Bobby Glennie when they stepped out of line at Hogmanay 1977 and found themselves fined and suspended by the manager.

Despite the trophy triumphs of Jock Wallace, the Rangers boss, it was Billy McNeill who was voted Scottish Manager of the Year, which was no more than due recognition of his rapid progress from the starting-block.

Inevitably, the mediocre performance of Celtic in season 1977–78 gave rise to speculation that the up-and-coming McNeill might not be too long delayed in succeeding his old boss, Jock Stein, as manager at Parkhead. The man himself brushed aside such talk and proceeded with the immediate task in hand. His efforts to bring tangible success to Aberdeen were not being overlooked on the terracings of Pittodrie and the finest display of the public's appreciation was to come on the day after the Scottish Cup Final when a dejected Aberdeen party set out from Perth, having stayed overnight at the Station Hotel. Win or lose, the plan had been to drive through the streets of Aberdeen, from the Bridge of Dee to Pittodrie, in an open-topped bus. In view of the massive disappointment of the previous day, however, the Dons players were privately dreading that nobody would turn out. They need not have feared.

The scenes in Aberdeen on that Sunday afternoon of 7 May 1978 were quite remarkable for their enthusiasm. Around 10,000 people were out to greet them along the route and a further 10,000 had crowded into Pittodrie, where the gates had been cast open for the occasion.

As that splendid captain Willie Miller and his players walked out to the arena in their red track-tops, the place erupted in a swell of emotionalism which would have been suitable acclaim for victorious heroes. If this was the sound of defeat, then what was victory! A sea of red scarves went up in solid salute as they chanted 'Aberdeen are magic!' with a loyalty which was prepared to overlook the fact that they had been very far from magic on the previous afternoon. But the thunderous vote of thanks went deeper than a day. It was the supporters' way of showing appreciation of a team which had given Pittodrie one of its most entertaining seasons in seventy-five years of contest. Player after player was singled out for chanted acclaim as they, along with Billy McNeill and his assistant John Clark, lined up at the Beach end to acknowledge the reception and to applaud the fans in return. Some players shed tears as they held out empty hands by way of an apology for the absence of a trophy.

But if the Aberdeen crowd were downhearted that sunny afternoon, they certainly were not showing it. And they responded to manager McNeill when he took over the microphone and said: 'Ladies and gentlemen, this reception is unbelievable. I am so disappointed for my players and for myself but most of all I am disappointed for you, the fans. All I can say is that we shall try very hard to bring you something next season.' It was all that the crowd wanted to hear, just as they had wanted Ally MacLeod to speak to them in the victory salute of 1976. McNeill had judged the mood more accurately and, in taking one of the rare opportunities for a manager to address the fans en masse, he enhanced his reputation still further.

At the end of the day, the Aberdeen players vowed that these fans must be rewarded at the earliest possible moment. Three of them – Bobby Clark, Stuart Kennedy and Joe Harper – were bound for Argentina as part of their old boss's World Cup squad and the others were due to fly off to a well-earned rest in the Majorcan sunshine. At a boardroom reception, the directors were expressing themselves well pleased with the impact of Billy McNeill and John Clark.

But alas, once more, that impact was never to know the test of time. The shock resignation of Jock Wallace as manager of Rangers on Tuesday 23 May heralded a chain of events which rather diverted public attention from the fact that the Scottish international party was already flying into Argentina for the finals of the World Cup. At home, John Greig's elevation from Rangers player to Rangers manager within twenty-four hours of Wallace's announcement seemed to hasten a shake-up at Celtic Park, where all was not well.

When Dick Donald lifted the telephone in the early morning of Friday 26 May, it was to be given due notice by the Parkhead board that they were about to offer their manager's chair to Billy McNeill in succession to the great Jock Stein, who was to be given another role. McNeill had settled happily into the life of the North-east but his regrets at leaving it so soon were outweighed by the temptation of a job which was, understandably, the peak of his personal ambition.

Within a few days it was all signed and sealed and the Aberdeen directors were back in the all-too-familiar position of finding a new man. Their enterprise deserved a better reward. However, they wasted no time in appointing Alex Ferguson of St Mirren, whose immediate task would be to instil in his players a belief that whatever had been achieved under Ally MacLeod and Billy McNeill could be improved under the new command.

34
ANNIVERSARY NIGHT

That dramatic week in the early summer of 1978, which brought managerial changes at Ibrox and Parkhead and left Aberdeen looking for Billy McNeill's replacement, also included the sacking of Alex Ferguson from the boss's job at Love Street, Paisley, amid bickering which ended in the public forum of an industrial tribunal.

A freshly sacked manager of St Mirren being engaged for what Aberdonians regarded as the more prestigious post at Pittodrie was scarcely going to stir enthusiasm in the approach to a new season. Dons supporters found more to cheer about at the Capitol Cinema one rain-swept night when the original version of this book was launched on a wave of nostalgia for better times remembered. The book was marking the seventy-fifth anniversary of Aberdeen Football Club – not that there was a great deal to celebrate in terms of silverware, with only five national trophies in all those years and nothing at all having been won in the first forty-three years! (Imagine the Pittodrie faithful tolerating that kind of barren existence today.) Yet the Dons' achievements were not inconsiderable when set in the context of those twin giants Rangers and Celtic, whose dominance down the century had cast all others in the role of cannon fodder.

Trophies were not everything in life, said the purists, and Aberdeen was celebrating a major milestone with a parade of names from the past, filing on to the stage of the Capitol to be greeted by a capacity audience of 2000, waving red scarves in the air. From every decade they came – Matt Forsyth and Stonewall Jackson of the twenties, Matt Armstrong and Willie Mills of the thirties, Archie Baird and Tony Harris of the forties and Fred Martin, Archie Glen, Harry Yorston and Jackie Hather of the fifties. It was a glorious night of music, merriment and reminiscence, with players recognising themselves in old newsreel films of Hampden occasions, and finishing off with a cocktail party in the restaurant area of the cinema.

At a more private gathering afterwards, in the Atholl Hotel, Alex Ferguson crept quietly upon the scene, taking it all in, acknowledging a past which had been well and truly celebrated that night – a past in which he had played no part at all – but indicating that his task would be to build on those memories. For all the rich history recalled that evening, who could have known that the real story of Pittodrie success was just about to be created? What a quirk of fate it was that the man sitting beside me with a drink in his hand, uttering modest platitudes, was destined to be the architect of that success, as well as the incomparable legend of the Pittodrie story.

Within a year that lonely figure, still reeling from the sacking notice of Love Street, would be inspiring a League Championship which was to be no more than the forerunner to the Golden Age of Aberdeen Football Club. Looking back from this final decade of the century, it is already an exquisite memory, distilled in history. On that launching night of 1978, that history still lay in the future. Such is the fascination of man's continuing story.

35
ENTER THE GOLDEN AGE

Alex Ferguson buckled down to his task at Pittodrie, at thirty-five one of the youngest managers in the game and with a margin between himself and the senior players which could prove perilously small. Indeed, there were said to be early signs of difficulty in establishing his authority. As a lad from the rough-and-tumble of Govan, however, he had learnt to look after himself in a career which had brought him to prominence as a player with Dunfermline Athletic and then with Rangers, for whom he had been part of a scooping up of Scotland's best players in a bid to counter the triumphs of Jock Stein as manager at Celtic Park in the 1960s. Ferguson had been manager at East Stirling and St Mirren, where he had fostered talents such as Tony Fitzpatrick and Frank McGarvey and, more significantly as it would turn out, young boys like Peter Weir, Dougie Bell and Billy Stark.

But now there was a sense of being in the bigger league of management as he surveyed the potential at Pittodrie and realised that the brief stewardships of Ally MacLeod and Billy McNeill had, between them, boosted morale and brought to the playing staffs such talent as Stuart Kennedy from Falkirk, Steve Archibald from Clyde and Gordon Strachan from Dundee. The basic wage of £80 a week could be doubled with bonuses but was still not the kind of money to hold top players. So Alex Ferguson set about improving the wage structure, which was further augmented for longer-serving players by the 'testimonial year' which had been established just before the manager's arrival, with goalkeeper Bobby Clark as the first recipient. That year of functions and a benefit match could amount to £20,000 in those earlier stages.

That first season of 1978–79 was overshadowed in Ferguson's life by the last illness of his father and the bad odour of his tribunal, claiming unfair dismissal from St Mirren. It turned out to be a season without merit in the Aberdeen performance, best remembered perhaps for the worst possible reason – a sending-off for big Doug Rougvie in the League Cup Final against Rangers at Hampden, following an incident with Derek Johnstone.

Rougvie and his team-mates accused the Rangers man of playing to get the foul and making the most of it, a view endorsed in his own book by Alex Ferguson. Aberdeen had taken the lead in that final through Duncan Davidson but Rangers equalised when Bobby Clark was awaiting attention for an injury. After Rougvie's dismissal, Colin Jackson (an Aberdonian to boot!) headed a last-minute winner.

Ferguson, who had already been abbreviated to the popular name of 'Fergie', appreciated a breather to gather his thoughts and resources and prepare for his second season at Pittodrie. For all the genius of Gordon Strachan, who arrived in Aberdeen at the age of twenty, he had taken time to establish himself in the team. But the new manager worked out his proper role and improved his confidence, and the player felt the better not only for Fergie's presence but for the arrival as assistant manager of Pat Stanton, his own personal hero from boyhood days following Hibernian in Edinburgh.

The Dons made an inauspicious start to the new season with defeat from Partick Thistle at Firhill and morale was not improved in December when, having reached the final of the League Cup – for the second time in the same calendar year, as it turned out – the Dons drew with Dundee United at Hampden and were thrashed 3–0 in the mid-week replay at Dundee, on a night of howling gale and lashing rain better suited to witches and warlocks than performing footballers.

That League Cup run, plus a severe winter, put the Dons well behind in their League fixtures as the nights began to stretch into the early spring of 1980. Celtic were out in front and seemed destined to stay there, opening up a gap of ten points at one stage, though Aberdeen had three games in hand. The Dons began their late charge and, with six games to play, were still three points behind Celtic, who then took a dramatic 5–1 defeat at Dens Park. Aberdeen had beaten Celtic at Parkhead on 5 April and, in trying to catch up with postponed fixtures, were due there again on Wednesday 23 April. Could it still be done?

A McCluskey penalty was cancelled by goals from Steve Archibald, Mark McGhee and Gordon Strachan and the football fat was now in the fire. The Dons still had four games to play, which began with a home win over St Mirren followed by three away fixtures. A draw with Dundee United on a Tuesday night was to tee up a situation where, if they could beat Hibs in Edinburgh on the Saturday – and if St Mirren could hold Celtic to a draw at Love Street on the same day – the Dons would almost certainly be the League Champions. What a setting for a grandstand finish!

All routes that day led to Easter Road, which had been proving an unhappy hunting ground for the Dons in recent years, in the knowledge that an away win was essential. As the action warmed up, Ian Scanlon, signed by Billy McNeill from Notts County, scored twice and Steve Archibald, Andy Watson and Mark McGhee brought the total to 5–0 in front of an audience which had its eyes on Easter Road and its ears on the transistors for news of the Love Street match, which was running minutes behind.

St Mirren were indeed holding Celtic to the necessary draw, but the Parkhead men were being awarded a penalty . . . no, wait for it . . . the referee was consulting a linesman and . . . it was a free kick outside the box! Hushed drama at Easter Road, where the final whistle had already gone. The Aberdeen players waited on the pitch for signals from the crowd. Yes, that was it! The final whistle had gone at Love Street. Unless Partick Thistle could beat the Dons next Tuesday by ten goals, the men from the North-east were Champions of Scotland for the first time in twenty-five years. Bedlam reigned. As I wrote in the *Daily Express*:

Oh what a day to be Aberdonian! I have lived through forty years of Pittodrie history but, make no mistake, this was their finest hour. Today's youngsters will tell their grandchildren about it. When the final whistle blew and the truth dawned through a mounting excitement, the whole frenzy of celebration exploded in a riot of red. There was Alex Ferguson running about the field in a mad delirium, crying like a baby and hugging his players in disbelief.

The coincidences began to dawn. It was fifteen years to the day that Bobby Clark, Aberdeen's most capped player [to date], had signed for the Dons. It had seemed that this prize would elude him. But now, just recovering from the sudden death of his father, Bobby was able to shed a tear which told its own story.

Willie Miller's mother, Jean, was recalling the amazing fact that her son had been born exactly twenty-five years ago – his birthday was the previous day – just as Aberdeen had been celebrating their only previous league championship, in 1955. Then came the champagne that flowed through the night and, yesterday, the most beautiful headache in the world!

The Dons fulfilled their remaining fixture, drawing 1–1 with Partick Thistle in a miserable anti-climax at Firhill, officially declared champions at the very ground where they had been beaten on the opening day of the season. What an unpredictable game is football. The team on that historic day at Easter Road read: Clark, Kennedy, Rougvie, Watson, McLeish, Miller, Strachan, Archibald, McGhee, McMaster, Scanlon.

Naturally, there were arguments about the respective merits of the teams which won in 1955 and 1980. Certainly the earlier team had names which would rank with the all-time greats of Pittodrie, from goalkeeper Fred Martin and Archie Glen to Graham Leggat, Harry Yorston, Paddy Buckley and Jackie Hather. The most significant comparison would have to be made on the quality of opposition. In 1955, each of fifteen opponents were played twice, so that once you were clear of Rangers and Celtic you could look forward to opponents like Falkirk, East Fife, Queen of the South, Raith Rovers, Stirling Albion and Clyde, all of which were in the top division of those days and, in fairness, of better quality than they are today. In the tighter set-up of 1980, the Dons had to play the nine best teams – and play them four times each. That must surely mean that the task of 1980 was the more formidable, though cynics might say that the regularity with which the Dons seemed to beat Rangers and Celtic made the 1980 task appear an easier one!

The point was that Alex Ferguson had made his breakthrough, winning the Premier Division Championship, while his neighbour at Dundee United, Jim McLean, had won the League Cup. Sports writers began to coin a phrase about the 'New Firm', meaning Aberdeen and United, as an east-coast threat to the dominance of the Old Firm. All neutral opinion in Scotland wished that it could be so.

Meanwhile the Dandy Dons arrived home to a tumultuous welcome which was red and royal, travelling down Union Street in their open-topped bus in what was to be the pattern for many similar scenes in the years ahead. The reception in the city centre was only a prelude to the demonstration at Pittodrie, where 20,000 people sunbathed for hours till the team arrived. One by one, the players were announced to the crowd as they trotted out to acknowledge individual acclaim. First, captain Willie Miller, then

Bobby Clark and so through the roll of special honour. The last player out was the man who had held a hero's place at Pittodrie for most of a decade. Alas, Joe Harper had been out of the picture with a bad injury but he was not forgotten as he ran out to the scene of his earlier glories. In that hour of triumph, there was a touch of sadness not just for Joe Harper but for the fact that the supporters were seeing Steve Archibald almost certainly for the last time in the club's colours. The dashing forward, who had blossomed towards international recognition since being signed by Billy McNeill from Clyde, would soon be on his way to the greater rewards of Tottenham Hotspur. The transfer was already in motion and the chants of 'Stevie must stay!' came more in hope than expectation.

If Stevie had ever had doubts about going to England, it must have been then. He looked embarrassed that he could not give the supporters the answer they wanted. On a gala day of informality, the Dons gave the crowd a sample of their training session, with Scotland's Player of the Year, Gordon Strachan, entertaining in goal.

With hindsight, we scribes should have kept a few superlatives in reserve, since what was happening that late spring day of 1980 was just the preliminary round of the Golden Age. We would need our hyperbole in the years to come; but who was to know? We lived for the moment, a truly glorious moment indeed. New forms of phraseology could test our talents at a later stage.

There was just one curious footnote to that memorable season, which was to surface much later. When Alex Ferguson came to write his lively memoirs, *A Light in the North*, he speculated on whether or not Aberdeen would still have won the League Championship if Joe Harper had been fit. While acknowledging the marvellous talents of the little buzz-bomb who had become one of the all-time folk heroes of Pittodrie, Ferguson went on to make an assessment which was surprising, to say the least. He wrote:

Personally, I don't think we would have won the League Championship with Joe in the side. He was a bit of a luxury at times, and away from home in particular. He wasn't the hardest worker and always had a bit of a weight problem – and we knew from the start of the season that the system we were playing would require a higher work-rate. Steve Archibald was a natural hard worker but I felt at the time that Steve was possibly doing more of Joe's work than Joe himself.

By then, Fergie had established himself as the greatest folk-hero of them all and his assessment no doubt had the benefit of wisdom and insight beyond the rest of us. But considering the wee man's pedestal position in the hearts of a generation, I wonder how many of them would have agreed with Fergie's view?

36
LIVERPOOL LESSON

If the dramatic events of 1980 gave promise of greater things to come, the surge towards the Golden Age of Pittodrie suffered a hiccup in the following season, which was disappointing at the time but, in retrospect, becomes part of a pattern not uncommon in such circumstances.

Season 1980–81 started up where the previous one had left off – on an emotional high which landed a trophy before the season had even properly begun. A compressed Drybrough Cup competition reached its final on the first Saturday of August with a Hampden occasion scarcely worthy of the name. A mere 7000 people saw the Dons take on St Mirren, who were leading by a penalty goal with only seventeen minutes left. Then Gordon Strachan took command, made ground on the right and crossed for Drew Jarvie to head the equaliser. The winner brought a moment of glory for Steve Cowan, one of Fergie's boys from his Love Street days, who scored against his old club with one of those long-range shots which delight the fans.

The next day the League Championship flag was unfurled at Pittodrie by Alex Fletcher, the government minister, as a preliminary to a match with Arsenal, who had come north to mark the official opening of the roofing for the south-side customers. The Gunners had recently been FA Cup finalists, suffering the double disappointment that season of being beaten at Wembley and also in the European Cup Winners' Cup Final – on penalties. The Dons added to the misery and gave a hint of their new-found aspirations by defeating them 2–1.

But that was as much as you could say about season 1980–81, except that it became a learning process for the future. Handing out the lesson was none other than Liverpool, who were to be the Dons' round-two opponents in the European Cup – a contest to which Aberdeen had been finally admitted, having been done out of the privilege exactly twenty-five years earlier when their right of entry as League Champions had been set aside in favour of Hibernian, a matter already discussed in an earlier chapter. In 1980 Austria Vienna had been overcome in the first round and the scene was set for the stiffest test of all, against the English supremos who included names like Clemence, Hansen, Dalglish and Souness.

Cup-tie fever, which had gripped the North-east in the build-up to the first-leg match at Pittodrie, turned swiftly to stunned silence when, during John McMaster's absence for treatment, Liverpool's McDermott chipped the ball past Jim Leighton for the only goal of the game. McMaster resumed and was starting on one of his mazy, diagonal runs towards the Beach end, beating one man after another, when he was felled by a high tackle from Ray Kennedy in what turned out to be one of the worst injuries in football history. Not only was McMaster put out of the game for a whole year but there were serious doubts if he would even walk properly again. Incredibly, Kennedy was not even booked for his indiscretion and his name retained unpleasant connotations with Aberdeen folk for many years. Before that decade was out, however, the poor man was deserving of sympathy and compassion himself when he fell victim to Parkinson's disease and faced a bleak future of disablement. Miraculously, John McMaster did recover in time to share the plaudits of another day.

Liverpool emphasised their superiority in the return leg at Anfield with a 4–0 win which left the Dons in some measure of despair. When you learn that that same season brought injury to long-serving goalkeeper Bobby Clark (making way for the twenty-year-old Jim Leighton) and that Gordon Strachan, quickly becoming the creative inspiration of the team, suffered an injury in December of 1980 which put him out of the game until the following season, you realise it was not Aberdeen's year, even if they did finish as runners-up to Celtic in the League.

37
ROBSON ROUTED

If Liverpool had been reigning supreme in English football, they were now being challenged by an Ipswich side fashioned by Bobby Robson. The men from Portman Road had just won the UEFA Cup and had taken over as leaders of the First Division when they found themselves defending their European trophy in a first-round tie with Aberdeen.

It was not a prospect to fill them with alarm but there was an element of surprise about the Robson eyebrows when his team was held to a 1–1 draw at Ipswich, the equalising goal for Aberdeen having come from the emerging talent of John Hewitt. With touches of that southern arrogance which irks the Scots, Bobby Robson expressed the view that he did not think Aberdeen could play any better. The conclusion must therefore be that he considered his own team would step up its performance and win through to the second round.

Pittodrie was beginning to gain a taste for the big occasion. In a buzz of excitement, the crowds streamed down Merkland Road East to see if the UEFA Cup holders could be toppled. Penalties from Gordon Strachan and John Wark maintained the deadlock at half-time but it is the second period which will linger long in North-east minds. Alex Ferguson had signed another of his Paisley discoveries, the greatly talented but highly sensitive Peter Weir, who had been struggling to shake off the yoke of his £300,000 transfer fee. Suddenly in that second period Weir began to show his real power, running at Mick Mills with such tantalising skills as to throw the international defender into total confusion. Thus Peter Weir scored for Aberdeen, a welcome event tempered only by the thought that an Ipswich equaliser would put them through on the away-goal rule. At a press conference afterwards Robson said he had been confident that that would still happen, even with only ten minutes to play. Peter Weir had different ideas. Running once more at Mills, he sealed the game for Aberdeen with a third goal which not only dismissed the Cup holders in the very first round but rang early bells across Europe that a team from the North-east of Scotland was on its way. The Liverpool lesson had not been wasted on Ferguson and his men.

Next came the Romanian team Arges Pitesti, which was despatched over the two legs but not before the Dons had had to retrieve a 2–0 deficit in the away game. John Hewitt scored in both legs.

The greatest test of that season was to come in the third round, from the strong-running Hamburg, favourites for the trophy now that Ipswich were out. Could Aberdeen repeat the medicine for the German team? Making his European debut, Eric Black scored first for Aberdeen at Pittodrie before a harmless throw-out from Leighton to Kennedy produced an incredible mix-up which let Hamburg through to equalise. Andy Watson and John Hewitt restored the Aberdeen lead, and it looked as if they might score more goals for a memorable victory, when Hamburg netted a second.

Though that goal put Aberdeen in a precarious position for the return match, Gordon Strachan was later to assess that Pittodrie night as the finest team performance in which he had ever been privileged to participate. Hamburg clinched the second leg by 3–1, spurred on by that immortal of the soccer stage, Franz Beckenbauer, who had been there with the German team in the 1966 World Cup Final at Wembley and was still in command on the European field fifteen years later.

Even though the Dons were out in the third round, their tidal ebb of the previous season had turned to flow a little further into the European experience of 1981–82. A new sense of ambition was running through the corridors of Pittodrie.

In view of the subsequent chain of events which would catapult Aberdeen into football history, it is interesting to pinpoint a January day of 1982 when it all began unexpectedly at Fir Park, Motherwell. That was the day Aberdeen set out on the Scottish Cup trail, in a match which would have been eminently forgettable except that this young man Hewitt set some kind of record by scoring the only goal of the game in just 9.6 seconds from kick-off. The second round brought Celtic to Pittodrie, where an incredible overhead kick by you-know-who sent the Dons on their way to further rounds with Kilmarnock and St Mirren before they prepared to face Rangers in the final.

As excitement built up in the customary way, the Dons players were training at Cruden Bay on the Thursday before the Cup Final when Alex McLeish gained possession on the edge of the penalty area and curved a beautiful shot into the far corner of the net. That was the stuff they needed for Saturday.

When the great day came – a day which would determine who would compete in the European Cup Winners' Cup of 1982–83 – John McDonald put Rangers ahead and sent the Ibrox legions into full song. As the Dons fought back, Alex McLeish appeared on the edge of the Rangers penalty area, with Gordon Strachan screaming for the pass. But no. Alex remembered Cruden Bay and, in an action replay of his training feat, he curved the ball past Jim Stewart for the equaliser. That was how it stood at full-time. So to extra time, an experience not relished by those who meet the Old Firm, with the thought that while Rangers had won the Scottish Cup many times, Aberdeen had won it only twice.

Three minutes after the re-start, however, Gordon Strachan lofted a ball into the path of Mark McGhee, who headed the Dons into the lead. Ten minutes later, the strong-running McGhee returned the compliment by jinking along the by-line, beating Alex Miller and nutmegging John McClelland before passing across goal to Gordon Strachan, who guided the ball into the net. His somersault of delight remains a precious memory with Dons fans. It was clearly Aberdeen's day and, as the Ibrox hordes began to drain away to their watering-holes, the result was sewn up in the craziest of fashions. As Colin Jackson made a short pass-back to Jim Stewart, the Rangers keeper had to run out to kick clear. His shot rebounded from the advancing Neale Cooper, spinning towards his own goal as the fair-haired Aberdonian ran past him and drove the fourth into an empty net.

The Dons had now won the Scottish Cup for the third time. The first success had been in 1947, under the captaincy of Frank Dunlop, when the score was 2–1 against Hibs; the second in 1970, when they were led by the twenty-one-year-old Martin Buchan to a 3–1 win over Celtic; and now in 1982, when the trophy was collected by Willie Miller. Ironically, the biggest victory of all, that 4–1 drubbing of Rangers, was the only one which had needed extra time. More important, however, was the fact that the Dons would be playing in next year's European Cup Winners' competition.

38
PITTODRIE'S GREATEST NIGHT

Apart from the natural optimism which tends to greet a new season, canny Aberdonians had very little sense of what might lie in store for them before the spring of 1983 was over. There is no crystal ball in football's locker, yet Alex Ferguson felt it in his bones that greatness beckoned.

For lesser mortals, the season kicked off on 17 August, more in hope than in expectation, with a League Cup match against the bogey team of Morton, a predictable 2–2 draw at Cappielow with an equalising goal from that inimitable character of Greenock, Andy Ritchie. The following week, the little-known Sion of Switzerland came to Pittodrie for a preliminary round of the European Cup Winners' Cup and, in a 7–0 drubbing, the scoring honours for Aberdeen were spread among Black, Strachan, Simpson, McGhee, Kennedy and Hewitt. At the start of what would be a historic season, it is worth looking at the composition of the Dons' team: Leighton, Kennedy, McMaster, Simpson, McLeish, Miller, Strachan, Black, McGhee, Bell, Hewitt, with Weir and Rougvie as substitutes.

The return leg in Switzerland was remembered less for Aberdeen's 4–1 win than for the fact that the team had never played in such a picturesque setting. Even the hard-nosed Fergie found time to reflect, with poetic eloquence, that his heart had been stirred by that Alpine splendour, with the twinkling lights of mountain villages providing a memorable backdrop to the progress of Aberdeen Football Club.

Fergie's poetic prose gave way to Anglo-Saxon bluntness on the Saturday, however, when the Dons kicked off their League programme with defeat at Tannadice. Before that season was finished, that same Dundee United team would dismiss Aberdeen from the League Cup and pip them by a single point for the Championship. But there were other glories on offer.

All attention that season would focus on the European scene where the Dons were drawn, in the first round proper, against Tirana, the capital city team from the hard-line communist country of Albania. John Hewitt, who was to become known as Super Sub for his uncanny ability to come off the bench and score vital goals, made it 1–0 at Pittodrie before a goalless draw in Albania took the Dons through to a second-round meeting with Lech Poznan of Poland.

Goals by Peter Weir and Mark McGhee at Pittodrie and Dougie Bell in Poland put Aberdeen into the quarter-finals of a European competition for the first time. Only now was there a sense of coming up against the elite of Europe, though there was to be a four-month gap from that November game in Poland until the next one in March. The December draw left plenty of time for planning ahead, not least for the supporters who might wish to be present on some foreign field in case a moment of history was about to be made. That wish was not diminished by the news that Aberdeen's opponents were the powerful Bayern Munich, with famous names like Augenthaler, Breitner, Hoeness and Rumminegge to feature in the match.

The first leg was in Munich and, if a 0–0 scoreline suggests something negative, the truth of that early March evening was very different. These are extracts from a report I sent to the *Sunday Standard*.

The lingering roar of celebration which rang around the great Olympic Stadium of Munich was more than the joyous expression of 1500 Aberdonians. It also marked the entry of Aberdeen FC into that upper echelon of continental football, with an announcement that the city which is already the oil capital of Europe is now set to take its place with the best of them.

All the years of promise and disappointment were finally put aside as the Dons took on the legendary Bayern Munich on their own ground and taught them a lesson in the arts of the game.

Of course, it was a night with an historical omen. The pitch on which this memorable game was played out marks the exact spot where Neville Chamberlain's plane touched down for his crucial meeting with Hitler in 1938. There may have been no 'peace in our time' for the Aberdeen defence as the Germans came at them in raids of growing desperation but, to quote Mr Chamberlain's successor, this was indeed their finest hour.

Curiously, against all the odds, you could sense the possibility of success from the time we all set out from Aberdeen on Tuesday morning. It was the first time the Dons had taken more than a plane-load of supporters to a foreign fixture and as they boarded four jets (suitably painted in the original black-and-gold of Aberdeen), a feeling of unusual optimism was buzzing all over Dyce Airport.

By Tuesday evening, the supporters had announced their arrival, not only in the beer-halls but, believe it or not, in the Bavarian State Opera House. Along with music buffs Robert Thomson and Bill Brown (Pittodrie season ticket-holders who live in Glasgow!) I found myself watching a spectacular production of Wagner's Lohengrin within the sheer opulence of an opera house where elegant ladies dripped with diamonds and flick-ered inside furs.

We crossed the street, from Opera House to Hofbrauhaus, Munich's most famous beer-hall where Hitler used to gather with his cronies when they were cooking up the Nazi Party in the 1920s. Lo and behold, that bustling beer-hall already belonged to the red-and-white scarves as Aber-donians raised their massive steins and sang 'The Northern Lights', as an alternative to the jolly rhythms of the oompah-oompah brass band. At least one puzzled German was hailed with the traditional North-east greet-ing 'Fit like, Fritz?'

As to the match itself, Aberdeen fans may not have seen their team move forward in the accustomed style. They may not have recognised the role of their current hero, Peter Weir. But who could argue with a team which not only stopped the great Bayern from scoring on their own ground but might well have scored themselves on at least three occasions?

After the match, the focal point was the Sheraton Hotel, where the players mixed with supporters in the lounge bar, enjoying a quiet glass of beer. Two American oilmen who had worked in Aberdeen and had flown in from Cairo and Tunisia for the night, paid their own tribute. It was the least they could do for 'mighty fine people', they said. There might still be a long way to go in the second leg but, in Munich at least, Aberdeen had won 0–0.

The scene was therefore set for what was potentially the greatest night Pittodrie had ever seen. Having reached the quarter-finals in Europe, one more game could take Aberdeen to the penultimate stage of the competition. Was it too much to expect? They had prevented Bayern from scoring at home, so why should they permit them greater licence elsewhere?

The excitement built up to unprecedented levels as the crowds converged on Pittodrie that March night of 1983. Within ten minutes, however, Bayern had shown what a dangerous team they could be when Breitner slipped a free kick to Augenthaler, whose thirty-yard shot merely touched Jim Leighton's fingers on the way to goal. Hopes were restored before half-time, however, when McGhee timed a perfect cross to Eric Black, whose header was blocked by Augenthaler. As Bayern's scorer made a second attempt at clearing, Neil Simpson ran in to equalise.

That half-time score would be enough to take the Germans through to the semi-finals, a possibility which increased in the second half when Pflugler scored with one of those long-range, swerving shots in which Continentals seem to specialise. Pittodrie went quiet. Heads went down. Not even an equalising goal would save Aberdeen now. It would take two to reach the semi-final and what kind of crazy optimist would bet on that possibility with only fifteen minutes left to play?

Alex Ferguson had already reacted by sending on his two substitutes, John McMaster and John Hewitt, replacing Stuart Kennedy and Neil Simpson. Without being wise after the event, Gordon Strachan maintained that he had a strong sense of something about to happen. Indeed, when you combined his own genius with that of John McMaster, something was always liable to happen anyway. This is how Strachan remembered the subsequent events.

With fifteen minutes left, I was fouled to the right of the German penalty area at the King Street end. As we placed the ball for the free kick, John McMaster and I remembered that, even though our double act was well known in Scotland, the Germans had probably never heard of it. Big Alex McLeish got the message and ran up to his spot in the penalty area.

John and I started our run, bumped together, pretended to blame each other then turned away as if in disarray. That's the moment when I turned quickly, apparently without looking where I was putting the ball, and chipped it to the spot where Alex McLeish was stationed. We had practised it dozens of times. With Bayern's defence still wondering what was happening, Alex rose like a bird and angled his header out of Muller's reach.

Pittodrie went wild. Back in business at 2–2, it would take just one more goal to see the Dons through. Were the gods on their side?

The answer came within a minute. From the re-start, John McMaster gained possession and prepared for one of his long, left-foot lobs towards the Bayern goal area. Eric Black was already in position to head towards Muller's right-hand side. If the keeper did well to reach the ball at all, he managed only to palm it towards . . . well, who else but the enigmatic John Hewitt, who could wander mysteriously out of a game but just as quickly appear from nowhere at the vital moment. With consummate skill, John brought the ball down and sent it through the legs of the keeper as he sought to recover balance.

Pittodrie erupted. There were still thirteen minutes to play, with at least one moment of anxiety when Rumminegge threatened to spoil the party. The game in Munich may have been the cool, technical victory but, when the referee drew breath for that final whistle, the grand old stadium witnessed an explosion of enthusiasm which confirmed that 16 March 1983 was beyond all measure of doubt Pittodrie's greatest-ever occasion. I tried to capture the essence of it at the time, perhaps with verbal excesses – but for these I offer no apology. This was the report:

When the Red Army of Aberdeen support had sorted out its delirium from its disbelief, there were so many burning topics awaiting attention that priorities became a problem. It went without saying that Wednesday's European epic produced the greatest, most emotional occasion in eighty years of Pittodrie history. Having danced in the streets until the early hours, wrung-out rags were trying to rehabilitate themselves as people and restore some rationale to a topsy-turvy world.

Thursday was for throat lozenges as even the most nostalgic die-hard conceded that, whatever periods of greatness had punctuated the Pittodrie story, no team from times remembered could stand comparison with the present squad. By the same token, their creator, Alex Ferguson, stands out as the most successful manager by far. Memorable talents like Charlie Cooke, Jimmy Smith and Zoltan Varga have peppered the Pittodrie story with artistry but no team has combined attractive football with the kind of drive, commitment and final achievement of these men of the eighties.

Behind that team and its manager lies a boardroom structure which could be taken as a model of how to run a football club. Indeed, after their 3–2 defeat on Wednesday, officials of Bayern Munich expressed envy at the tightly run, three-man board arrangement, with its own compact ground, providing more noise and atmosphere from a 25,000 crowd than they can muster from 50,000 in the vast Olympic Stadium, where they are only sharing tenants.

With native shrewdness, millionaire Dick Donald runs the show quietly and efficiently, with vice-chairman Chris Anderson and Dick's own son, Ian, all former professional footballers, providing able support. The talents are wholly complementary. As the men of vision who have given Aberdeen the first all-seated-and-covered stadium in Britain and many other innovations as well, they took the congratulations of Wednesday evening with the genuine modesty of men who know their business.

But even they were showing beads of sweat in the aftermath of that European classic. And little wonder. For this was the kind of night to be talked about in fifty years from now, the night when people all over Europe were trying to find Aberdeen on the map, curious about a side which could arise from the dead, with fifteen minutes to play, and deliver a killer punch to the legendary Bayern of Munich. For those of us seeking to distil the memory of a great Scottish occasion, assorted pictures keep flitting across the video-screen of the mind, like half-remembered dreams and nightmares. Shall we ever forget the cool, Teutonic precision of the Munich machine with its chilling art of suddenly converting half a chance into a lethal shot? What about the inspiration of Alex Ferguson in bringing on that footballing genius, John McMaster, as the substitute who changed the course of the game? Or the hunch which made him produce young John Hewitt as another replacement to forge delirium from despair with the winning goal? When it was all over, we stayed to demand a lap of honour and to cling to one of football's finer moments. As the joy eventually flooded through the streets of the Granite City in rivulets of red, one of the focal points of celebration was the pub of former Dons player Jimmy Wilson, who was holding a fund-raising night for the blind. Within that pub it was a fair measure of the exclusive preoccupation of an incredible night that the gyrations of a sexy lady disrobing to the raucous rasp of 'The Stripper' was hard put to divert doughty men from their Pittodrie post-mortems. But in the end the analyses were exhausted, the emotions truly spent. Grown men who had long believed that Roy of the Rovers belonged to fiction might have disputed the fact, if only they could have raised the energy. It would be time enough in the morning, after a restless sleep of action replays, to accept that their team had really joined the European elite.

We tend to suffer for euphoria in this life and the Dons came bumping back to earth on the Saturday with a home defeat from Dundee United, followed by a last-gasp win against Morton and a further home defeat from St Mirren. It was hardly the best preparation for the semi-finals of the European Cup Winners' Cup, in which the Dons had been drawn against one of the lesser-known names in Europe, Waterschei of Belgium. From the town of Genk, they had quietly built a workmanlike side which was making up in effectiveness what it lacked in glamour. They had come a long way from their origins in the 1920s, when they were founded by local coal-miners, but were breaking into the European scene only in the 1980s. Good reports preceded them, and Aberdeen were faced not only with a slump in their own performance but the secret fear of going out to an unfashionable team when they had already disposed of a giant.

For the first leg, which was to be at Pittodrie, Alex Ferguson decided to bring back Dougie Bell, prompted by a slight twinge of conscience at having left him out of the second Bayern match when the gangling, mercurial wizard of dribble had performed so well in the first. Fergie's instincts triumphed again. No sooner had the game started than Bell, with that sergeant-major gait of his, gained possession and proceeded to take on the Waterschei defence on his own. There are still doubts as to whether his parting ball was meant as a pass or a shot. Either way, it streaked diagonally for the right-hand post at the King Street end and Eric Black arrived in time to slide home the first goal. Before Waterschei had time to draw breath, the Dons scored again through the sheer determination of Neil Simpson, who survived three tackles to send a low shot into the net. The game had been running for only four minutes. The Belgians stabilised the situation until the interval and showed how dangerous a side they could be. In the second half, however, Doug Bell launched himself on another of his extraordinary forays, leaving Mark McGhee to complete the third goal. Waterschei scored before Peter Weir restored the three-goal lead, and the final score was settled at 5–1 during an incredible goalmouth scramble, when the ball seemed net-bound on four occasions before McGhee, now lying on the ground, managed to scoop it in.

No one doubted then that Aberdeen were set for the greatest event in their eighty years of history. The return tie in Belgium would surely be a formality but before then the Dons had to face Celtic in the semi-final of the Scottish Cup. The Celts were battling for both League and Cup, eventually losing out in both, so there was a lot of Parkhead pride to play for that day at Hampden. It turned into a rough-house of an occasion with Aberdeen, just three days away from the Waterschei match, sustaining injuries to Gordon Strachan, Eric Black, Dougie Bell and Neale Cooper. Cooper had to be taken to Glasgow Victoria Infirmary, while Bell's injury was to have a disastrous effect on his European hopes. All four missed out on the Belgian game, which Aberdeen lost 1–0, a minor matter which niggled as the only defeat on that European adventure but did nothing to alter the most exciting football prospect Aberdonians had ever known. The Dons were in a European final for the very first time!

39
GOTHENBURG GLORY

Well before the semi-final had been completed, Aberdonians were making their arrangements for the European final. 'Are ye gyan tae Gothenburg?' became the most common question around the North-east and even far beyond, as the Dons had gathered an amazing number of new-found supporters.

Yes, they were going to Gothenburg all right, with much perusal of Scandinavian maps to see exactly where the damned place was. The majority would go by air – fifty plane-loads as it turned out – while the P and O ferry *St Clair* was drafted in to cruise across the North Sea with 500 supporters. Many went by car and coach, using the English ferry crossings to the Continent before heading north to Scandinavia. Personal stories abounded. An Aberdonian policeman in Edinburgh, Bryan Farquharson, a fanatical Dons supporter, had a typical story to tell. With a car-load of friends, he set out from Edinburgh at 5 p.m. on the Monday, heading for Ramsgate and the Tuesday-morning ferry to Dunkirk. A strike diverted them to the Dover–Calais crossing and Bryan was navigating his driver through Belgium, Holland and Germany towards Denmark when he realised they were running short of time to catch the ferry to Sweden. As the car accelerated, under the direction of the policeman, they ran into a speed trap and were fined £70 on the spot by the local bobbies! Worse still, they missed the ferry – although they managed to catch the last possible crossing to be in time for the match.

In the euphoric exodus, there was time to spare a thought for two men who had played a significant part in the Aberdeen advance of recent years. Dougie Bell, exciting ball-player with a temperament for the big occasion, was virtually out of contention for the final. The injury news was even worse for right-back Stuart Kennedy, a forceful character of the Pittodrie dressing room, who had seriously damaged his knee against Waterschei in Belgium. In one single stroke of misfortune, Stuart's career with Aberdeen came abruptly to an end. Such is the cruelty of fate. Alex Ferguson put him on the bench at Gothenburg, to give him the chance of a European medal. The substitutes' bench could not hold a second invalid, however, and the manager thought that Bell might at least have another chance. Medals would therefore be going to some who had as yet played no part in the campaign at all and that seemed a poor sort of justice.

The sense of an army on the move gathered momentum that May weekend as the North-east prepared for the trip to Gothenburg. Before flying out on the very first plane from Dyce on the Monday morning, just ahead of the team, I was asked to set the scene for the *Evening Express*. This is an excerpt:

As we stand on the eve of Gothenburg, by far the greatest event in the eighty years of Aberdeen Football Club, I doubt if too many of us have really grasped the full significance of where we are going and what we are doing. For this is no mere walk to Pittodrie or even the lengthy bus journey to darkest Glasgow.

This is the day when we set out in our thousands by aeroplane, ferry-boat or warship, as well as car, bus and bicycle, to meet the greatest club name in the history of world football – at a level of the game where few Scottish players have been privileged to compete.

To say we are poised for the greatest occasion many of us will ever know may be tempting providence and running against the grain of North-east caution, which generally counsels us to 'flee laich, flee lang'. But to hell with caution! What time is this to 'flee laich' when we have already flown into the heights of the European elite and may be standing just ninety minutes away from the applause of a television audience estimated at around 800 million?

Of course the Dons may lose but if we don't savour the moment now, when can we ever? It is wonderful just to be there. If someone had told us in September that the glamorous Cup Winners of Europe, all the way from Scotland to the Soviet Union, from the Baltic to the Mediterranean, would knock each other out in furious competition and that the great Real Madrid would be left to face the Dons in the final, we would have directed him to a good psychiatrist. But it happened . . . and now I'm on my way to Dyce. Gothenburg, here we come!

Aberdeen Airport, that Monday morning, was a seething mass of red and white, a concourse of throbbing anticipation as one plane-load after another was called to the departure lounge and duty-free allowances were bought up for the great spree ahead. The Gothenburg airlift was on its way, a modest journey which soon had us flying over Scandinavian forests and losing height on the approaches to the airport.

In that *Express* article I had paused to remember absent friends, those who had followed the Dons all their days but had not lived to see this. What would the late Jimmy Forbes of the *Evening Express* have been writing on this historic occasion? What would that other memorable colleague, George Chrystal (Chrys), have been preparing for his lovable cartoon creation, Wee Alickie?

Among those who later responded with their own experiences, none expressed the feeling better than Mrs Mary Gardner from Gray Street, Aberdeen. In this condensed version of her graphic letter to me, she gives a striking picture of the occasion as seen through the eyes of a woman:

In deciding we were going to the final, there was no thought in our minds as to who would look after the children, how we could afford it and so on. We were going, come what may! From the moment we touched down in that lovely city, the welcome the Swedes gave us was quite overwhelming. Shouts of 'Hej Abidane' rang out from enthusiastic young-sters who were already wearing red and white scarves. There was no doubt who they would be supporting at the Ullevi Stadium. Our first stop on arrival had to be at that stadium, to savour of the place. Workmen were putting finishing touches here and there and, as we watched, it was hard to imagine how this eerie, empty stadium would generate an electrifying excitement.

Wednesday came and the centre of Gothenburg was hotting up with the arrival of more fans. Familiar songs were being sung in the shopping precincts, new friends were being made, old acquaintances renewed. There was a continuous cluster of interest around the window of the bank where the coveted European trophy was on display. By the time afternoon arrived, the brief shopping spree was behind us (I had bought a tear-proof mascara, which could come in handy that night!). I tried to grab a few hours' rest in preparation for the big match but sleep was impossible through sheer excitement.

I had been too young to understand and only now, in thinking of my late father, was I becoming aware of what a huge part this Aberdeen Football Club had played in his life. What would he have had to say today about a daughter of his going all the way to Sweden to follow the game which had deprived her of so much of his attention all those years ago? I smiled a quiet smile and felt I was here for him too.

That was how Gothenburg affected people. On the day before the match I wandered out on the pitch of Ullevi, an oddly designed stadium which was built for the World Cup Finals held in Sweden in 1958. As the Dons players went through a training session on a pleasant afternoon, onlookers took snapshots of casual little groups. My album contains one in the company of Dons vice-chairman Chris Anderson, *Observer* writer Hugh McIlvanney and Scotland manager Jock Stein, who was lending a quiet word of advice here and there to Alex Ferguson, giving the benefit of his vast experience. Everyone, it seemed, had come to Gothenburg on this family outing. North-east journalist Jim Naughtie had managed to flee the confines of Westminster to appear at the bar of the Europa Hotel, which was the centre of all Aberdeen activity. My youngest son had finished his Highers in Glasgow on the Tuesday, jumped on a bus north and caught the last plane from Aberdeen Airport to Gothenburg.

The carnival atmosphere built up until there was no doubt that the Swedish city belonged to Aberdeen. Locals stood back, mesmerised by the good-humoured invasion, then joined up with the tidal wave of red and white which seemed to generate a conviction that there could be only one result on the night. That matter, however, would be resolved in the football arena and nowhere else. On second thoughts, privately entertained, were Aberdeen really capable of keeping this kind of company? That thought was allowed to drown in the deluge which descended from dark and thunderous skies as the hour of the match drew near.

The Aberdeen party was already on its way to the stadium by coach, tense and tight as bowstrings, some cutting themselves off from reality with Sony Walkman headsets, listening to the music and glancing nervously at the lightning which flashed across an ugly sky. As the fans made their way to Ullevi, the 12,000 Aberdonians outnumbering the Spaniards by about four to one, groundsmen began to haul away the massive tarpaulins which had surely saved the match from being postponed that night. As articulate in his words as he was in football artistry, Gordon Strachan neatly observed the dressing-room situation when he said:

In strange surroundings, we changed into our familiar strip and realised that the great moment was ever so near now. An unusual hush descended on the dressing room as everyone went into his own thoughts, maybe his own prayers, and we just sat looking at each other.

It was not until five minutes before we were due to take the field that reality returned. That was the moment when we all started screaming and shouting, like a bunch of schoolboys. Alex McLeish is always shouting. The lads began to shake hands and wish each other all the best. My style is to tell the boys to enjoy themselves above all else. I looked at the lads – Neale Cooper, Neil Simpson, Eric Black and John Hewitt – and wondered what was going through their young minds. They were showing no nerves but it must have been affecting them on the inside. The boss gave us his final words. All the planning was over now, he said. It was up to us, out there in the Ullevi Stadium of Gothenburg. Suddenly a bell rang and that was our signal to leave the dressing room. Out we trooped to line up in the tunnel and that was a curious experience. For we were standing just an arm's length from the Real Madrid team, across the passage, side by side, casting an odd glance at each other but never exchanging as much as a smile. This was time for serious battle. No time to be fraternising with the enemy.

Out they came, the all-red of Aberdeen, all-white of Real Madrid, in that parallel procession which brings a lump to the throat on great occasions. The formalities over, the game was soon in progress and in seven minutes the Dons were a goal ahead. Strachan took a corner on the right, McLeish came up to power the ball towards goal with his head; it was blocked near the line but Eric Black swung round to drive it into the net.

The joy was short-lived. In attempting a pass-back to Jim Leighton, Alex McLeish misjudged the heavy ground and the ball drew up in the water. The dashing Santillana appeared from nowhere to accept the gift and was brought down in the box by the desperate efforts of Leighton. Juanito scored from the penalty spot and the rest of normal time was fought out on that basis. Real were managed by their former playing star, Alfredo di Stefano, whose rather cynical approach to the game was revealed in his subsequent criticism of his own players. During extra time, he said, Real had attacked too much: 'They did not do what I told them to do. What I was hoping for was a result for us through penalities.'

Though Aberdeen had played well enough to win, the experienced Spaniards were generally regarded as favourites if it came to a penalty shoot-out. Matters seemed to be going their way when the teams started the second period of extra time. Just fifteen minutes left to avoid the sudden-death decision. Eric Black had gone off limping and on came the man who symbolised memorable moments in cup dramas, young John Hewitt himself. Could he do it again?

In some ways, this had been Peter Weir's night. Once again, the cultured left-winger managed to draw the attention of three Real players as he hovered near the dug-out. Then off he set, beating two of them before chipping a perfect ball to Mark McGhee down the left touchline. To the great credit of his skill, strength and determination, he rounded his marker and crossed into the penalty box. The Real goalkeeper, Augustin, came out to intercept the square-cut cross, missed it by inches – and who was running in on his own to head into an empty net but the man of destiny himself, twenty-year-old John Hewitt. As he wheeled to the right, performing a Middlefield version of the Highland Fling, he was acclaimed by the crowd as a hero yet again. He had started it all on a January day in 1982, with that nine-second goal at Motherwell, and he had finished the job sixteen months later in the faraway venue of Gothenburg.

There were still eight minutes to go and Real were soon awarded a free kick just outside the Dons' penalty area. The ball was blocked but the referee gave them a second chance because they hadn't waited for his whistle. This would surely be the last chance to secure their penalty shoot-out and the Aberdeen players lined up, desperate to foil them. Gordon Strachan was suddenly aware of a prayer being intoned behind him: 'Please God, don't let them score. They don't deserve it!' In his infinite mercy, the good Lord cast down favours upon the red sea of support and answered the prayer of the man called Peter, who sought no more than justice. The Real player shot past the post and there was time for only a goal kick before the referee blew his whistle.

The Dandy Dons of Pittodrie had done it! Whereas they had once reached only for the heights of Scottish football – and arrived there very rarely – they had now adjusted their sights to the pinnacles of Europe and beaten the best that that great continent could provide. More immediately, they had sparked off such a celebration as no Aberdonian had ever seen before. In those gaunt stands of Ullevi we danced and sang and shouted and hugged and sought new ways of expressing ecstasy. Out there on the field, the players enjoyed their own frenzied performance as Willie Miller received the European Cup Winners' Cup and came with his team-mates to salute those faithful thousands who had come to share in their finest hour.

Bedlam broke loose in that Swedish city as carefree Aberdonians splashed in the fountains. They were drenched already by the rain so what did it matter? It was reminiscent of VE Night in 1945; indeed, this *was* their VE Night – a Victory in Europe which had come the way of Aberdeen Football Club for the first time ever and might not be repeated in a lifetime. That tear-proof mascara came in handy for Mary Gardner.

When we had wrung the last ounce of joyous expression from wilting bodies and drifted briefly into a sleep where dreams could not better reality, there were the stirrings of a grey dawn and a fleet of aeroplanes awaiting the red army which would return to the home shores like foot soldiers back from a victorious war.

My report for the *Sunday Standard* that weekend said:

As the city of Gothenburg sank out of sight and I sipped champagne from that cup on the team plane home, it was time to close an eye and seek to clarify the dream of a thousand memories.

Finally convinced that there would be no waking up to some cruel joke of reality, I could still see those 12,000 magnificent fans singing in the rain, dancing in the streets, putting the final touches to the greatest night of their lives.

I remember the agonies of those final minutes when injustice was still a possibility, and then the final explosion of relief, a moment when Aberdeen's biggest bookmaker, Bobby Morrison, stood beside me with tears in his eyes, not because of the money he had lost but through genuine emotion – no more than a symbol of all those granite men around him now, unashamedly admitting the softness of their hearts.

But when they dimmed the lights of Ullevi Stadium around 11 o'clock on Wednesday night and the Pittodrie party returned to their village headquarters of Farshatt Hotel, outside Gothenburg, it was there that some gems came dancing out as a gift to the collector of memories. For here was a scene of controlled celebration, totally in keeping with the reservation of the Aberdeen character. When the players arrived back with the trophy, hotel guests suspended everything to form a guard of honour and applauded as Alex Ferguson and his men proceeded to the banqueting room.

Here was a Government Minister, Alex Fletcher, proposing the toast and a leading European official talking from knowledge of the great clubs of the world and saying he had never known a team with such a wonderful family atmosphere as Aberdeen.

Here was vice-chairman Chris Anderson, one of the great architects of football administration, moving about from table to table in the role of discreet host. Here, too, was Dick Donald, who first arrived at Pittodrie as a player in 1928 and, fifty-five years later, was savouring his finest moment. He had not had a chance to speak to his captain, Willie Miller, and as they came together at the self-serving buffet table, I strained to hear their first exchange, wondering if there might be some historic words on this, the greatest night of their respective lives.

Without breaking stride or diverting from the business of shovelling on a slice of ham, some salad and tatties, the doughty Dick said: 'Well well, Willie, it's been quite a night.' To which the inscrutable Willie replied: 'Ay, so it has.' Two unflappable men of sterling character had surely said it all.

Others were less restrained and, when we touched down at Dyce, emotions which were already spent had to be quickly revived to meet a welcome which defied description. I remember as a boy running up Union Street, reaching out to touch Winston Churchill as he sat in an open car after the victory of World War II. But Winnie had nothing on this day, when Aberdeen laid down its tools and formed a crowd of at least 100,000 welcomes.

Like Pied Pipers of Pittodrie, the Dons team drew thousands in their triumphal wake to the ground they call home. Among those waiting to greet them was an old man with a wistful look in his eye. The great Stonewall Jackson, now 83, was playing for the Dons sixty years ago and has lived through almost all there is to tell about the club. Doctors no longer allow him to attend a match but there he was, holding out his hand to young Eric Black, who clasped it with a respect and courtesy and admiration which spoke volumes for the character of the boy.

What a moment that was. Two men representing the opposite ends of the Aberdeen story but united in a simple scene which told you everything about what is good and civilised at Pittodrie. That was the final lump in the throat for those who dreamed a dream and woke up to find it was all true.

228

40
BEST IN EUROPE

Aberdonians had been to the zenith of their footballing experience, rounded off with those truly amazing scenes of the following day when the city went on unofficial holiday and filled every inch of the triumphal route, from the airport right through Bucksburn and Woodside, up Anderson Drive and down Queen's Road and Albyn Place to Union Street. Aberdeen had never seen anything like it. The scenes continued down King Street to Pittodrie itself, a homecoming where, perhaps for the first time, a certain truth began to dawn.

For those unaccustomed to it, ecstasy needs a soft landing. When you have just been to the top, the immediate and obvious prospect is that lesser experiences must prevail. Nothing else would be reasonable. Even a repeat of the ecstasy would not feel the same without an interval and may never again have quite the same flavour as that first occasion. The immediate prospect at Pittodrie on the homecoming was a League game with Hibernian two days later, the last League fixture of the season, when it would still be possible to become Premier Division Champions if Dundee United lost on the same day.

The carnival revived on the Saturday, with the Hibs team forming a guard of honour for the new Cup Champions of Europe as they ran out for their first competitive appearance since the great night. The Dons proceeded to win 5–0 but, in the event, Dundee United went through that afternoon to win their first ever Scottish League Championship by a single point over Aberdeen and Celtic, confirming the impression that the balance of power in Scottish football had at last moved eastward to the so-called New Firm.

On the following Saturday there was still the Scottish Cup Final to look forward to, the finale to the Dons' most memorable season of all. The Gothenburg eleven lined up against a Rangers team which still had an all-Scottish look about it, before the advent of manager Graeme Souness, and contained one name which would yet figure in Pittodrie's scheme of things: McCloy, Dawson, McClelland, McPherson, Paterson, Bett, Cooper, McKinnon, Clark, Russell, McDonald. It turned out to be one of the most disappointing of Cup Finals, with Aberdeen coasting to a 1–0 victory through an Eric Black goal in extra time. All things are relative, no doubt, but it seemed so tame in the week after Gothenburg and the indifferent quality of the play left a curious feeling of deflation. Yet the team had won the Scottish Cup, something they had done only three times in the previous eighty years of the club. And they had beaten Rangers into the bargain. What more could people ask for? Clearly, Aberdeen had reached new plains of expectation, tasted the exquisite flavour of life at the top, and things might never seem quite the same again.

The mediocrity of the play that day brought a public outburst from Alex Ferguson, who felt that only Willie Miller and Alex McLeish had played as he wanted, and the party repaired to the Old Course Hotel at St Andrews for a reception which seemed more like a wake than a celebration. Upset by the manager's tirade, Gordon Strachan made his own protest that night by getting up and leaving the function, an act which was carefully noted by the manager who later fined him £250 for the discourtesy. Strachan apologised but made the very fair point that the players had given of their best against Rangers although, quite frankly, after a season like that there wasn't very much left to give. Some of them were due to leave immediately to join the Scottish party for the home internationals, to be followed by a Scottish tour of Canada and an Aberdeen tour of Germany. It was all too much. Alex Ferguson had the grace to apologise to his players after breakfast the next morning, not having fully appreciated how the emotion of Gothenburg had affected them.

The summer passed by and before that extraordinary year of 1983 was out the Dons had been voted Best Team in Europe in the annual award made by the sports manufacturers Adidas and the magazine *France Football*. What's more, they had been given the chance to prove it in that fixture between the holders of the European Cup and the Cup Winners' Cup, by which final supremacy can be established. The opponents in this Super Cup contest would be Hamburg, who had beaten Juventus of Italy in the final of the European Cup and had shown their greater experience when knocking Aberdeen out of the UEFA Cup in 1981.

Aberdeen's development as a team was to be tested as they set out for Germany in November 1983. Forcing a non-scoring draw in Hamburg, they prepared for another of those great Pittodrie nights when a full house was assured, promising a possible belated moment of glory for those fans who had not gone to Gothenburg.

On a wet night, Peter Weir took control and one of his surging, left-wing runs towards the King Street end produced the cross which was cut back by John Hewitt for Neil Simpson to score. A corner kick from Weir and Willie Miller side-footed the ball to Mark McGhee, who made it two. With the bandwagon rolling, it could have been five or six but the 2–0 scoreline remained and Pittodrie had produced another of its phenomenal European nights – one of the rare occasions when the winning silverware could actually be presented at the home ground.

By then the Dons had recovered from the emotional strains of Gothenburg and its anti-climax and were now sitting at the top of the Premier Division. Even with having mastered all the giants of European football, by winning the Cup Winners' Cup and the Super Cup, there was still the target of the European Cup itself, which had been won by a British club for the first time in 1967, when Celtic triumphed over Inter Milan in Lisbon.

The passport to that trophy would be the Premier Division Championship, which must now be the main ambition. The Dons strode through that season majestically, winning the League by seven clear points over Celtic and conceding only eighteen goals up to the last game. Jim Leighton was set for a League defensive record if he conceded no more than two goals but Alex Ferguson put out half a reserve team for the final fixture at Love Street and St Mirren won 3–2, still leaving the Dons with a shared defensive record but rather taking the gloss off Leighton's magnificent performance. Next season they would be poised for that European Cup contest but success was now such a familiar element at Pittodrie that there was still much to achieve in 1983–84.

Back to defend their Cup Winners' Cup of the previous season, the Dons progressed with wins over Akranes of Iceland, Beveren of Belgium and Ujpest Dosza of Hungary to find themselves, by April of 1984, once more in the semi-final. Blasé though the supporters had tended to become, there was a rekindling of enthusiasm with the realisation that only one more team stood between the Dons and another European final.

Where was it being held this year, we all began to ask. When do they start booking the flights? The Portuguese team, Porto, brought a 1–0 lead from the first leg to the deciding night at Pittodrie. That seemed no great obstacle for an Aberdeen squad which had learnt to rescue deficits and turn them into triumphs as a matter of course. Alas, the Portuguese managed another 1–0 victory at Pittodrie and those hopes of a repeat performance disappeared in the sea mists that night.

But one exciting goal still lay ahead. Aberdeen had never won the League and Cup double and, with the League title safely tucked away, they were due to meet Celtic in the Scottish Cup Final at Hampden on 19 May. Eric Black put Aberdeen in the mood with an opening goal before the game was marred by an ugly incident. Roy Aitken made such a lunge at Mark McGhee that he was sent off and the Dons faced ten determined Celts, always a difficult challenge. In the way these patterns work, Paul McStay scored a deserved equaliser with four minutes to go and the match went into extra time. Appropriately, it was Mark McGhee, victim of the earlier incident, who scored the Dons' winner, which would also prove to be his last goal for the club.

That season's end brought the expiry of several contracts, with Gordon Strachan considered the likeliest player to test his skills at a more lucrative level. Indeed, Alex Ferguson had already anticipated his star play-maker's departure by signing Billy Stark from St Mirren, another of the players he had nurtured in his Love Street days. After much sniffing around by those agents who seek to make a living from shaking football's kaleidoscope, Strachan was diverted from some confusion about a move to Cologne and landed instead with Manchester United, in time to be part of its FA Cup-winning team of 1985. Mark McGhee was also rumoured to be on his way, a matter which was mishandled by Alex Ferguson, and he did indeed end up with Hamburg.

Clearly, the Dons players had reached their moment of greatest European exposure, with a shop-window value which was likely to be at its highest. Strachan and McGhee were free agents, with special talents which would be much in demand. Big Doug Rougvie hardly came into that category but he proved to be the third member of the Gothenburg team to depart in that close season of 1984, a matter to be examined at a later stage.

So the Dons had won the much-coveted double for the first time in their history and faced season 1984–85 with such new players as Frank McDougall from St Mirren and Tommy McQueen from Clyde, joining up with Billy Stark, who had already taken his place in the team, and another significant player for the future, Stewart McKimmie from Dundee FC. An Aberdeen lad, McKimmie had been signed during the previous season, in time to win a European Super Cup medal in his very first week as a Dons player, and would take over the raiding right-back role formerly held by Stuart Kennedy (by now forced into premature retirement) and latterly by big Doug Rougvie.

The Aberdeen team in that Scottish Cup Final against Celtic had still retained the highly recognisable look of: Leighton, McKimmie, Rougvie, Cooper, McLeish, Miller, Strachan, Simpson, McGhee, Black, Weir. But the departure of three Gothenburg heroes alone would have altered the shape of the team and we were soon having to accustom ourselves to the sound of new permutations. In the autumn of 1984, the team was liable to read: Leighton, McKimmie, McQueen, Stark, McLeish, Miller, Black, Simpson, McDougall, Bell, Falconer. Other variations made room for people such as Brian Mitchell, Ian Angus, Ian Porteous, Steve Cowan and, of course, Neale Cooper, Peter Weir and John Hewitt.

No matter the permutations, however, the Dons struck front from the first day of the season, and by the beginning of December had won fifteen of their seventeen League games, with another one drawn. The form was quite devastating, with victories by a four-goal margin not uncommon, including a 5–1 drubbing of Rangers at Pittodrie. So it went on until the last day of the season when they established a new Premier Division record of fifty-nine points, having gone two better than the fifty-seven points record which they themselves had created in the previous season.

Curiously, that stunning performance in the League was some-how at the expense of all else that season. On a bleak August night at Broomfield, the Dons were sent spinning out of the League Cup in a first-round defeat from humble Airdrie, by now under the managership of the effervescent Ally MacLeod, an occasion best remembered by Dons fans for the fact that they were given their first sight of a promising new signing from Stirling Albion, Brian Grant.

The Dons did manage to reach the semi-final of the Scottish Cup, only to be despatched by Dundee United. And the high hopes of reaching for the European Cup took a disastrous turn in the very first round, after they had taken a 2–1 lead against Dynamo Berlin at Pittodrie. The Germans reversed the score on their home ground and after extra time the matter went to penalties. Glued to their radios, Aberdeen fans went through the agonies of hearing the Germans missing one of their kicks and knowing that the next Aberdeen goal would take them through to the second round. Courageous as ever, Willie Miller stepped up to take the vital kick. It was saved – and Dynamo went on to win the extended shoot-out.

Despite the European disappointment, however, there was a sense of astonishment that Alex Ferguson had somehow managed to ride out the inevitable destruction of his Gothenburg team to come up with a fresh combination which could take them to another Premier Division Championship within a year. Did the man have access to some kind of magic? If so, it had not produced the potion for winning the League Cup, the only trophy which had eluded the Dons manager in his remarkable career at Pittodrie. That missing piece of the Ferguson jigsaw, however, was supplied in the early weeks of season 1985–86 when Aberdeen carved their way through the League Cup contest, beating Ayr United, St Johnstone and Hearts before gaining sweet revenge on Dundee United, who had thwarted their efforts far too often in this competition. It all led up to the final at Hampden Park on Sunday 27 October, when they met Hibernian.

Within twelve minutes, the inimitable John Hewitt had laid on two goals for Eric Black and Billy Stark and a second one by Black rounded off a victory which meant that the Dons had scored thirteen times during that Cup run without conceding a single goal.

That Hampden day was particularly poignant for the club's vice-chairman and former player Chris Anderson, whose description of it appears in a later chapter. For Chris, a superbly fit man still in his fifties, had been shattered with the news that he was suffering from the incurable motor neurone disease. In the previous month, Alex Ferguson had been assisting Jock Stein in Scotland's bid to qualify for the 1986 World Cup Finals when, in the moment of victory at Ninian Park, Cardiff, the Scots manager had collapsed and died. Stein had been without doubt the greatest figure in the entire history of Scottish football, mainly as manager of the Celtic team which won the European Cup.

Now, in the hour of tragedy, the Aberdeen board agreed that

their own manager, who had been developing in the Stein mould, should take on the dual role of running the Dons and taking Scotland to the World Cup Finals in Mexico. It was a generous gesture by the directors, offered in the national interest, but it worked to the disadvantage of the club, as Alex Ferguson now admits. Though still top of the League table in December, the Dons began to slip and ended up in fourth place that season. Fortunes were revived for the Scottish Cup, however, when the Dons reached the final without travelling further than the Tay, having beaten Montrose, Arbroath and Dundee on the way to the semi-final against Hibs, which was also played at Dens Park. This had looked like being the year of the Hearts, who seemed to be coasting to a League Championship and a Scottish Cup Final in their finest season for a long time. They had taken their cue from Aberdeen's successes and all neutrals wished them well. But a last-game defeat at Dundee, plus a high-scoring win for Celtic at St Mirren, pipped them for the Championship on goal difference. In a day of tearful deflation, one sensed that their misery was not yet over.

Fate plays many a cruel hand and Aberdonians went south for the Hampden final wishing they were playing some other team. It took John Hewitt just five minutes to score and the Gothenburg hero added another before the stylish Billy Stark emphasised Aberdeen's superiority with a third goal. Poor Hearts went home with no more than a cup of woe and much sympathy from football people everywhere, including Aberdeen. Their noble attempt to join the Dons and Dundee United in trying to spread the honours more evenly around Scotland had suffered a double blow and one wondered how long it would take them to get over the disappointment.

Meanwhile, Aberdonians pondered the extraordinary fact that, in the seven seasons between 1980 and 1986, the Dons had carried off no fewer than ten major trophies, had been declared the Best Team in Europe and were dominating events in Scottish football. They had brought a much-needed breath of fresh air into a game which had been crying out for someone to crack the mould of Rangers and Celtic. In the continuing imbalance of wealth and power, it was always going to take a superhuman effort to achieve it; so most fair-minded people rejoiced in what Aberdeen had done.

Honours had been coming so thick and fast that it was a temptation for the supporters to become blasé about success. That last League Championship had meant another entry to the European

Cup in 1985–86 and the Dons set out to erase the nightmarish memory of the Berlin shoot-out. Akranes of Iceland, European opponents of two years earlier, were duly despatched in the first round and Servette of Switzerland in the second. When the quarter-finals came along in the early spring of 1986, one wondered if there was some kind of omen in the fact that Aberdeen had been drawn against Gothenburg of Sweden. Ah, those magical memories! Three years had now elapsed since the great night and this time they would be playing the team which actually belonged to that cur-vaceous stadium of Ullevi.

The Swedes came to Pittodrie for the first leg and the crowd stood in a tribute of silence to their Prime Minister, Olaf Palme, who had just been assassinated. The Dons were leading 2–1 when the great Johnny Ekstrom equalised in the very last minute. That score would take the Swedes through if there were no more goals in the return leg and it was perhaps with a certain fear of tarnishing the memory of 1983 that the supporters, a much smaller band of us this time, flew out to Gothenburg. It was March instead of May and the bulldozers were clearing snow into murky mountains by the roadside. From a different seating angle, the Ullevi looked another place and I found my attention wandering from the match as I tried to regain my bearings and superimpose upon the stadium the memory of an exquisite night.

It would have taken only one goal to see the Dons through to the European Cup semi-final – and who knows what beyond that? Jim Bett very nearly achieved it but the match ended without a score and the Dons were out of Europe. We drank quietly in our hotel that night, knowing it had been an unreasonable expectation that Gothenburg could reproduce its magic.

Jim Bett, a Hamilton lad, had been signed from the Belgian club Lokeren that season, having previously played for Rangers, though it would take him a few more years to emerge as a major figure in the plans of both Aberdeen and Scotland. In that same season, the big-game favourite of Pittodrie crowds, Doug Bell, was transferred to Rangers and, bit by bit, the elements of the Fergie era were being whittled away.

41
CHRIS BOWS OUT

Despite the continuing habit of winning trophies, there was a general sense of running down at Pittodrie, as if the successes were now being gained more by reflex than renewed inspiration. That mood of malaise was strangely symbolised by the death of Chris Anderson, whose fight against the dreaded Motor Neurone Disease had finally ended. It was a sad day for football in general and Aberdeen in particular and this is an excerpt from what I wrote about him in the *Glasgow Herald*:

Scotland could ill afford to lose Chris Anderson, vice-chairman of Aberdeen Football Club and one of the game's ablest adminstrators, who has died, at the age of sixty, from the same Motor Neurone Disease which claimed film star David Niven.

Chris Anderson was the fair face of sport, an intelligent and articulate spokesman and the brain behind so much of the change, not only at Pittodrie but throughout the game of football. Destined to be the next chairman of the Dons, he told me, in a deeply moving interview not long before he died, about his sadness at being robbed of the chance to lead the club towards the 21st century.

He was well aware of his fate and, with a courage which had characterised him as player and man, he told me of his last visit to Hampden Park and how he looked around and knew he was seeing the great stadium for the last time.

The public knew less perhaps of his work as chief executive at one of Britain's leading polytechnics, Robert Gordon's Institute of Technology, where he took immense pride in the provision of higher education for talented youngsters in the North-east. Indeed, his OBE was awarded for both his service to sport and education.

But it was football which brought wider recognition, first as an Aberdeen player in the post-war era and then as the director who masterminded much of his club's off-the-field success, like building an all-seated, all-covered stadium with executive boxes and so on. He played just as big a part in laying the foundations of Aberdeen's rise to dominance of Scottish football in the eighties, leading to the success as Cup Champions of Europe in 1983.

For the greater good of the game, he led the way to the creation of a Premier Division in 1975 and was advocating a British Cup and a Scottish National Soccer League when few could envisage the ideas. But a cruel twist of fate struck at Chris Anderson soon after he took early retirement from his college post at the age of fifty-eight.

While still able to communicate, he talked to me very frankly about how it all happened. I leave it to the man himself to make his last public utterances:

'Now that I was taking early retirement, I looked forward to fulfilling my two remaining ambitions. I wanted to spend more time travelling the world with my wife, Christine, who is a great tennis buff, and to take Aberdeen Football Club into the 21st century as its chairman. I have always had strength. I had some money but I never had the time. Now I was making some time for myself.

'Always superbly fit, I could be found in the gymnasium at Gordon's College twice a week, even after retirement, playing head tennis, or running along the beach at Barra, where I was in August, 1984. I was always a fast mover, I suppose the fittest man for my age in the whole of Aberdeen, a teetotaller and non-smoker.

'In September, 1984, I had to go into hospital for a hernia operation but recovered from that. By the end of the year, however, I began to feel a stiffness in my right leg and hand. There was a lack of thrust. I was also beginning to lose too many games of head tennis! The trouble was diagnosed as Motor Neurone Disease – and there was no known cure. Damage or disease of the central nervous system apparently affects the nerve fibres, which then fail to energise the muscles of the body. So the muscles waste. Naturally, we were shattered but decided not to tell anyone at that stage. We didn't want to upset people. So I soldiered on through last Spring, getting stiffer and more restricted in my movement but still able to get about.

'In July I went to Switzerland for the European Cup draw but things were getting more difficult and my condition was becoming apparent. So, in August, I told my family and friends that I had this disease and was heading towards being unable to move physically. There was total disbelief. They were so devastated that I found myself having to cheer them up.

'I had also been trying to avoid creating any alarm at Pittodrie but, of course, I had to tell the chairman, Dick Donald, and our manager, Alex Ferguson, who were both shattered. When I discovered there was nothing that could be done for me in Aberdeen I began to find out what else might be done and that was how I came to visit Newcastle, which is a major centre for this kind of disease.

'I learned about research going on in Boston – and that there are between 4000 and 5000 sufferers in the United Kingdom. I found a pattern beginning to emerge, showing that the victims are generally fit and athletic people and that the trouble often arise after an operation. All along I felt some reaction to my hernia operation was triggered off in the body. The medical people say they might crack this disease in two or three years but time is not on my side.

'Anyhow, I have faced up to my situation and, when people ask if I feel any bitterness, I can only reply that I do not. If it hadn't been me it would have been someone else. My mind is clear but I am now faced with the frustration of not being able to move and feeling I'm a burden on other people. I was always such an independent kind of North-east person.'

We talked about the golden age of Aberdeen Football Club, starting with the managership of Ally MacLeod in 1975, continuing briefly with Billy McNeill and brought to fruition by Alex Ferguson.

'What we have done is succeeded in shifting the football base from Glasgow to the east coast,' said Chris Anderson. 'In my illness, I have been deeply touched by the reaction of the younger players at Pittodrie, who have sent me cards of encouragement.

'When I went to Hampden for the League Cup Final in October and Willie Miller stepped up to receive the trophy, I found myself looking round the great stadium and knowing it was the last time I would see it. Afterwards, I went to congratulate the players and found I could face them all with one exception. Somehow, I choked up when I came face to face with Eric Black. And so did he. It wasn't just that he had scored twice that day or that he set us on our way to victory in Gothenburg. I'm sure it was because he epitomised for me all that was good in football. He seemed to stand for all that Aberdeen had done in recent years.'

Though too ill to see Aberdeen in the Scottish Cup Final against Hearts, Chris watched on television and tapped out his prediction of the result. It was: Aberdeen 3 – Hearts 0 (the correct score).

In facing up to his greatest battle so courageously, Chris Anderson remained conscious till his very last day. But he was trapped inside an immobile body without means of communication, except for the flap of an eyelid.

The man who loved fitness and freedom was finally a prisoner. And, in the fading minutes of Tuesday night, he was mercifully given his release.

42
FERGIE LOOKS BACK

Before that year was out, the living legend of Pittodrie, Alex Ferguson, went on his way to the greater challenge of Manchester United, claimed by many as the top managerial job in Britain. That fine old club, which had lost its famous Busby Babes in the Munich air disaster of 1958, arose from the ashes to produce another great team exactly ten years later, when Matt Busby himself came back from the threshold of death to lead his side to the European Championship, with legendary names like George Best and Bobby Charlton (Aberdeen's own Denis Law missing out through injury).

By the time Ferguson took over as manager in 1986, United had gone for nearly twenty years without winning the English League. Liverpool's dominance in that period went down very badly with Manchester supporters and one manager after another had been sacrificed in the frustration of seeking a new Messiah. Ron Atkinson had just led them to an FA Cup victory with the team which included Gordon Strachan but that did not prevent him from being displaced soon afterwards. Alex Ferguson took up the challenge but was still struggling for his first taste of victory in England into the last decade of the century. It was a hard and demanding task of almost impossible dimensions. His reward came, however, in the FA Cup Final of 1990, when United managed to equalise in extra time, against Crystal Palace, before winning the replay at Wembley.

On the day that Scotland clinched her place in the 1990 World Cup Finals in Italy, beating Norway at Hampden, I collected Alex Ferguson at Glasgow Airport and we sat down to relive his eight glorious years at Pittodrie. We later drove through his native Govan towards Hampden, where he began his senior career with Queen's Park. As a player, he came first to prominence with Dunfermline in the 1960s before he was snapped up by Rangers in their bid to counter Jock Stein's all-conquering Celtic. His managerial teeth had been cut at East Stirling and St Mirren, where he built the best team that Love Street had ever seen. So to Pittodrie in the summer of 1978. How did it all seem now, I wondered, as he looked back on the eight most eventful years of his life? He explained:

After the part-time set-up at Love Street, the most important thing in coming to Pittodrie was the feeling of security. We keep on saying there was a great chairman and vice-chairman but you cannot appreciate that unless you worked for them. Dick Donald just said to me, 'You make your own decisions about the team and you will never get interference from us.' And that was how it remained. It was also quite important because I wasn't long there when the *Press and Journal* carried out one of those 'What's wrong at Pittodrie?' stories, seeking the views of the public. I was said to have had a fight with Willie Miller and this was looked upon as an issue.

The truth is that the team was not playing the way I wanted and I did have arguments with individuals. I had a disagreement with Willie Miller. I felt his defence was staying far too much in the penalty area. It wasn't easy at the beginning and things were not helped by one or two personal problems, like my father's last illness and the fact that I went ahead with my case against St Mirren for unfair dismissal. The Aberdeen directors advised me against going to the tribunal but I was impulsive in those days and only later realised that it was a stupid thing to do. I have learned to curb that side of myself.

In that first October, we played Fortuna Dusseldorf in the Cup Winners' Cup and lost 3–0 in Germany. I was still trying to bridge the gap between the players and myself and, inadvisedly, I listened to their request for a night out after the match. I softened and let them go. Well, they must have had a night out! On the Saturday they played Hearts at Pittodrie and were awful. After a 2–1 defeat, I went into the dressing room and rounded on Alex McLeish, who was one of the younger players. Willie Miller spoke up and said, 'Why don't you get on to the older ones?' That started an argument but Willie did later apologise. We ended up fourth in the League that season and, at the end of it, I told the players, 'If anyone wants to leave this club, they can go. Just come and see me tomorrow.' Only one player came in. He was Willie Garner, who knew his place was in jeopardy anyway.

Ferguson had established his authority, shown who was boss around here. If they didn't want to be part of it, they could be on their way. The matter was now settled.

He proceeded to look around for the team he wanted to build. His first purchase, in the early spring of 1979, was Mark McGhee from Newcastle. Gradually he got to grips with people and situations, as he revealed in this rare insight into the private world of a football manager:

As a young manager, I worked by intuition and instinct. You just had a smell for things. I have always tried to have certain guidelines, trying to judge, decide and act quickly. If you have an injury on a Friday, for example, and the players are sitting there waiting to hear the team, you must go right in and tell them. You must not show hesitancy or fear.

It was wonderful to have the backing of a man like the Aberdeen chairman. I found the main strength of Dick Donald to be that he didn't care what people thought of him. He had a great strength, capable of making a decision and sticking by it. At first, we would discuss bonuses for a forthcoming match and I might state a figure, to which he would say 'Ridiculous!' But he would go away and come back and say either 'OK' or 'Too much'. Latterly, he found he could leave it to me. But he had a wonderful way. He would say, before a Cup Final perhaps, 'It won't be the end of the world if we lose this one. The players are getting a bit carried away.' It was his way of saying to me, 'Don't worry if you lose. Your job is safe.' Dick would sit around in the team hotel and just watch. He was a great observer.

Chris Anderson was the balancing factor in the club, a complete contrast to Dick Donald. Chris was looking forward all the time. For example, he could see the way ahead for the televising of football. I may not always have agreed with his views but he was the kind of man we needed. We needed him at the SFA, though he was not keen to go at first. Chris had big ideas for the club and wanted to promote it – and he was a great supporter of the players.

Willie Miller was my mirror on the park, as well as the best penalty-box player I have ever had anything to do with. He and Bryan Robson at Manchester United are identical types, the best two players I have dealt with. Alex McLeish is also coming to acquire their qualities. I would say Willie Miller is the best player to emerge in Scotland in the fifteen years from the early 1970s to the late 1980s.

Success gave him presence and authority and he capitalised on that by dominating the scene for a number of years. The fact that Rangers and Celtic players were afraid of his presence was a measure of the figure he had become in Scottish football. As a captain, he has to come into the class of John Greig and Billy McNeil, the three most successful team captains we have seen. It is difficult for me to judge people like George Young of Rangers before that.

Willie Miller was the single factor at Aberdeen but he was surrounded by players of character, people like Stuart Kennedy, Drew Jarvie, Mark McGhee, Gordon Strachan. Big Doug Rougvie was a character of a different type, well loved and part of the balancing act. So the team was full of characters, who combined to overcome the Rangers–Celtic dominance.

What about that great day at Easter Road in 1980? Did he really mean that that championship could not have been achieved with Joe Harper in the team that season?

Yes, I meant it. We wouldn't have won it with Joe there. He was not a worker. In fact, I was trying to find ways of getting rid of him. He could score goals at home but not away from home.

Bobby Clark was a great influence around the club. He instilled discipline in other goalkeepers, like Jim Leighton and Brian Gunn. Bobby was like a sergeant-major and had a fiery temper. But he started a tradition of goalkeepers gathering around after a match. They are a breed by themselves; they don't criticise each other. Bobby was a very good organiser but, in the end, the man he helped so much, Jim Leighton, became a better goalkeeper.

So we won the League and gained entry to the European Cup. That Liverpool experience and the embarrassment of it was the big lesson. The players didn't really have the experience of Europe. I had had eight years of it with Dunfermline and Rangers. They lost that game in Dusseldorf because they could not take in the message of how you play the game in Europe.

At what point did Alex Ferguson begin to realise that his team might be going places in Europe?

I realised it when we beat Rangers in the Scottish Cup Final of 1982. To go to Hampden and dominate an Old Firm team gives you reason to believe you have a decent team. The players sprouted wings then. Jock Stein was recognising their capabilities and by 1984 he had five of the players in the Scottish team – Leighton, Miller, McLeish, Strachan and McGhee. Jock played as big a part as anyone by doing that. Willie Miller had started getting his place over Alan Hansen and Gordon McQueen.

It is interesting to analyse the team which was building up to that European Final night in Gothenburg. Six of the twelve who took the field that night were at Pittodrie before Ferguson arrived: Leighton, Rougvie, McMaster, McLeish, Miller and Strachan. All but Strachan were home-grown talents. The other six were Ferguson's own choices. McGhee, who had gone from Morton to Newcastle, came to Aberdeen for £70,000 and his other purchase was Peter Weir, who came from St Mirren for £300,000. The remaining four were part of the crop of youngsters he himself had developed: Neale Cooper, Neil Simpson, Eric Black and John Hewitt. Others in that group who were playing their various parts included Brian Gunn, the goalkeeper, Steve Cowan, Dougie Bell and Ian Angus. Fergie was in reminiscent mood, recalling players at random:

Stuart Kennedy was a brilliant player but what a tragedy that he went out of the game as he did. He had that great belief in himself – as the best back in the world! He was also the barrack-room lawyer at Pittodrie and a bit of a Pied Piper. People seemed to follow him around. John McMaster had genius which was electrifying. Before that disastrous Liverpool game, Jock Stein had told me, 'I am going to pick McMaster for Scotland. But don't tell him unless you think it would do you good.' Well, we all know what happened that Liverpool night. But he fought back and made it to Gothenburg. John had magnificent vision and stroked his left foot with all the smoothness of an artist's brush. You could have set it to music.

Peter Weir could be mercurial. But when he played, the whole team played, as witness Gothenburg, where he made so much of it happen. I thought Neale Cooper had a lot of promise but he should have turned out to be a better player than he did. He was a good tackler and aggressive, and he and Neil Simpson protected the back four. In the end, however, I would have to say that Simpson was a better player than Cooper. Neither had great vision but they did have dynamism and natural enthusiasm.

Mark McGhee had tremendous resilience as a player and when he was leaving I remember standing on the park with Willie Miller one day and remarking how much we were going to miss him. In fact, Mark was a bigger loss to the team than either Gordon Strachan or Doug Rougvie. John Hewitt was the scorer of big-game goals and Eric Black was at his best in the air as well as being a good finisher. But both Black and Hewitt were influenced by McGhee's game.

The Gothenburg team grew up together and stayed together and, when you combine that with ability and character, there is only one way to go. If they had stayed together beyond the Gothenburg time, it is difficult to assess what damage they could have done to the Old Firm, perhaps for three more years. It used to get me annoyed but there were times when I knew they were playing to only sixty per cent of their capabilities – and still winning. In heading towards Gothenburg, we were also throwing away the League title, by only one point as it turned out.

In that next season, when we won the League and Cup double, we knew that Gordon Strachan was going to leave us. He needed a new motivation. In the summer after Gothenburg there were lots of inquiries about Gordon. Then they became fewer and fewer. Dick Donald suggested we phone Manchester United to see if they were interested in him at £500,000. Yes, they were interested, but Ron Atkinson came back to tell us there was a problem – he discovered that Gordon had already signed for Cologne! Evidently he had signed some kind of contract and we didn't know. I could have killed him! The matter was resolved, however, and he went to Old Trafford.

In offering re-signing terms, we were not prepared to go daft with money. We tried to have a strict financial set-up at Pittodrie but perhaps we took it all a bit for granted. After Gothenburg, Mark McGhee had given me his demands, saying how much he thought he was worth to stay. I said he must be joking. The season went on that way and I left it too late. It was really my fault that we lost Mark. It wasn't worth quibbling over the extra £5000 or £10,000. It would have been worth paying it to keep him. By the time March came round, Mark had decided to go and I knew I had made a mess of it.

In the case of Doug Rougvie, I made him what I thought was a good offer. But what he wanted was the same as Willie Miller. I said I would take it to the directors, who then asked me if I could perhaps improve the offer. By the time I went back, Doug had left for London to sign for Chelsea but I think he made a terrible mistake in leaving Aberdeen. He may have done all right financially but he could still have been there, into the 1990s, the folk hero which he had already become. [Rougvie's own version of events comes in a later chapter.]

As to my own career, there is no doubt that Aberdeen made me as a manager and I keep a very special place in my heart for Pittodrie. They were eight great years. When I left, I thought the choice of Ian Porterfield was a ridiculous decision. Do you know, he never once phoned me about anything? Alex Smith was the right type to choose.

Can the Ferguson era ever be repeated? Have we seen our moment of glory for this century?

I have to say that the chemistry which brought together that particular kind of talent and character might well turn out to be a once-in-a-lifetime happening. Luck entered into it. It is possible that the Dons will never reach that place in Europe again. When Willie Miller goes, you wonder if Aberdeen will ever be the same again. Look at Manchester United, who have been waiting for well over twenty years to find another Charlton or a Best. Celtic are still waiting for another Lisbon Lions of 1967. Rangers are waiting to repeat their Cup Winners' triumph of 1972. Of course Aberdeen will continue to have success in Scotland but that is not the criterion any more. Having won in Europe whets your appetite.

Fergie as pessimist or realist? It will be up to Alex Smith and other managers of the future to prove his prediction wrong. Time alone will tell.

43
END OF AN ERA

When Aberdeen generously decided to let Alex Ferguson divide his time between club and country, after the sudden death of Jock Stein, his commitment to the club was almost bound to suffer. And it did. In all truth, the era of Alex Ferguson had run its course. The supporters felt less conscious of his presence. Everyone sensed it was only a matter of time before he moved on to a club like Manchester United, which still craved a return to the success of its illustrious past. So much of what goes on behind the scenes will always remain private property but it was known to his friends that Ferguson felt he had not been well enough paid at Pittodrie, though he has never said so publicly.

As in all things in life, there is a time to come and a time to go and, while it is hard to say so about your greatest-ever legend, Fergie's hour had arrived. His loyal and energetic assistant, Archie Knox, had meantime left to be manager of Dundee but was brought back as assistant, with thoughts that he would be the ready-made replacement, no doubt. In the event, Knox chose to accompany Ferguson as assistant at Old Trafford, a move which incurred the displeasure of the supporters who felt, understandably, that if he did not intend to stay as manager, he should perhaps not have returned from Dundee.

In November 1986, Aberdeen were therefore left without a manager and eventually settled on the surprise choice of Ian Porterfield, the former Raith Rovers player who was best known as the man who had scored the winning goal for Sunderland in the FA Cup Final against Leeds United at Wembley in 1973. Almost immediately, Porterfield ran into some tabloid publicity about his private life and, for all his drive and dedication to the game, he was never fully accepted by the supporters. He will be best remembered in Aberdeen for his Nicholas signings – Charlie from Arsenal for

£425,000, and Peter from Luton for £320,000. His big moment on the field was the Skol League Cup Final of 1987, when Aberdeen were beaten by Rangers in a penalty shoot-out, the culprit being the ever-popular and highly skilful Peter Nicholas, who missed his scoring chance. Peter went back south for family reasons, joined Chelsea and became their captain in the 1989–90 season, when the Stamford Bridge club made an early challenge for the English title.

Porterfield's time ran out in the spring of 1988. He, too, went to Chelsea as assistant manager, before moving to Reading as manager. After his divorce, he married a daughter of the memorable Jack Allister, a hero of the Dons' championship team of the 1950s.

Hereabouts, history repeated one of its strange quirks. Just as Alex Ferguson had been sacked by St Mirren in the week when Aberdeen needed a replacement for Billy McNeill, so was Alex Smith sacked by St Mirren not long before they needed a replacement for Ian Porterfield. In fact, the latter had invited Smith to come and help out with coaching at Pittodrie just before he himself reached the point of resigning by what amounted to mutual consent. Smith, who had always been a student of Alex Ferguson and a regular attender at Pittodrie's European specials, was therefore a ready-made successor, and the Dons board did not waste much time in confirming his appointment. He was asked to form a management team which brought back to Pittodrie old favourites Jocky Scott, who gave up his management job at Dundee to be co-manager at Aberdeen, and Drew Jarvie, who also returned from Dundee to be coach.

In his first few months, Alex Smith ran into a repetition of Ian Porterfield's misfortune with the Skol Cup Final. Once again it was Rangers who were the opponents and this time they managed a 3–2 victory without the agonies of a penalty-kick decider. The rest of that 1988–89 season left the supporters reserving judgement on the new management team. Smith was working away quietly in the background, however.

Having lost Jim Leighton to Manchester United, he took a tip from his predecessor, Alex Ferguson, that there was a surplus of good keepers in Holland. Fergie also suggested to Smith that, while over looking for a goalkeeper, he might give him a report on a Merseyside lad playing for Groningen. His name was Paul Mason. When Smith arrived to cast an eye over the FC Twente goalkeeper, Theo Snelders, the big man had called off with an injury. In the opposing team, Mason did indeed impress Smith, though not as the full-back Ferguson had been looking for. He passed on his report and, when the former Dons manager took no further action, Smith stepped in and signed Mason for a different role.

He did, of course, catch up with Mr Snelders and brought off a double Dutch coup which proved what a shrewd judge of a player he could be. Within a short time it was hard to find an Aberdeen supporter who would have exchanged Snelders for Jim Leighton, fine servant though he had been. The Dutchman became an instant hero at Pittodrie, a stylish giant of a man with a superior bearing, who could make goalkeeping look so easy that he was voted Scotland's Player of the Year by his fellow professionals in his very first season.

Nor was Smith finished with the Dutch connection. He paid £300,000 for the gigantic Willem van der Ark, a 6 ft 5 in striker from the Willem II club, and followed that up with what looked like the most spectacular signing of them all. A tip from a contact in Holland brought the news that Hans Gillhaus of PSV Eindhoven might be available. Back went Smith to buy him for £650,000, a record fee for an Aberdeen signing. Gillhaus (the G is pronounced as an H) first appeared against Dunfermline at East End Park in November 1989, a dream debut in which he scored twice in the first sixteen minutes, the first being a spectacular overhead hitch-kick which sent the travelling support into raptures. On the following Wednesday, he made his home debut when Rangers came to Pittodrie and fought an even battle. But they were beaten by another spectacular goal from the Dutchman, by now being acclaimed as the best of the foreign imports in a period when clubs like Celtic, Dundee United, Hearts and Dunfermline had been finding players in Poland, Hungary and Yugoslavia as well as Scandinavia.

All of a sudden the stimulating presence of Gillhaus seemed to electrify Pittodrie, players as well as spectators, with Charlie Nicholas rekindling his enthusiasm in the company of a kindred spirit. Hopes of a new inspiration, reminiscent of the days of Zoltan Varga, were dampened when the Dutch player became an early victim of heavy tackling but no one doubted that he was someone with a special talent to offer.

Before then, however, Aberdeen had already signalled their intentions for the new season by winning the Skol League Cup in another exciting final against Rangers, the third successive meeting between the clubs in the same competition. Having lost out in 1987 and 1988, Aberdeen seemed determined to see justice restored.

They had gone to Hampden for the semi-final and beaten Celtic, with a spectacularly long-range goal from Ian Cameron, another of Aberdeen's signings from Smith's former club, St Mirren. Cameron, an honours graduate of Glasgow University whose culture extended to his feet, was injured before the final; but the cudgels were taken up by Paul Mason, now quickly establishing himself as a valuable member of the squad, who scored the first goal. Before half-time, however, Ally McCoist had backed into Willie Miller and been awarded the kind of penalty which would not have been claimed by the most diehard Rangers supporter. All were agreed that referee George Smith had suffered some kind of aberration and, in the process, had given the initiative back to the Ibrox club. Was this to be yet another Skol Cup victory for Rangers? Happily, justice was finally done when the same Paul Mason shot home the winner – and Aberdeen had scored their first trophy success for three years.

Those barren years which followed the departure of Alex Ferguson were over at last and the sheer delight of the support was reflected best of all on the face of Willie Miller, not a man to display emotion but confirming that it was one of his most satisfying moments. The Dons were back in business. The success of the Fergie era, which had threatened to become an albatross around the necks of the Aberdeen players, had finally been shaken off. They were playing good football and success would surely follow.

It did. Season 1989–90 ended in dramatic fashion when the Dons, having accounted for Partick Thistle, Morton, Hearts and Dundee United, reached a Scottish Cup Final in which, with no scoring after extra time, the penalty shoot-out was introduced to this competition. Still level after the five regulation kicks, the teams went to a sudden-death decision and, with Anton Rogan's kick brilliantly saved by Theo Snelders, it all came down to Brian Irvine. Hampden had never known a moment like it.

Big Brian, taking over from a semi-fit Willie Miller, strode majestically to the spot and sent the cup to Pittodrie on a nail-biting 9–8 margin. He said afterwards that God was with him as he took the kick. So too was the racing heart of every living Aberdonian.

One could reflect with sympathy that Ian Porterfield had occupied the buffer position after Alex Ferguson. It had taken yet another manager to inspire a fresh initiative and that man was Alex Smith, with the back-up team of Jocky Scott and Drew Jarvie.

44
THE NEW REGIME

Alex Smith was born in the coal-mining community of Cowie, near Stirling, bred from mining stock though his father spent a large part of his life as a regular soldier and distinguished piper in the Argyll and Sutherland Highlanders. Alex served his time as a glazier in Stirling and, in football terms, had captained Stirlingshire schools and played for the local juvenile team, Gowanhill United, where his team-mate and close friend was Billy Bremner, at whose wedding he was best man.

When Bremner went to Leeds United, Smith joined Kilmarnock, in the days of Jimmy Brown, Frank Beattie, Willie Toner, Gerry Mays and Joe McBride. Failing to make the first team, he settled for the bread-and-butter end of the game, an experience of learning the hard way which prepared him for the rough-and-tumble of management. He played for Stenhousemuir and Stirling Albion but a knee injury put him out of the game for two years. He started his own business in 1964 but returned to football with Albion Rovers before becoming the first-ever manager of Stenhousemuir in 1969. Life at the bottom of the Second Division was raw experience but after five years he received a call from the general manager of Stirling Albion, Bob Shankly, inviting him to be the club's manager. Shankly may have lived in the shadow of brother Bill at Liverpool but there are plenty of witnesses to his own ability. Says Smith:

I learned more about football management from him in six months than anything else I have learned. I was there for eight years before he died and left me a legacy of how to organize things, how to treat people and get the best out of players. He was a strong and honest man.

I brought in players like John Colquhoun, Willie Irvine and Brian Grant and knew that, for Stirling to survive, I had to produce a player every year who could be sold for upwards of £60,000. In one such deal I sold Brian Grant to Aberdeen for £35,000, with another £25,000 to come when he had reached forty first-team appearances.

Smith was coming up quietly through the hard school, regretting that his own playing career had not taken better shape but determined to make good the deficiency through management. He became a qualified SFA coach of such reputation as to be appointed assistant to Andy Roxburgh with Scotland's professional youth team and later as manager of the Scottish Under-19 team. Smith had already been a manager for seventeen years when he stepped into the Premier arena with his appointment as St Mirren boss in December 1986.

Within five months he had led the Love Street team to a famous victory over Dundee United in the Scottish Cup Final, en route to the European Cup Winners' Cup, and brought in more than £400,000 for the sale of Steve Clark to Chelsea. With Ian Ferguson then determined to join Rangers, he haggled for a deal which was worth £920,000 to St Mirren; but he was running into conflict over one of his players, Frank McGarvey, and assistant manager Jimmy Bone, who was sacked by the board.

Just as Alex Ferguson was sacked by St Mirren in the spring of 1978, so was Alex Smith sacked by the same club in the spring of 1988. In similar manner, he arrived in Aberdeen within a short time, despite an offer to join Graeme Souness at Ibrox. It had been a frenetic period in his life. 'I used to come up here in the days of Alex Ferguson and Archie Knox and became friendly with them,' he recalled. 'I became familiar with the place but never believed I would ever be manager at Pittodrie. Now I have the biggest job in Scotland, outside Rangers and Celtic, and I'm sure their managements must be envious of the position here, so free of the bigotries.'

Leaving to others the running of his Smith's Restaurant in Stirling, Alex headed north to take over the Pittodrie job at the age of forty-eight, the first bachelor ever to manage Aberdeen. Having learned to delegate responsibility, he left the coaching to Jocky Scott and Drew Jarvie, local heroes of Aberdeen's League Cup victory in 1976, but was always in the background as the boss. He explained it like this:

I devote my whole life to football, often from eight o'clock in the morning till midnight. Jocky, Drew and I have all had to adjust, but the arrangement has worked very well. The three of us have open discussions about players' abilities, possible signings and team selection and sometimes they can become heated. But there is always a decision to be made and sometimes I will lean the way of Jocky or Drew.

We came to a club which already had professional discipline. There were players like Miller, McLeish, McKimmie, Bett, Connor, Grant, Nicholas and David Robertson and we had to complement them with more quality, while trying to groom our own. So we bought players like Snelders, Mason and Gillhaus and introduced young talent like Eoin Jess, Steve Wright, Gregg Watson, Scott Booth, Andy Roddie and Michael Watt, the goalkeeper.

What Aberdeen achieved in the eighties was fantastic but we have to guard against that becoming a burden on our shoulders in the nineties. It happened to Hibs with the Famous Five, to Hearts with Conn–Bauld–Wardhaugh and to Manchester United with the Busby Babes. We have to make sure we create our own history. That was why, after three barren years at Pittodrie, we were delighted to break the duck and win the Skol League Cup in 1989. It was a very significant victory, having gone to Glasgow to beat Celtic in the semi-final and Rangers in the final. It was significant because it proved that Aberdeen were still a potent force in Scottish football. People had begun to doubt it. The signing of Gillhaus prepared us for further challenge, provided a new dimension and gave an already talented squad an extra confidence.

It may be true that there will never be another Miller or McLeish but there will be other quality players. Jim Bett showed signs of becoming another Gordon Strachan. McKimmie and Robertson are superb fullbacks. The important thing is that Aberdeen Football Club has a structure which is right, very much like Liverpool. Because it is there, I have found it much easier to manage the Dons than I would have imagined.

45
LOYALTY OF TED

Continuity and loyalty in any football club rest, in the final analysis, with people who are not on the payroll, mainly directors and supporters. Not unreasonably, players and even managers must put their own livelihoods first. It happens all the time in the modern world. You hear of a manager struggling to retain players and uttering platitudes about loyalty. The next you know is that the manager has undermined his own argument by moving on himself. Alex Ferguson was no exception. For all his attachment to Aberdeen FC and the people of the North-east, his admiration and respect for Dick Donald, he knew that the offer of a job from Manchester United would be enough to lure him away. Indeed, it was to his credit that he resisted the attempts of Rangers to take him to Ibrox. So it all comes back to the supporters and a board like Aberdeen's, which takes no financial recompense from the club at all. It is truly a labour of love.

Having said that, you come upon an occasional employee who shows such touching loyalty as to put him in a special category. Two names spring to mind. As already mentioned in this book, Willie Cooper was one of the most capable full-backs Scottish football has ever seen, the man who told me that, in all his twenty-one years as a Dons player, he never once contemplated leaving his native city. He was just glad to be signing on for the kind of wage which was not available to most of his friends outside football.

The other name which comes to mind, of course, is Teddy Scott, something of a legend at Pittodrie, with thirty-five years of service by the time he had reached the age of sixty – and still going strong. Teddy has been player, trainer, valet, as well as guide, friend and philosopher to every young player at Pittodrie since the 1950s. On top of all that, he represents the archetypal North-east man, a solid, hard-working, genuine, decent, likeable human being who does nothing but good for those around him. Such people are as indispensable as they are unfashionable.

His value was best summed up, perhaps, by the quick wit of Gordon Strachan when the Dons went to play Sion of Switzerland and arrived with the wrong pants. Alex Ferguson said in mock seriousness that he would have to sack Teddy Scott. Up piped Strachan: 'And where are you going to get the ten people to replace him?' That was not far off the mark.

Teddy Scott was born in Ellon in 1929, one of eight children whose father died before the last one was born. He left school at thirteen to work in the Ellon boot factory and played for Caley Thistle, along with two other Dons of the future, Kenny Thomson and Billy Smith. During his National Service he played for Bournemouth but returned to join Sunnybank in time to become a part of history. For in 1954, Sunnybank became the first-ever Aberdeen team to win the Scottish Junior Cup and Teddy was the centre-half.

By then twenty-five, he was signed by Aberdeen in the very season when they were coasting towards their first Scottish League Championship. He was therefore competing for a place with stalwarts such as Alec Young and Jim Clunie and, in fact, made it to the first team only once. Teddy played one season with Elgin City in the Highland League, worked as an uncertificated PE teacher in Buchan and gave up playing the game in 1958 to rejoin Aberdeen as trainer. He was still only twenty-nine.

Legend has it that Teddy leaves Ellon on the first bus every morning and arrives home on the last one at night, devoting his entire life to Aberdeen Football Club. Legend is very nearly correct, except that he now has a motor car and feels the loss of contact with his cronies on the bus and in the streets as he walked down to Pittodrie.

Incredibly, Teddy has served under ten of the twelve managers who have run Aberdeen FC since 1903. When he joined the reserves, his team-mates included names like Ian Macfarlane, Ian McNeill, George Kelly, Joe O'Neil, Hughie Hay, Norman Davidson, Reggie Morrison and Jimmy Hogg. Teddy's recollections are an insight into Pittodrie's past:

Though I started with Davie Halliday as the boss, Davie Shaw was manager when I came back as trainer but he let young players go and that created a gap. Then came Tommy Pearson, another former Dons player, who talked a good game but didn't take part in training. He used to hold a team meeting on the Friday to discuss last week's match and tomorrow's one. I always remember, there were ashtrays on the table and the players sat there smoking! Eddie Turnbull was our first track-suit manager – and a very good one at that. His number two, Jimmy Bonthrone, who succeeded him, was a good tactician but hardness was not in his nature.

Then came Ally MacLeod, a great personality and enthusiast who got the supporters going. He also brought Stuart Kennedy from Falkirk. But I always regarded his tactics as dodgy and never rated him as a manager. Billy McNeill was a gentleman, as well as a good manager and tactician. I believe that, if he had stayed at Pittodrie, he would have achieved much the same as his successor, Alex Ferguson. Alex, of course, deserves most credit for what happened in the eighties. He was the best of all the managers to that point and he and Archie Knox were a good combination.

Down the years, I have had the advantage of being with the reserves and seeing the youngsters coming through. Names which come back to me include young talent like Tommy Craig, Jimmy Smith, John Hewitt, Neale Cooper, Neil Simpson, Eric Black, Martin Buchan and, of course, Willie Miller, who turned out to be the greatest of them all. Eric Black would have been a lazy player in any other team but it was Stuart Kennedy who made him work. Your mind roams over names like Peter Weir, who could hold the ball so well; Doug Rougvie, who was such a character; and who could forget John McMaster? I remember him coming from Greenock and being anxious to work through the close season, on the ground staff, just to make a bob or two. Boys come from all kinds of homes and I can recall some well-known names arriving here with holes in the soles of their shoes.

You try to teach the youngsters good habits, as well as skills, and hope that they will still be around when the club can reap the benefit. I had high hopes of Paul Wright, for example, but he was off to Queen's Park Rangers on freedom of contract. We may never again see the kind of loyalty shown by Willie Miller and Alex McLeish. Looking back over the years, the names which spring to mind as exceptional players are people like George Hamilton, Archie Glen, Alec Young, Gordon Strachan. Mark McGhee did a lot of work here.

In the build-up towards Gothenburg, the secret was that Alex Ferguson and Archie Knox planned everything correctly. Archie would go to watch foreign teams and he was brilliant at remembering names and what they could do. The pair of them were thorough in all they did and deserved their success. They were followed by Ian Porterfield, a nice man, but he was out of touch with Scottish football, after his years in England, and was never right for Aberdeen.

Teddy Scott gives great credit to an unexpected quarter for Aberdeen's success in the 1980s. Andy Roxburgh, he says, helped the Dons tremendously when he began the practice of taking Scotland's boys to youth tournaments on the Continent. It gave added confidence to youngsters like Cooper, Simpson and Hewitt. Aberdeen then picked up the habit and went to such tournaments on their own.

Teddy keeps an eye on Pittodrie's playing staff of forty players, who perform in three leagues – the Premier Division, the Reserve League and the Reserve League East, which takes in the second strings of teams such as East Fife, Raith Rovers and Arbroath. Jimmy Carswell, who was right-hand man to Bobby Calder, is now the chief scout, having performed a sterling task for Aberdeen Football Club down the years.

As for Teddy Scott, he acknowledges that Gothenburg was the greatest moment in the life of every Dons fan. In his own book, however, the great event must share the honours with another – that day in 1954 when he won a Scottish Junior Cup medal with Sunnybank at Hampden Park, Glasgow!

46
MILLER THE IMMORTAL

When all the assessments of Aberdeen's history have been exhausted, there will be one man above all who will emerge, by common consent, as the most important Dons player of all time. He is, of course, Willie Miller, for two decades an Aberdeen player and the captain who led them through the glory years to Gothenburg and beyond. The fact that managers like Alex Ferguson have described him as the best penalty-box player in the world is a measure of Miller's status in terms of international football, a stalwart of steel who had become a legend before his playing career was over.

Willie Miller grew up near Bridgeton Cross, Glasgow, not far from Celtic Park yet a Rangers stronghold to be found in the east end of the city nevertheless. There was no background of football and the boy wasn't even interested in the game during his early life. At primary school they needed a goalkeeper and the young Miller obliged, ending up as the keeper chosen for the Glasgow Schools Select to visit the United States.

Back home, he became bored with goalkeeping and thought he would try his luck in the outfield, perhaps as a centre-forward. That was where he was spotted by Dons scout Jimmy Carswell, while playing for Eastercraigs, and it was as a goal-scorer that he was signed on an S-form at the age of fourteen. Two years later, in 1971, he arrived at Pittodrie and was farmed out to Peterhead, where he proceeded to score twenty-three goals in the Highland League. Recalled to the Dons' reserve team, he remembers being greatly helped by George Murray, Bobby Clark and the inevitable Teddy Scott. Indeed, it was Teddy who suggested a move back to defence, having spotted his potential in a vastly different role. 'It clicked straight away,' Miller recalled, 'and I knew this was going to be my position from now on. Teddy has been so important to all the young players in the time I have been there.'

Miller made his debut in the Dons' first team against Morton at Cappielow Park on Saturday 28 April 1973, when he came on as substitute for Arthur Graham. Aberdeen won 2–1 that day and the team was: Clark, Williamson, Hermiston, Thomson, Young, Boel, Joe Smith, Taylor, Jarvie, Varga, Graham.

His first honour in an Aberdeen jersey was a League Cup medal with Ally MacLeod's team of 1976, when the Dons beat Celtic 2–1 at Hampden Park. The semi-final had seen the 5–1 demolition of Rangers, with that hat-trick from Jocky Scott and goals by Jarvie and Harper. It was in that final that Jarvie equalised a Kenny Dalglish penalty and Davie Robb scored the winner three minutes into extra time.

But Miller's greatest years lay ahead in the 1980s, after the arrival of Alex Ferguson as manager. As two very positive personalities, it has already been established that Ferguson and Miller did not hit it off at first, though reports of their conflicts were greatly exaggerated. Willie explains:

When he came at first, he used to keep on referring to his St Mirren players and that annoyed me. He had his ideas on how the game should be played and I had mine but we saw each other's point of view and there was compromise. Through the arguments, we had a couple of head-ons and I felt the better for it. His aggressive style of man-management didn't bother me; in fact, it helped. Perhaps he should have changed the style for other players who couldn't take it. His great strengths were his tactical ability and his motivation. He knew how to play the European teams and had the knack of choosing the players for the occasion, Dougie Bell being the classic example.

When Willie Miller's contract was at an end in 1981, he went south to discuss terms with Sunderland, well remembered by a previous generation as an extremely wealthy and ambitious club. Miller revealed:

I would have been substantially better off but I didn't like the place. It was a big club but it was like a mausoleum. They were living in the past and mainly on the memory of winning the FA Cup in 1973 – with a goal scored by a player called Ian Porterfield!

So I stayed with Aberdeen and have never regretted my decision. The success we have had has been more important than money. That success culminated in Gothenburg and it is only later that you realise how important it is to win a European trophy. You build up a reputation, become accepted in Europe; and it doesn't go away overnight.

Willie Miller's reputation will never disappear. In a game which lives by its generated emotion, he rarely shows a trace of it, on or off the field. How does he reconcile this? 'I do have the emotion inside me all right,' he explained. 'But I channel it into my football.' There, in succinct terms, we have an interesting insight into the character and being of Willie Miller.

Now he has taken his place as a businessman in Aberdeen, running the Parkway pub at the Bridge of Don as well as a number of nursing homes. He married Claire, a member of the well-known amusements family of Codora, and became the North-east's most famous adopted son. The name of Willie Miller, quiet lad from the east end of Glasgow who grew into the stature of a soccer giant, is engraved for ever in the history of Scottish football, most of all in the hearts of Aberdonians, who followed his leadership to the most unforgettable experience of their lives.

47
THE CASUALS

It would be simple (and very tempting) to ignore completely the one black chapter which threatened to tarnish the Golden Age of Pittodrie. But history takes in warts and all, and that is the category to which we must consign the so-called Casuals, a group of marauding juveniles who began to make their objectionable presence felt in the early 1980s.

There had been crowd trouble on the terracings of England throughout the seventies and the Scottish Cup Final of 1980, between Rangers and Celtic, had produced one of Hampden's ugliest scenes, with mounted police separating fans who came to meet each other across the pitch. But no one had ever associated Aberdeen with hooliganism. (Those demonstrations in the earlier part of the century had all been related to events on the field.) Suddenly there was a new breed of football troublemaker declaring war on the football slopes of Britain, which had nothing to do with what was happening on the field of play – and, of all places, it seemed to have originated in Aberdeen.

This was gang warfare attaching itself to football, finding a ready-made structure of enemies within the framework of soccer and travelling great lager-laden distances for the sheer excitement of kicking in heads. They called themselves the Casuals, taken from their expensive Pringle or Lyle and Scott casual sweaters. For this was no set of under-privileged, unemployed youths kicking against an unjust society. They were the swaggering well-heeled, proud of their trendy image with its Burberry and Lacoste fashions and total absence of the club colours. Thus camouflaged, they could more easily infiltrate the ranks of the 'enemy' at away games, then suddenly reveal themselves, like troops from the Trojan Horse.

The average Dons fan was bewildered by the early antics and took some time to understand the mentality of this new breed of hooligan. If identities were hidden, much was revealed in 1989 when one of their leaders emerged from a prison sentence in Craiginches to write a book about his adventures. He turned out to be no common-or-garden hooligan but a member of a prominent North-east family which had always taken some pride in its leadership qualities.

David Jay Alexander Allan (called Jay after the popular Scottish heavyweight athlete, Jay Scott) was the son of Charlie Allan, farmer and broadcaster from Little Ardo of Methlick, and a grandson of that distinguished North-east writer, John R. Allan, who ranks second only to Lewis Grassic Gibbon. His father's uncles included Sir Maitland Mackie, who became Lord Lieutenant of the county, and two of his brothers who took their seats in the House of Lords. None of that made Jay Allan any less of a hooligan. It was just a more interesting background, proving that attempts at leadership don't always turn you into the Queen's representative.

Here was this boy of privileged upbringing (and there were others like him) giving us the sordid story of violence played out in the name of city and club, with such mindless naivety as to be disappointed that there was not greater recognition of the fact that they had put Aberdeen in the headlines! The thrills of violence were evidently akin to skiing or diving off the high board at the Bon Accord Baths – and better than sex. In this sorry catalogue of misguided energy, there are two points on which I do agree with Jay Allan. In another age, I suspect, he would have been off to war with the Gordon Highlanders. 'My generation didn't have a war,' he seeks to rationalise, 'so perhaps what we were doing was inventing our own.'

Of the forty-seven Casuals arrested when they tried to ambush Motherwell supporters (and they themselves were ambushed by Grampian Police), only five were unemployed. Most came from good backgrounds with settled, professional parents, Allan reveals, ruling out the hackneyed argument of social workers and psychologists about deprivation and lack of prospects. Jay Allan himself was coming off the oil-rigs with good money, heading off with his fighting mob to the Dons' away games, sometimes carrying an umbrella in case it rained! His narrative contains some interesting self-assessments. As the gates of Craiginches clanged behind him, he suddenly wondered what he was doing there. 'I'm not jail material,' he said to himself. Oh no? Try telling that to a North-east jury!

When he left prison, he went home to help his father on the farm at Methlick and to write his book. Then he set off on continental travels, ending up in Tenerife where he was supplying barmen and bouncers for pubs, taking the stage himself for a spot of disco-dancing – and supporting the local football team.

His book, called *Bloody Casuals – Diary of a Football Hooligan*, was not written as a warning to other youngsters and even proposes a 'battling area' where thugs could knock hell out of each other during a game. It is the ludicrous conclusion of a book which seeks to rationalise the appalling behaviour and states that organised hooliganism is partly the attempt of some fans to seek a closer identity with their heroes on the field. 'Nothing made us so proud as when the mob from little Aberdeen made the main national news,' he boasts.

Jay Allan may have gone but some of his Casuals are still there, though much less in evidence through better policing. (The supporters' association has a dossier of names who are banned from membership.) His 'national news' is something Aberdeen and Aberdonians can do without. By now, it must surely be penetrating that the mindless violence is something for which players, officials and the overwhelming mass of the support have nothing but contempt.

48
WHAT PRICE PITTODRIE?

Aberdeen Football Club has retained the structure of a private limited company, with 166 people owning between them the 100,000 shares, which have a face value of £1 each. A share value of £100,000 must seem like a nonsense to the supporter in the street, who knows that you pay more than that for an average-sized villa in Aberdeen. But, as vice-chairman Ian Donald says: 'How do you value a football club? It has no value for any purpose other than playing football.' (Clearly the people who bought Hibernian FC in the late 1980s saw matters differently, as they talked on television about Easter Road's value as a commercial development.)

Most of Pittodrie's 100,000 shares are held for sentimental reasons, with the result that very few come on the market. When they do, arrangements are made privately and the buyer has to be approved by the directors, who are not obliged to give a reason for their veto of a transaction. In this age of rampant democratisation, this might seem like an anachronism which has outlived its day. The other side of the argument is that Aberdeen FC, for all its board-room autocracy, remains a model of how to run a football club, a fact acknowledged on all sides of the game.

Though the shares have a face value of £1, in reality they were changing hands for anything up to £20 in the late 1980s and, if the club ever decided to go public, as happened to Tottenham Hotspur and Millwall, they would reach much higher still. It would not be unreasonable to expect a club valuation of £10 million, which would still be short of Millwall's £12 million.

It is an interesting subject for debate and, however one views the situation, it says much for the integrity of the Donald family that they react with a measure of indignation at any suggestion of going public. They are, of course, a wealthy family outwith football but consider their financial gain if the club followed Tottenham to the stock market. Chairman Dick Donald, his son Ian and son-in-law Stewart Spence hold between them, a total of 24,000 shares. At a single stroke, that nominal value of £24,000 (nearly one-quarter of the share value) would be multiplied many times over.

Others would benefit in proportion. The next largest shareholder is the well-known Aberdeen fish merchant Alex Whyte, who holds 8900 shares, and he is followed by the descendants of the late Charles B. Forbes, former headmaster of Middlefield School and chairman of the Dons. The family of the late Chris Anderson, vice-chairman until his death in 1986, hold 5500.

If the argument about the proper value of a football club confuses the man in the Paddock, he is liable to be further baffled by the fact that the value of the players does not normally appear on football balance-sheets, even though the buying and selling of them is part of the trading operation of the business.

As an interesting footnote to this topic, every Dons manager, from Tommy Pearson in the 1950s to Alex Ferguson in the 1980s (that takes in Eddie Turnbull, Jimmy Bonthrone, Ally MacLeod and Billy McNeill), has remained a shareholder of the club. That tradition goes back even earlier, to the late Davie Halliday, manager from 1938 to 1955, whose family still hold his shares. The only ex-manager who does not possess Dons shares is Ian Porterfield.

After the death of Chris Anderson, the directors co-opted the well-known Aberdeen bookmaker, Bobby Morrison, to the board. Soon after his days at Holburn Street School, Mr Morrison suffered serious ill health but by the age of twenty-two he had recovered sufficiently to launch himself as a bookmaker in the city. It was the start of a highly successful career which culminated in selling out to William Hill in 1985. As well as his chain of bookie's shops, he was also the owner of some prominent racehorses, sometimes in partnership with his business friend, Peter Cameron.

Bobby Morrison's interest in the Dons goes back to 1938 and one of his most treasured memories is of the Scottish Cup Final of 1947 when he was one of a small, brave band of people who paid £5 each to fly to the match in one of Gander Dower's planes from Dyce! He owns 900 Dons shares. As the Dons chairman approached his eightieth year, and the demand on directors' time and energies increased, the board decided to co-opt a fourth member. He was the well-known Aberdeen stockbroker, Denis Miller, senior partner in Abercromby and Stott, who took early retirement in 1988 before becoming a director of the expanding investment company, Aberdeen Fund Managers. He owns 1320 shares but had the backing of Alex Whyte.

Denis Miller left Hilton Academy in 1944, at the age of fourteen, and became a clerk with the London and North-Eastern Railway at Waterloo Station, alongside a senior figure he remembers as a mathematical genius – and who turned out to be the father of Buff Hardie, of 'Scotland the What?' Mr Miller was a railway clerk at Maud and Ballindalloch and returned to Kittybrewster after National Service, during which he played football for Maidstone in the Southern League. He then joined Abercromby and Stott as a young clerk and rose to lead the firm, which later merged with Parsons.

Looking forward, with his reinforced board, Mr Ian Donald said: 'We have been ahead of the game in the 1980s, in matters like the all-seated, covered stadium, computerised turnstiles and so on, and we aim to stay ahead. We are looking at possibilities like an indoor centre, perhaps across from the main stand, which would involve the city as well as ourselves. It could provide facilities not only for our own training but for tennis, badminton and basketball.' Mr Donald emphasised the point about Aberdeen's ability to compete with the best in a playing sense, while not being in the top league from a financial point of view. With freedom of contract now well established, he thought it unlikely that clubs would retain the loyalty of a Willie Miller or an Alex McLeish in the next generation.

It was fairly typical of Aberdeen FC's sensible approach to life that the directors resisted the temptation of big-money sponsorship if it meant players advertising alcohol on their jerseys. Weren't there enough lager louts already? Instead, they have a deal with Abtrust, a local financial group, worth up to £1 million over three years.

Meanwhile, the administration of the club is led by Ian Taggart, who grew up in the northern town of Golspie, of Aberdeen parents, before returning to the city to train as an accountant. After a spell with an oil-related company, he joined the Dons in 1976. Acting as link between the playing side and directors, Ian Taggart supervises a non-playing staff of seventeen people. He is assisted by Barbara Cook, who runs the clerical side of the club, Ashley Reid, who is in charge of tickets, and his own secretary, Jean Sandham. The club has now appointed a commercial executive, David Johnston, formerly with Dundee, whose enterprise will have a vital part to play in the future of the club.

Executive boxes have now taken their serious place in the financial reckoning of football clubs and the Dons provide that facility in a line of well-appointed suites along the back of the main stand. The Fifty Club retains its role as an executive type of supporters' club, in which more than a hundred people pay £330 a year for their own premises at Pittodrie, with direct access to their own reserved seats, free car-parking, programmes and so on.

In the wider sphere of support, Mrs Isobel Fyfe from Dyce co-ordinates the association of forty-five clubs, which embrace between 7000 and 8000 members, indicating a healthy measure of enthusiasm. These supporters' clubs range all the way from Scotland to Australia, where the Melbourne branch has close ties with two well-remembered names, Jim Hermiston and Derek 'Cup-Tie' McKay. The largest branch is to be found in Orkney, with 450 members, and the arrival of Dutch players is reflected in a thirty-strong branch in Holland. The popularity of the Dutch goalkeeper can be seen in the existence of a Theo Snelders No. 1 club in Glasgow! That popularity was further displayed in season 1988–89 when the big keeper was voted Scotland's Player of the Year by his fellow professionals. The opinion was endorsed by the supporters' association and, when the Dutchman came to accept his award at a function in the Treetops Hotel, he delighted the fans with an introductory salute of 'Fit like?'

So there is a well-integrated structure, both inside and beyond the portals of Pittodrie, which serves every need of a modern football club. The general well-being of soccer limbs is in the hands of Dr Leslie Forbes, son of the former chairman, who is assisted by Dr Derek Gray. The orthopaedic surgeon who regularly examines players is Mr Tom Scotland, whose operations have included those on Willie Miller's knee.

49
WHERE ARE THEY NOW?

In winning the Cup Winners' Cup in 1983 and beating Hamburg in the European Super Cup, Aberdeen did of course prove themselves the best team in Europe at that time. The paradox was that, while they could compete with the very best in a footballing sense, the club was never likely to be in the top bracket financially. The giants of Madrid, Milan or Munich – even Merseyside or Ibrox, with twice the Pittodrie capacity – can generate funds which belong to a different plain. There is a very strict limit to what a club like Aberdeen can pay its players, particularly since the directors pride themselves in a reputation for good housekeeping which avoids all debt.

As we enter the final decade of the century, matters have improved to the extent that it is possible for an Aberdeen player to gross £100,000 a year, according to vice-chairman Ian Donald. As recently as 1983, however, the men who declared themselves the best in Europe were lucky to have reached £40,000 for their season's efforts. In prosperous Aberdeen, there were many people would could look forward to a lifetime of earnings at that level, against a footballer's few years at the top. When Alex Ferguson was sacked by St Mirren in 1978, he was actually earning more than the £12,000 he received as a starting salary at Pittodrie. At that stage, the players were on a basic wage of around £80 a week.

Prosperity in the Fergie era improved that situation dramatically but after Gothenburg the disparities began to show. The departure of Doug Rougvie is a case in point, revealing too that Alex Ferguson may have had a thing or two to learn about man-management. The gigantic Rougvie, who arrived from Dunfermline United in 1972, may not have been the most sophisticated talent in the Gothenburg team but he was certainly one of Pittodrie's greatest favourites, capable of responding to the crowd's chant of 'Roog-vee, Roog-vee' with an inspired surge to tingle the blood of everyone – except perhaps the manager, who might be wondering where he was off to now!

When Rougvie went to discuss a new contract in 1984, after twelve years with the club, he asked for a signing-on fee of £15,000 and an increase in basic wage from £275 to £375 a week. For his long service, he was due a testimonial but missed out because recent poor attendances had caused the club to set aside that means of reward. When the manager did not meet his demands, the full-back went to London to discuss an offer from Chelsea, who were not only prepared to meet his £15,000 signing-on fee but were offering £600 a week, plus £6000 a year for each year of service. That was tantamount to a weekly wage of £720. When he came back to report that, despite the Chelsea terms, he would be happy to stay with Aberdeen at £375 a week, he claims that the manager accused him of playing one against the other and told him bluntly where to go. 'He kicked me out of his office and, on the following week, wouldn't let me inside the Pittodrie door,' said Rougvie later. 'He slaughtered me in the press but I didn't respond. I must admit I was hurt, though. My heart was at Pittodrie and I didn't want to leave. I have every respect for Mr Ferguson as a football manager but not for the way he managed people.'

I found that a sad postscript to the glory days. Doug Rougvie went on to play a hundred matches in three years at Chelsea and moved on to Brighton, Shrewsbury and Fulham before returning to his native Fife and the Dunfermline Athletic club to which his original boys' team had been affiliated. But Doug and his Aberdonian wife Brenda had a house built at Kingswells in preparation for their return to the North-east they hadn't wanted to leave.

So, as we enter the last decade of the century, where are the other Gothenburg heroes now? Jim Leighton followed Alex Ferguson to Manchester United, a reunion which did little to relieve that great club of its continuing misery. John McMaster went back to his native Greenock and is coaching Morton. Neale Cooper had an ill-fated spell with Aston Villa before returning north to play for Rangers and struggling to find a place. Alex McLeish, Willie Miller and Neil Simpson remain as the only survivors at Pittodrie, big Alex growing in stature with every game and establishing himself not only as Aberdeen's most-capped player of all time but second only to Kenny Dalglish in the entire history of Scottish football. Gordon Strachan parted company with his former Dons manager at Manchester and found a new lease of life as captain of Leeds United, leading that club back towards the English First Division in 1990.

After a spell with the mighty Hamburg, Mark McGhee came home to join Celtic, then went full circle and returned to Newcastle United, from where he had been signed by Aberdeen in the first place. Eric Black went to the French club Metz and Peter Weir was allowed to go to Leicester City and later nearly returned to Pittodrie but the English club blocked the deal. He was diverted instead to his starting-point of St Mirren.

Finally, of the twelve men of Ullevi, John Hewitt was still at Pittodrie in 1989 but, curiously, for all his heroic feats at vital moments, never fully established himself in the Dons team. Eventually he tired of the 'Super Sub' label and sought a move, which landed him at Celtic Park, after having carved for himself a very special niche in the history of Pittodrie as the man who set Aberdeen on the road to Gothenburg and rounded off the journey in fairy-tale fashion.

In later years, it was a strange experience to see McGhee and Hewitt returning to Pittodrie in the Celtic jersey, Neale Cooper in a Rangers one, Doug Rougvie in Dunfermline's and Peter Weir in St Mirren's. There was something ill-fitting about the garb, which stirred memories of their previous incarnations – to which, one felt, they more properly belonged. Their glory days had slipped quietly into these pages of history and, as we bit our lips and swallowed hard, it was time to acknowledge Grassic Gibbon's truism that nothing in this world abides. Nothing at all is for ever.

50
THE NORTHERN LIGHT

So the Dons have survived through nine decades of ups and downs, establishing themselves as by far the biggest single source of public entertainment in the North-east of Scotland. Football may no longer have a monopoly on Saturday-afternoon leisure but it is still an attraction which draws out men, women and children in search of a spectacle. Players and managers, even directors, must come and go but the supporters remain the most constant factor in the life of any football club. The crowds who flock down King Street have invested a part of their lives in Pittodrie, in the hope that there will be a dividend of satisfaction and an occasional bonus of joy. The clicking sound of the turnstile propels them into another world, the woes of the week shut out behind, and there they air their lungs, free their frustrations and come away with a sense of pleasure or punishment, according to the success or failure of their team. They raise their own heroes and villains and talk of them with close familiarity whereas, in the majority of cases, they never come as close as to say 'Hello'.

But they march through the history of football together, players and supporters, reflecting the styles and fashions and moods of their particular day. The middle parting and the baggy pants will fix us in the 1920s or 1930s, just as the clean-cut image of a George Hamilton or an Archie Baird will tell us about wartime's young men. When the heavy beat of rock 'n' roll produced Elvis Presley in America and Tommy Steele in Britain, it sparked off a new vitality which was bound to show elsewhere. In that same year of 1956, when the fair-haired Steele was introducing the new craze at the Capitol Cinema, Aberdeen, that other fair-haired lad called Denis Law, from Powis School, was starting to symbolise that same vitality on the football field, albeit at the distance of Huddersfield. Similarly, the Beatles of the mid 1960s were reflected in football terms by George Best, while the Bay City Rollers of the 1970s spread their influence more widely on the terracing, spawning an army of youngsters in big boots, tee-shirts and half-mast denims. Like life itself, football was undergoing a revolution, with new styles and formations to baffle the innocent. Some of it has worked and some of it has not. Much of it has ended up in a fankle of fancy names and boring formulae, expressed in a jargon of gibberish.

Stan Williams and Paddy Buckley spent all those years darting through the middle and scoring goals without ever knowing that they were 'front-runners' or 'strikers', and feeling none the worse for it, I'm sure. George Taylor and Andy Cowie, forging between defence and attack with George Hamilton and Archie Baird, were blissfully ignorant of the fact that they were 'link men', while that dashing full-back Pat McKenna could come through on his own without the encumbrance of knowing that he was 'overlapping'.

From the 1960s onwards, there has been an attempt to present football as a kind of science whereas, I believe, it is nothing of the sort. At its best, football is an art, not a science, a form of co-ordinated movement with the creative freedom of weaving spontaneous patterns. There is no set script. It is like a competitive ballet, performed on a stage of turf to the choral accompaniment of 'We'll Support You Evermore' or, in the case of the Dons, 'The Northern Lights of Old Aberdeen'. An interest in football is the average man's search for an art form, as surely as other people look to the theatre or the concert hall. A sustained piece of skilful play, even by an opposing team, can draw a round of applause because it has touched man's longing for perfection.

In the Pittodrie experience, we have savoured those moments of perfection all the way from Willie Lennie and Donald Colman through to the days of Joe Harper and Drew Jarvie, Gordon Strachan and Willie Miller. Memories arise and linger with us for ever.

As our story draws to a close for the moment, may these merry-dancing Dons perform on our northern horizons for many a day, stirring the imagination of youth, gladdening old men's souls and sending the great battalion of Pittodrie faithfuls pounding their homeward way up Merkland Road East with a spring in their step and a song in their hearts. A song which will echo from the green fields of Buchan to the oilfields of the North Sea for as long as little boys will wish to kick a stone or an old tin-can down a cobbled city street or a dubby country road.

FACTS AND FIGURES

Aberdeen Football Club founded 1903

Honours

European Cup Winners' Cup: Winners 1983

European Super Cup: Winners 1983

Scottish League Champions: 1954–55, 1979–80, 1983–84, 1984–85
Runners-up: 1911, 1937, 1956, 1971, 1972, 1978, 1981, 1982, 1989, 1990

Scottish Cup Winners: 1947, 1970, 1982, 1983, 1984, 1986, 1990
Scottish Cup Finalists: 1937, 1953, 1954, 1959, 1967, 1978

Scottish League Cup Winners: 1946, 1955, 1976, 1986, 1989
Scottish League Cup Finalists: 1947, 1979, 1980, 1987, 1988

Drybrough Cup Winners: 1971, 1980

Directors in 1990

Chairman: Richard M. Donald

Vice-chairman: Ian R. Donald

Directors: Robert Morrison, Denis Miller

Managers

Jimmy Philip 1903–24

Paddy Travers 1924–38

David Halliday 1938–55

David Shaw 1955–59

Tommy Pearson 1959–65

Eddie Turnbull 1965–71

Jimmy Bonthrone 1971–75

Ally MacLeod 1975–77

Billy McNeill 1977–78

Alex Ferguson 1978–86

Ian Porterfield 1986–88

Alex Smith, Jocky Scott (joint) 1988–

Payroll at Pittodrie in 1990

Managers: Alex Smith, Jocky Scott
Assistant manager: Drew Jarvie
Trainer: Teddy Scott
Physiotherapist: David Wylie
Youth coach: Len Taylor

Players: Willem van der Ark, Jim Bett, Scott Booth, Paul
Bridgeford, Euan Brydson, Ian Cameron, Robert Connor, John
Dickson, Ian Downie, Thomas Fallon, Graeme Ferguson, Lee
Gardner, Andrew Gibson, Hans Gillhaus, Brian Grant, Scott
Harvie, Mark Humphries, Brian Irvine, Eoin Jess, Stewart
McKimmie, James McCarron, Stephen McAnespie, Alex
McLeish, Andrew McLeod, Colin McRonald, Paul Mason, Willie
Miller, Charlie Nicholas, Craig Robertson, David Robertson,
Ian Robertson, Vincent Rae, Andrew Roddie, Neil Simpson,
David Smith, Theo Snelders, Derek Stillie, Malcolm Thomson,
Graham Watson, Gregg Watson, Michael Watt, Stephen Wright,
Robert Zagorski. Part-time: Brian Lithgow.
Scouts: Jim Carswell (chief), Robert Weir, Archie Rose, Stewart
Taylor, Peter Brain, John Murphy, George Campbell, Jim
Summers, Jim Whyte, Alex Rae, Ian Cumming, Billy Kerr.

Secretary: Ian Taggart
Commercial executive: David Johnston
General office: Barbara Cook, Jean Sandham
Ticket office: Ashley Reid, Pat Forrest, Carol Brett
Lottery promoter: Fred Booth
Lotteries: Peggy Petrie
Cook: Olive Furness

Cleaner: Jessie Carr
Outside staff – Groundsman: Jim Warrender; Maintenance: Sandy Robertson, Eric McCulloch; Boot room: George Perry, Charlie McKay; Cleaners: Alex Taylor, Jim Bain, Kenneth Cumming, Charles Dowall, Clarence Cownie, Robert Burnett, Richard Evans, James McSloy, James Park, William Perry, Herbert Smith, Luigi Spoggi, John Flint

First player capped

Willie Lennie, 1908

Most-capped player

Alex McLeish – 66 full caps to end of 1989
(That also made Alex the second most capped player in the entire history of Scottish football, surpassed only by Kenny Dalglish of Celtic and Liverpool.)

All-time top scorer

Joe Harper – 199 goals

Top scorer in one season

Benny Yorston – 46 League and Cup goals, 1929–30

Top scorers in one game

Paddy Moore scored six against Falkirk, 1932
Alex Merrie scored six against Hibernian, 1930
Ian Rodger scored seven in reserve game with Leith Athletic, 1952
Dod Ritchie once scored seven in reserve game with Aberdeen University

Record score

Aberdeen 13   Peterhead 0 (Scottish Cup, third round, 1923)

Record crowd at Dons game

146,433 – at Scottish Cup Final 1937 *v* Celtic (the biggest crowd ever to watch a club football match in Britain, a record unlikely to be equalled)

Record crowd at Pittodrie

45,061 – at Scottish Cup fourth-round tie with Hearts, 13 March 1954

First game

On 15 August 1903 *v* Stenhousemuir in the old Northern League

Jerseys

Aberdeen wore white in 1903
Changed to black and gold in 1904
Red jerseys first worn on 18 March 1939
Numbered jerseys first worn on 16 November 1946

Internationals at Pittodrie

3 February 1900	*Scotland* 5 (Hamilton 2, Bell, Wilson, Smith)	*Wales* 2 (Parry, Butler) Attendance: 12,000
12 February 1921	*Scotland* 2 (Andy Wilson 2)	*Wales* 1 (Collier) Attendance: 20,824
21 November 1935	*Scotland* 3 (Napier 2, Duncan)	*Wales* 2 (Phillips, Astley) Attendance: 26,334
10 November 1938	*Scotland* 1 (Jimmy Simpson)	*Ireland* 1 (Peter Doherty) Attendance: 21,878
10 November 1971	*Scotland* 1 (John O'Hare)	*Belgium* 0 Attendance: 36,500
16 May 1990	*Scotland* 1 (Ally McCoist)	*Egypt* 3 (Abdelhamid, Hassan, Yousef) Attendance: 23,000

That Scotland team of 1900 included R. S. McColl, of Queen's Park, later famous for his sweetie shops
The 1935 team included Aberdonian Dally Duncan of Derby County
The 1971 team included three Dons – Bobby Clark, Martin Buchan and Steve Murray

INDEX

279